Learning to Teach Religious Education in the Secondary School

A companion to school experience

Edited by

Andrew Wright and Ann-Marie Brandom

RoutledgeFalmer
Taylor & Francis Group

LONDON AND NEW YORK

First published 2000
by RoutledgeFalmer
2 Park Square, Milton Park, Abingdon, Oxon OX14 4RN

Simultaneously published in the USA and Canada
by RoutledgeFalmer
270 Madison Avenue, New York, NY 10016

Reprinted 2002, 2003, 2004, 2005

RoutledgeFalmer is an imprint of the Taylor & Francis Group

Typeset in Bembo by
J&L Composition Ltd, Filey, North Yorkshire
Printed and bound in Great Britain by
TJ International Ltd, Padstow, Cornwall

British Library Cataloguing in Publication Data
A catalogue record for this book is available from the British Library

Library of Congress Cataloging in Publication Data
A catalogue record has been requested

ISBN 0-415-19436-9

Contents

Illustrations

FIGURES

TASKS

Contributors

Andy Angel is studying for ordination into the Church of England at St John's College, Nottingham. Until recently, he was Head of Religious Education at Brentwood School in Essex for four years. Before that he taught RE and drama at Trinity School, Croydon, for five years. He holds degrees in Theology and Educational Studies from Oxford and Surrey Universities. His research interests in Educational Studies have been twofold: RE and indoctrination, and the introduction of theology and philosophy to RE in Key Stage 4.

Jo Backus is Senior Lecturer in the Study of Religion and Religious Education at Bath Spa University College. She holds degrees in Philosophy and Theology and in Religious Studies. Before moving into higher education she taught RE in secondary schools and ran a Department of Religious and Social Studies. She has considerable experience in initial teacher education, both as school mentor and as PGCE RE Programme Director. A practising Buddhist, she is completing her PhD research, focusing on issues surrounding the representation of Buddhism in the classroom, at King's College London.

Ann-Marie Brandom is Lecturer in Religious Education at King's College London, where she co-ordinates the PGCE RE course and contributes to the MA RE programme. She was a visiting lecturer at Goldsmiths' College, University of London, providing RE input on the Primary BEd course. Before that she was a teacher of RE and a head of department in an Inner London comprehensive for ten years. She is undertaking research into the cognitive abilities of students in relation to religious and theological understanding.

Andrew Clutterbuck is Senior Lecturer in the Study of Religion at the University of Hertfordshire. A former teacher of RE and head of department in a comprehensive school, he now contributes to BA and BEd Study of Religion and Religious Studies courses. His previous publications include *Growing up in Sikhism* and articles in the *International Journal of Human Computer Interaction* and *The Reader's Guide to Women's Studies*. He is completing a PhD study in ICT and the elicitation and representation of religious concepts.

Trevor Cooling is head of the Stapleford Centre, a Christian centre which supports RE teaching and the promotion of spiritual and moral development in schools. Before that he was Head of Religious Education in a large secondary school, having converted from being a biology teacher. He is a Special Lecturer in the School of Education at the University of Nottingham and course leader for the range of distance learning courses for RE teachers provided by St John's College.

Clive Erricker is Reader in the Study of Religions at University College, Chichester. He is the author of, contributor to and editor of a number of publications in the area of RE and spiritual education. He is co-director of the Children and Worldviews Project and co-editor of the *International Journal of Children's Spirituality*.

Jane Erricker is Research Officer in the School of Education, King Alfred's College, Winchester, and lectures in Education Studies and Science Education. She has contributed to and edited a number of publications in the fields of spiritual and moral education and RE. She is co-director of the Children and Worldviews Project and co-editor of the *International Journal of Children's Spirituality*.

Jean Harris is studying for an MA in RE at King's College London. She holds a BA Hons in English from the University of North London. Jean was Head of Religious Education at Ashburton High School for two and a half years, and is now RE co-ordinator at Rosemary Musker High School, Thetford. She has worked on producing multi-media CD-ROMS about various faith groups, and sees this as an extension of her interest in inter-faith work. Other interests include how language develops and can change both conceptions and perceptions of religions.

Fred Hughes is Head of the School of Theology and Religious Studies, Cheltenham and Gloucester College of Higher Education. He teaches RE on the BA, MA and Secondary PGCE courses. He has an MEd and PhD from Nottingham University and is a member of the Gloucestershire SACRE. He has taught RE in Essex, Gloucestershire, Leicester and Uganda. He is author of *What Do You Mean? Christian Education* (Paternoster, 1992). From 1993 to 1998 he was an OFSTED Team Inspector for Religious Education. He trained for Section 23 Inspections of Religious Education and Collective Worship in church schools and has carried out inspections in several schools in the Diocese of Gloucester.

Taira Mohammed is Head of Religious Education at Nower Hill High School in Harrow. She is co-tutoring on the Institute of Education's Secondary PGCE RE course with Angela Wright. For several years she has been part of the Institute's Initial Teacher Education Partnership, mentoring and assessing trainee and newly qualified teachers. She is a member of the Institute of Education PGCE Advisory Group.

Vanessa Ogden qualified as a Religious Education teacher in 1993 and is now Senior Teacher with responsibility for teaching and learning across the curriculum at Hurlingham and Chelsea School in the London borough of Hammersmith and

Fulham. As Sir Halley Stewart Teacher Fellow she undertook full-time research into post-16 RE in 1996–7. Over the last few years she has taught on a consultancy basis at universities and national conferences, and she currently lectures and supervises on the MA (Ed) course in RE at the Institute of Education, London University. She has been part of working parties for QCA on cultural development, RE and work-related learning, and post-16 RE.

Joanne Reed has a degree in Social Sciences from the Polytechnic of Central London and an MA in Theology and Education from King's College London. She worked as a freelance journalist for several years before training to become an RE teacher at the Roehampton Institute in west London. She then worked for three years at Blackheath Bluecoat School, in south-east London. She is Head of the Religious Education Department in a secondary school in Kent.

John Rudge is a PGCE tutor and freelance writer and consultant. From 1988 to 1997 he was Director of the Westhill Religious Education Centre, Westhill College, Birmingham.

Linda Rudge is the Director of the Keswick Hall Centre for Research and Development in Religious Education at the University of East Anglia in Norwich. She is Chair of the Conference of University Lecturers in Religious Education. She was a secondary RE teacher and head of Department between 1980 and 1990, and an Essex LEA curriculum adviser on RE between 1990 and 1993. Her research interests are the history and politics of RE, the professional lives of RE teachers and the relevance of RE to the 'silent majority.'

Alison Seaman is Director of the National Society's Religious Education Centre in London, where she is involved in a comprehensive programme of in-service training and is responsible for the centre's extensive collection of resource materials. She also co-ordinates its advisory and information service. She taught for many years in a range of primary schools where she developed a particular interest in RE and spiritual development in the primary and early years. She is author of a variety of RE resources, including books about Christianity for pupils at Key Stages 1 and 2.

Derek Webster is Reader in Education in the School of Education, University of Hull, and an Anglican priest working in the Diocese of Lincoln. A former teacher, he taught in colleges of education in London, Leeds and West Yorkshire before being appointed to his university post in 1972. His most recent book is *Our Time Now: The Lincoln Cycle of Prayer* (Kenelm Press, 1997). Forthcoming is a fourth volume in his desert spirituality series entitled *Spirit in the Desert*.

Joy White is the Religious Education Adviser in the London Borough of Croydon. She is an experienced secondary school teacher and previous Head of Religious Education. With Ann Lovelace she is co-author *of Beliefs, Values and Traditions* (Heinemann, 1996). Joy has contributed regularly to a number of secondary PGCE courses, both as external examiner and as visiting lecturer. She has been a director of a series of St Gabriel's Trust-sponsored Action Research Initiatives developed jointly by Croydon LEA and King's College London.

Andrew Wright is Lecturer in Religious and Theological Education at King's College London, where he is Programme Director of the MA in RE and co-ordinator of RE PhD research students. He has been in charge of PGCE RE courses at King's College, the Roehampton Institute and the London Institute of Education. Prior to his move into higher education he was head of the RE departments in three contrasting secondary schools. Among his publications are *Religious Education in the Secondary School* (Fulton, 1993), *Spiritual Pedagogy* (Culham, 1998) and *Discerning the Spirit* (Culham, 1999). His current research is concerned with hermeneutics and religious literacy.

Angela Wright is the RE PGCE Tutor at the Institute of Education, University of London. Prior to that she taught RE in two London schools. In 1995 she was awarded the Sir Halley Stewart Fellowship for Religious Education and spent the year investigating the whole issue of teaching RE at Key Stage 4. This coincided with the development of the new GCSE short courses, in which she was involved. She is part of the team of authors who have written *Religion in Focus*, the textbook series devoted to the teaching of the short courses published by John Murray. She is also Resources Officer at the National Society's Religious Education Resource Centre in Pimlico.

Acknowledgements

Sincere and grateful thanks are due: to all the contributors for all their hard work, enthusiasm and support in the face of what must have at times felt like an increasingly irritating editorial duo; to Tony Turner, who proved to be the perfect mentor and guide; to Mike Totterdell, who first floated the idea; to Sudi Ansari-nia, who looked after our administration at King's College; to the PGCE Religious Education class of 1996–7 at King's College; and to Andrew's sister Angela, who once spent a rather curious three hours in a bar on Paddington Station helping to compile a list of potential contributors, in the process failing miserably in her attempts to exclude herself from the roster!

Abbreviations

AREIAC Association of Religious Education Inspectors, Advisers and Consultants
ACT Association of Christian Teachers
ACCT Association of Church College Trusts
AS Agreed Syllabus
ASC Agreed Syllabus Conference
AT Attainment Target
BECTa British Educational Communications and Technology Agency
BFBS British and Foreign Bible Society
BHA British Humanist Association
BJRE *British Journal of Religious Education*
CEM Christian Education Movement
CTC City Technology College
CULRE Conference of University Lecturers in Religious Education
DES Department of Education and Science
DFE Department for Education
DfEE Department for Education and Employment
EA Education Act
EBD Emotional and Behavioural Difficulties
EFTRE European Forum of Teachers in Religious Education
ERA Education Reform Act
FE Further Education
GCE General Certificate of Education
GCSE General Certificate of Secondary Education
GM Grant-maintained
GNVQ General National Vocational Qualification

HEI Higher Education Institute
ICT Information and Communications Technology
IEP Individual Education Plan
IHE Institution of Higher Education
INSET In-service Education for Teachers
IT Information Technology
ITE Initial Teacher Education
KS Key Stage
LEA Local Education Authority
ME Moral Education
MLD Moderate Learning Difficulties
NASACRE National Association of SACREs
NASEN National Association of Special Educational Needs
NCC National Curriculum Council
NCET National Council for Educational Technology
NGfL National Grid for Learning
NQT Newly Qualified Teacher
NS National Society (Church of England) for Promoting Religious Education
NVF National Values Forum
NVQ National Vocational Qualification
OFSTED Office for Standards in Education
OHP Overhead Projector
PCfRE Professional Council for Religious Education
PGCE Postgraduate Certificate of Education
PRU Pupil Referral Unit
PSE Personal and Social Education
QCA Qualifications and Curriculum Authority
QTS Qualified Teacher Status
RE Religious Education
REC Religious Education Council of England and Wales
RI Religious Instruction
SACRE Standing Advisory Council on Religious Education
SCAA Schools Curriculum and Assessment Authority
SEN Special Educational Needs
SENCO Special Educational Needs Co-ordinator
SLD Severe Learning Difficulties
SMSC Spiritual, Moral, Social and Cultural
TES *Times Educational Supplement*
TTA Teacher Training Agency
WREP Warwick Religious Education Project
WWW World Wide Web

Introduction to the series

This book *Learning to Teach Religious Education in the Secondary School* is one of a series of books entitled *Learning to Teach* (subject) *in the Secondary School: A Companion to School Experience* covering most subjects in the secondary school curriculum. The books in this series support and complement *Learning to Teach in the Secondary School: A Companion to School Experience* (Capel, Leask and Turner, first edition 1995, second edition 1999). These books are designed for student teachers learning to teach on different types of initial teacher education courses and in different places. However, it is hoped that they will be equally useful to tutors and mentors in their work with student teachers. In 1997 a complementary book was published entitled *Starting to Teach in the Secondary School: A Companion for the Newly Qualified Teacher* (Capel, Leask and Turner, 1997). That second book was designed to support newly qualified teachers in their first post and covered aspects of teaching which are likely to be of concern in the first year of teaching.

The information in the subject books does not repeat that in *Learning to Teach*, rather, the content of that book is adapted and extended to address the needs of student teachers learning to teach a specific subject. In each of the subject books, therefore, reference is made to *Learning to Teach in the Secondary School*, where appropriate. It is recommended that you have both books so that you can cross-reference when needed.

The positive feedback on *Learning to Teach*, particularly the way it has supported the learning of student teachers in their development into effective, reflective teachers, has encouraged us to retain the main features of that book in the subject series. Thus, the subject books are designed so that elements of appropriate theory introduce each behaviour or issue. Recent research into teaching and learning is incorporated into the text. This material is interwoven with tasks designed to help you identify key features of the behaviour or issue and apply these to your own practice.

Although the basic content of each subject book is similar, each book is designed to address the unique nature of each subject. In this book, for example, the key role of Religious Education within the whole curriculum is given particular attention. Despite its often controversial past outdated perceptions of irrelevance and accusations of indoctrination have gradually given way to an increasing recognition of the important role the subject can play in the personal, social and intellectual development of the whole child. Particular attention is paid to methods of teaching that encourage the emergence of religious literacy and spiritual sensitivity. The controversial aspects of religion are not glossed over, and pupils are encouraged to develop informed responses to both religious and secular belief systems. Special attention is given to the professional development of teachers, with an emphasis on reflective practice and classroom based curriculum development.

We, as editors to the series, have found this project to be exciting. We hope that you find that this book is useful and supports your development into an effective, reflective religious education teacher.

Susan Capel, Marilyn Leask and Tony Turner
September 1999

Introduction: Becoming a Religious Education Teacher

Andrew Wright and Ann-Marie Brandom

Religious Education is flourishing: brash, bold and self-confident. The old assumption that the subject is no more than a missionary wing of the Christian churches is fading fast. Those still subscribing to such a dogma must rely increasingly on memory rather than appeal to current reality in sustaining their argument. Similarly the misplaced reaction against RE as Christian nurture, which led to the reduction of the subject to forms of personal and social education, is itself quickly becoming a thing of the past. Admittedly not without effort, RE has learnt to resist the temptation to replace religion with mere morality The last quarter of a century has seen the emergence of a third way, in the form of a modern RE committed to the integrity of its subject matter and to the professionalism of the task of teaching religion. This book is designed to support PGCE students at secondary level who, recognising the sea change that has swept the subject, have chosen to embark on a professional career as teachers of RE. It is also hoped that it will contain much of value for established professionals.

Learning to Teach Religious Education in the Secondary School takes its place within the Learning to Teach Subjects in the Secondary School series, which has established itself as offering a key range of standard texts for many PGCE courses. RE students using this book are strongly urged to read it in conjunction with the lead book in the series, *Learning to Teach in the Secondary School* (Capel et al. 1995).

THE ART, CRAFT AND CHARISMA OF TEACHING

One popular, though misplaced, view of the teaching profession subscribes to the theory of 'personal charisma'. Good teaching is dependent on the possession of an effervescent personality, able to enthuse and motivate otherwise reluctant pupils. If you embark on your teaching career committed to this particular myth you will find yourself looking up enviously at fellow students who are simply more charismatic than you are, and rather smugly down at those grey colleagues who you know instinctively are not going to make the grade. It is important to ditch this myth at an early stage in your initial teacher education (ITE). Though it possibly contains a fragment of truth it remains ultimately flawed.

The vast majority of good teachers ground their professional credentials not on force of personality but in hard graft. As a student teacher you must learn the craft of the classroom by becoming an apprentice to experienced mentors. The way to establish yourself as a teacher is by the observation and imitation of those who, with years of experience behind them, know how to operate effectively in the classroom.

However, the model of learning to teach as a craft is again only part of the story. Teaching is a profession, and becoming a professional teacher is all about becoming a 'reflective practitioner'. The profession of teaching goes far beyond mere imitation and transcends the mere passing on of traditional wisdom. As a teacher you must become critically aware and responsible in your role, capable of using your insights into the nature of education to take initiatives to develop and transform your practice.

Responsibility for ITE is shared between schools and higher education institutions (HEIs). This partnership reflects an understanding of the teaching profession rooted in the dual models of teaching as a 'craft' and the teacher as 'reflective practitioner'. As a student teacher you must learn both the craft of teaching from your school-based mentors and the art of critical reflection from your HEI tutors. Of course the holistic nature of teaching means that you must also beware of too strong a division of labour here. Your school-based mentor will also help you become a reflective practitioner, and your HEI tutor will help you learn the craft of teaching. Perhaps the key issue is the recognition that craft without reflection, and reflection without craft, will both lead to the diminishing of your competence as an effective RE teacher.

ABOUT 'LEARNING TO TEACH RE'

The contributors to this book have been selected to reflect the ITE partnership between school and HEI, and the crucial balance between craft and reflection. They are all either established and effective classroom teachers of RE with experience of mentoring students, or experienced HEI tutors on PGCE courses. In many cases both roles are combined.

The brief given to each contributor was to support and enhance the teaching and mentoring that takes place on PGCE RE courses by:

- providing a clear and balanced introductory survey of the designated topic of their chapter;
- highlighting those areas of dispute and contention which form the cutting edges of contemporary developments in the subject;
- offering their own specific opinion or slant on their topic so as to encourage critical reading on the part of students.

In setting down these ground rules for contributors we hoped to ensure two things: (1) that you will be provided with clear and balanced introductions to key themes and issues facing the contemporary RE teacher; (2) that at the same time you will be confronted with the need to read the book critically, acknowledging that the particular standpoint of an author does not necessarily reflect any general consensus in the RE world, thereby enhancing the development of your reflective practice.

We have tried to ensure that each chapter is self-contained, and can be read independently, without reference to any other chapter. Inevitably this has led to a limited amount of overlap and repetition. This reflects the pedagogical concept of the spiral curriculum: the notion that we learn not in linear fashion along a straight line, but by constantly spiralling back to a topic at a higher level so as increasingly to develop new insight.

THE STRUCTURE OF THE BOOK

Though each chapter in this book is self-contained there is, nevertheless, a coherent structure and flow to the text as a whole.

Part I: The context of RE

This first part sets out to locate the task of teaching RE at the beginning of the third millennium within its broad educational setting. In Chapter 1, 'The Place of Religious Education in the Curriculum', Linda Rudge maps the contours of the subject's increasingly successful struggle to secure its proper place within the school timetable and generate a sense of its own identity and integrity. In Chapter 2 Fred Hughes considers the place of 'Religious Education in State and Faith Community Schools', underlining the importance of recognising that the increasingly diverse range of types of school available in the UK will both demand and create a plurality of approaches to the teaching of RE.

Part II: Teaching and learning

The second major part takes us to the heart of the pedagogical process: teaching and learning itself. In Chapter 3 Jo Backus offers guidance on the process of preparation and planning for teaching through 'Developing Programmes of Study'. In Chapter 4 Trevor Cooling addresses the process of 'Pupil Learning', paying particular attention to his pioneering model of 'concept cracking' as a means of enabling pupils to grapple effectively with religious questions.

Part III: Classroom issues

Here a range of classroom issues that will inevitably arise once you have become familiar with the context of curriculum and schooling, and begun to learn the craft of teaching and learning, are addressed. Ann-Marie Brandom explores the importance of teaching for religious literacy in Chapter 5, 'The Role of Language in Religious Education'. John Rudge guides us through the minefield of pupil and programme 'Assessment in Religious Education' in Chapter 6. In Chapter 7 Jean Harris reminds us of the importance of attending to the responsibilities of 'Teaching Children with Special Educational Needs'. The third major section of the book concludes with two chapters looking at key stages in secondary RE which present their own range of specific issues: In Chapter 8 Angela Wright and Taira Mohammed explore 'Religious Education at Key Stage 4', paying particular attention to GCSE teaching. Finally Chapter 9 finds Vanessa Ogden unpacking 'Religious Education at 16-plus', and reminding us that there is much more going on here than just A Level studies.

Part IV: RE and the whole school

In this fourth major part we recognise the fact that RE exists only alongside, and in intimate relation with, the broader curriculum of the school. Here three areas of overlap with the educational task facing the whole school are explored. In Chapter 10 Clive and Jane Erricker guide us through an issue that has been more significant than most in recent years: 'Spirituality in the Classroom'. Derek Webster cautions against dismissing the educational value of 'Collective Worship' too lightly in Chapter 11. Finally Andy Angel invites us to take a fresh look at the relationship between 'Religious Education and Moral Education' in Chapter 12.

Part V: Supporting professional development

A PGCE can provide no more than an *initial* teacher education. Learning to teach is an ongoing, indeed lifelong, task. Consequently in this final part we look at ways of supporting and resourcing your professional development, both during your PGCE and beyond. In Chapter 13 Joanne Reed explores the issue of 'Resources for Religious Education'. Andrew Clutterbuck, in Chapter 14, unpacks one of the most significant growth areas in recent years: 'Information and Communications Technology'. Finally in Chapter 15 Joy White offers pearls of wisdom concerning your 'Professional Development' as a reflective practitioner of the craft of teaching religion in future years when your present PGCE course is nothing but a distant memory!

FURTHER READING

Baumann, A.S., Bloomfield, A. and Roughton, L. (1997) *Becoming a Secondary School Teacher*, London: Hodder & Stoughton. Designed to help support PGCE students achieve Qualified Teacher Status, this balanced and practical text is likely to fulfil its intention of helping you 'on that journey from novice to expert'.

Capel, S., Leask, M. and Turner, T. (1995) *Learning to Teach in the Secondary School*, London: Routledge. The indispensable foundation stone of the Learning to Teach series, of which the present book is part.

Watson, B. (1993) *The Effective Teaching of Religious Education*, London: Longman. A balanced and insightful book, and as good a place as any to begin your own exploration of the contours of RE.

Wright, A. (1993) *Religious Education in the Secondary School: Prospects for Religious Literacy*, London: David Fulton. A basic introduction to the key issues facing RE teachers today.

Part I

The context of Religious Education

1 The Place of Religious Education in the Curriculum

Linda Rudge

> No boy or girl can be counted as properly educated unless he or she has been made aware of the fact of the existence of a religious interpretation of life.
>
> (Spens Report, 1938 (Cox and Cairns 1989, p. 5))

> Who said that religion was dead – or that religious education has no part to play in a secular society? Where is this secular society anyway?
>
> (David Pascall, Chair of the NCC, 1992 (Copley 1997, p. 172))

> The Government's aim . . . is to improve the quality of the religious education curriculum.
>
> (Department for Education (DFE 1994a, para.5))

> My dream for the future of RE has to be earthed in answering the challenges of the three Ts – time, teachers and training.
>
> (Ian Wragg, HMI (ret.) (Copley 1998, p. 5))

This chapter begins with an overview of a range of factors influencing the place of RE in the curriculum. It then explores some controversial aspects of RE's development, exemplified by the fact that the subject is both compulsory but optional and local but national. The ownership of RE, the subject's aims and its relationship with religion(s) are noted, as the origins of current realities are explored. The concluding section considers current and future possibilities for RE as it finds a place in the new revised curriculum.

Any review of RE's place in the curriculum has to take account of wider debates about the whole curriculum in state schooling, from the early years of education to (and through) adulthood. The perceived purposes of education affect RE's position. The main focus of the legal framework described in this chapter is RE in the maintained (county) secondary school curriculum in England, with some references to Welsh provision. School collective worship is mentioned, but only as part of RE's history. The chapter explores the maze of structures, people, and their communities, that are intended to support the subject in a variety of different schools. The intention is to reach the centre of the maze, the pupil, and hence the heart of RE.

OBJECTIVES

By the end of this chapter you should:

- understand some of the debates surrounding the purpose of RE and its position in the curriculum;
- be familiar with aspects of Agreed Syllabus construction, and the aims of RE;
- know about the legal requirements which affect RE teachers;
- be able to formulate a justification of RE's place in the school curriculum.

RELIGIOUS EDUCATION: REALITIES AND RUMOURS

RE's place in the curriculum presents new teachers with many possibilities and, inevitably, some problems. Here are five possible aims for the subject, though there are many more possibilities. RE can:

- be an important contributor to personal development, enabling pupils to develop their own beliefs and values, and to consider thoughtfully those of others;
- provide an academic and rigorous way of understanding the world(s) in which we live, introducing pupils to the fascinating realm of rituals, ceremonies, symbols and lifestyles;
- help develop critical thinking and skills of communication and expression, providing a literacy for dealing with religious questions and experiences;
- offer pupils a chance to reflect on the ultimate questions in life, and so open doors to worlds known and unknown;
- stimulate interfaith dialogue and understanding, and offer an interface between the secular and the spiritual.

A tall order? Some, or all, of the above claims for RE may have been why you decided to become an RE teacher. This chapter is not only about RE's place in the curriculum, and how it is kept there, it is also about aims for RE and for RE teachers. As you develop a rationale for the subject, and for your teaching methods, you will need to consider where that rationale has come from, and what alternatives exist.

You also need to be hard-headed about the realities. How is it possible to fulfil any of these aims given the complexity of the task and, if government guidelines are actually met, a mere 5 per cent of curriculum time is available (Dearing 1994)?

Task 1.1 Developing a professional rationale for RE teaching

Before you read any further, think about the question 'What is RE?' During the course of your career you will encounter many definitions and models of RE, and you may find yourself identifying with one or more of them. Despite this diversity most good RE teachers will work with a clear understanding of, and commitment to, their own personal rationale for the subject.

- Look at the five suggested aims of RE outlined above, and try to place them in descending order of importance according to your own developing approach to the subject.
- Are there any possible aims you would like to add to the list?
- Write down a summary of your professional aims as an RE teacher and share your perspectives with those of your colleagues.
- Seal your summary in an envelope and put it in a safe place. In a year's time go back to it and consider how your views have changed.

RE is a comparatively new subject, although it has many ancient and contemporary relatives, such as Theology and Religious Studies. RE was effectively created by teachers and other educators during the period between 1944 and 1988, and it was legally recognised and given its current name by the 1988 Education Reform Act. During those forty-four years it was also officially (if inadvertently) divorced from its partner, collective worship. RE, like all school subjects, continues to evolve and develop, reflecting the changing nature of society and of schooling. In thirty years, between 1945 and 1975, the subject changed (at different speeds in individual schools and regions) from semi-confessional religious instruction, usually based on Christian Bible study, through thematic approaches to social and ethical issues usually addressed from a Christian viewpoint, to a multifaith experience in which pupils became engaged in the phenomenological study of religion(s). After 1975, the year of publication of the ground-breaking Birmingham Agreed Syllabus and its accompanying teacher's handbook *Living Together*, the stage was set for the developments and debates about RE's place in the curriculum described in the rest of this chapter (City of Birmingham Education Committee 1975). By 1988, RE had to be reviewed alongside the dramatic proposals for a state National Curriculum and broader intentions for schooling as a whole.

The Education Reform Act 1988 sets out as the central aim for the school curriculum that it should promote the spiritual, moral, cultural, mental and physical development of pupils and of society, and prepare

> pupils for the opportunities, responsibilities and experiences of adult
> life.
>
> (DFE 1994a, para. 1)

A curriculum is a programme for learning within and across subjects, and outside them. There is a curriculum in each school, and there is a basic formal curriculum that educators, politicians and others refer to in discussions about schools, their purpose and their effects. Part of this basic curriculum is the National Curriculum, another part is RE.

> RE is required to be included, alongside the National Curriculum, in the
> basic curriculum which all maintained schools must provide for their
> registered pupils . . . The special status of RE as part of the basic but not
> National Curriculum is important. It ensures that RE has equal standing
> in relation to National Curriculum subjects within a school's curriculum.
>
> (DFE 1994a, para. 20)

The current realities affecting RE's place in this curriculum are presented below in some detail. The detail is provided so that you can become professionally informed about RE, and be able to deal accurately with rumours which you may encounter. These realities have to be seen as a whole picture; none is fixed for ever, but they are certainly the givens which impact upon the place of the subject, its aims, and its rationale.

The teacher of RE

Teachers of any subject immediately affect its place in the curriculum as perceived by others. Professional standards, combined with personality, values and attitudes send messages about the subject, its aims and content. They affect the religious education of your pupils. The formal standards you have to reach to become a teacher, published by the Teacher Training Agency (TTA) and the Department for Education and Employment (DfEE) in 1997 and revised in 1998, emphasise this central role of the teacher. RE teachers face specific challenges in their training, because the subject is not organised through one set of national Statutory Orders (DfEE 1998a). In certain circumstances, teachers can decline to teach RE (DFE 1994a, paras 141, 144) but as a specialist teacher of the subject your future employers will assume that you will not use that right (DFE 1994a, para. 145).

The pupils, their families and their communities

Attitudes to religion in society inevitably influence attitudes to RE. At a time when secularism, individualism and religious diversity have increased, public and professional perceptions of the subject are often confused and contradictory. Consider the following broad range of opinions: RE should

- teach children to be religious;
- mould them into good Christians;
- teach pupils about religions;
- encourage them to learn from religion(s);
- educate them in religion, or spirituality.

RE can be inspiring, interesting and relevant, but given this broad spectrum of opinion it is not surprising that some of the expectations are not met. Most pupils and teachers can be loosely affiliated to the 'religion of the silent majority': that is, those in society whose religious beliefs and attitudes are often implicit and even invisible, being related primarily to forms of civic and common religion rather than formal religious institutions (Wolffe, in Parsons 1993, p. 309; cf. Rudge 1998a); they too have a share in RE's place in the curriculum. There will, however, be pupils in your lessons who come from families and communities where formalised religious belief and activity are still a central part of life.

Just as teachers have a right not to teach RE, parents and guardians have the right to withdraw their family members (even in sixth-form school education, Years 12 and 13) from all or part of RE (DFE 1994a, para. 44). The withdrawal clauses are theoretically the most damaging challenge to the integrity of RE, and their existence has been questioned in recent years (Copley 1997, p. 207). However, in practice, the number of secondary school withdrawals is very small compared with the total school population. Nevertheless you may find yourself having to deal with a parental request for a child to be withdrawn from your lessons, in which case your school will advise you on the correct procedure.

Task 1.2 Investigating changing attitudes to RE

Identify a group of adults, including if possible colleagues from any subject in your PGCE year, teachers in schools, family, friends and acquaintances. Try to ensure that the group embraces a broad age range capable of reflecting changing attitudes towards the subject.
   Ask each member of your selected sample to:

- recall their own primary or secondary religious education;
- express their attitudes and feelings towards their experiences;
- outline their perceptions of the nature and purpose of contemporary religious education.

Consider the responses as a whole. What patterns emerge? Which issues constantly push themselves centre stage?
   Do the members of your sample have a fair and balanced understanding of your chosen professional role? Or are you misunderstood? Is, in your judgement, your sample typical of public understanding of RE? How should you and your colleagues respond to public perceptions of RE?

Pupils contribute to RE's place in the curriculum by their attitudes and responses to it, and by their use of their religious education in their wider communities. They help mould the identity of RE together with their teachers and their peers. Their lives, and the lives of teachers, are part of the substance of the RE curriculum itself (Copley 1998, p. 39).

The RE department

The department with delegated responsibility for RE usually has a head of department and other staff working with them. Sometimes RE is organised through a Humanities faculty or PSE team. The staff teaching RE will have a range of qualifications and experience, and you must expect to find yourself working alongside non-specialists, some of whom may be unwilling conscripts to the team. The department's schemes of work, the resources it deploys, and the school's internal syllabus for RE, with its interpretation of the local Agreed Syllabus, all affect RE's place in the curriculum of individual schools. Standards in departments across the country will also affect national policy and so help determine RE's future.

> Every school must by law provide religious education and daily collective worship for all its pupils . . . It is a matter of deep concern that in many schools these activities do not take place with the frequency required or to the standards which pupils deserve.
>
> (DFE 1994a, para. 5)

The school

RE takes place in a variety of types of schools, including special schools (DFE 1994a, Annex B). This chapter focuses on state-maintained or 'county' schools, although some of its discussion is relevant to teachers in denominational schools. The place of RE in the secondary school curriculum has to take account of developments in primary education, and standards for Qualified Teacher Status require you to consider issues of continuity and progression in RE. The variety and types of schools have had a complicating effect on these matters. However, reports from the Office of Standards in Education indicate that standards of RE in primary schools have risen, and that Key Stage 3 RE is gradually following the trend (OFSTED 1997). The type of school, its relationship with feeder primary schools, its management and ethos have a far-reaching effect on RE's place in its curriculum.

The RE syllabus

> The 1988 Act requires all syllabuses to reflect the fact that the religious traditions in Great Britain are in the main Christian whilst taking account

of the teaching and practices of the other principal religions represented
in Great Britain.

> (DFE 1994a, para. 31, referring to section 8.3 of ERA 1988)

Religious education in schools should seek: to develop pupils' knowledge,
understanding and awareness of Christianity, as the predominant religion
in Great Britain, and the other principal religions represented in the
country; to encourage respect for those holding different beliefs; and to
help pupils' spiritual, moral, social and cultural development.

> (DFE 1994a, para.16)

RE aims to help pupils to: acquire and develop knowledge and
understanding of Christianity and other principal religions represented in
Great Britain; develop an understanding of the influence of beliefs, values
and traditions on individuals, communities, society and cultures; develop
the ability to make reasoned and informed judgements about religious and
moral issues with reference to principal religions represented in Great
Britain; enhance their spiritual, moral, social and cultural development;
develop positive attitudes towards other people, respecting their right to
hold different beliefs from their own, and towards living in a society of
diverse religions.

> (SCAA 1994a, p. 3)

RE is part of a broader process of education which helps children and
young people to make sense of the world and how they relate to it.

> (Clwyd Agreed Syllabus, 1996, quoted in UEA 1996–99)

It is important to be aware that, apart from the requirement to address Christianity
and other principal religions represented in Britain, there is no stated aim for RE in
national law and no prescribed curriculum content. Unlike subjects in the National
Curriculum, the aims and material content of RE are determined locally. Most
pupils in England and Wales in state education encounter their RE through school
schemes of work based, as the law requires, on locally Agreed Syllabuses, issued by
each Local Education Authority (LEA). There are separate arrangements regarding
the scope and content of RE in controlled, aided and grant-maintained schools
(DFE 1994a, paras 22–3). You will find these dealt with in detail in Chapter 3.

   Historically the legal requirement that RE should be provided for all pupils, from
nursery to tertiary stages of education, has tended to flounder in the face of the
demands of public examinations at Key Stage 4. Many schools struggled to find sufficient curriculum space to enable pupils to follow GCSE RE, thereby consigning
the subject to the graveyard status of a compulsory non-examination subject. A
recent innovation has been the introduction of short courses in RE at GCSE level,
requiring 50 per cent teaching time of a standard GCSE. The first entry in 1997 of
12,244 rose dramatically to 79,291 in 1998 (QCA 1998b). The new short course means
that pupil effort and achievement at Key Stage 4 can now be recognised nationally.

   A syllabus is a tool for planning; its reception by teachers affects the RE of the pupils in individual schools and the place of RE in the curriculum as a whole. Although there are no national Statutory Orders for RE, the relevant clauses in the Education Reform Act, and subsequent legislation and advice (DFE 1994a), have provided a national basis for syllabus development in LEAs. The publication of national Model Syllabuses in RE as advice to LEAs and Standing Advisory Councils on Religious Education (SACREs) (SCAA 1994a, b) was intended to homogenise RE syllabuses around England and Wales, but diversity and variety still dominate the picture, as more LEAs have created their own syllabus rather than adopt those of other LEAs (Keswick Hall RE Centre 1997; UEA 1996–99). When you go into schools, remember that many RE teachers will not have seen these Model Syllabuses.

The majority of Agreed Syllabuses are now saying similar things about RE. It is the way they say it, and the philosophy and education model that underpin the design, that make an Agreed Syllabus distinctive. Some emphasise the importance of spiritual development in their aims and approach, others the exploration and/or systematic study of beliefs and values, and others the opportunities RE provides for pupils to explore, and respond to, religion. Each syllabus either prescribes or offers schools choice concerning which religions are to form the basis of study for the achievement of these aims. Some include detailed schemes of work, programmes of study, attainment targets and assessment procedures, while others are less detailed (DFE 1994a, para. 37).

Although there could be 126 locally Agreed Syllabuses in England and Wales, it has never happened, as local government reviews, SACRE recommendations and local elections mean that syllabuses are always at different stages of development. It was not until 1993 that LEAs were required by law to review their syllabuses to check that they were in line with 1988 legislation and national government advice. Since the 1993 legislation, syllabuses have to be reviewed every five years following their adoption, if not requested to do so sooner by SACRE (DFE 1994a, para. 29).

An LEA adopts a syllabus after taking the advice of an Agreed Syllabus Conference (ASC). An ASC may recommend adopting an existing syllabus from another LEA, choose to revise the syllabus currently in use, or opt to write a new one. The ASC is made up of committees representing various sectors (including religious ones) of the local community, education and local government. The ASC meets only at the direction of an LEA, after a recommendation by its SACRE, and can have an active life ranging from days through months to years. However, its only official function is to recommend a syllabus (DFE 1994a, para. 24). ASC membership is supposed to represent the 'proportionate strength' of religions and denominations (other than the Church of England) in a local area (DFE 1994a, para. 103). Since 1993 representatives of 'belief systems' such as humanism can no longer be included on the committee representing religions or religious denominations (DFE 1994a, para. 104).

The quality of LEA syllabuses is directly affected by the procedures and expertise of this conference. Agreed Syllabuses have an impact on RE in the curriculum both at a national level, via debates about aims and standards, and in each school as teachers use them in their day-to-day planning (UEA 1996–99). The focus in the last decade on the syllabus *content* of RE, on what pupils are to study and learn about, has provided most of the ammunition for a clash of interests and cultures between teachers, educators, faith communities and politicians which is still being resolved (DFE 1994a, paras 31–7).

Task 1.3 Exploring the aims of RE

Collect a sample range of current locally Agreed Syllabuses, the internal syllabuses used in your teaching practice schools, together with the SCAA/QCA Model Syllabuses.

- Identify and record in outline the various aims and objectives set out by these documents.
- Note how the form, structure and language through which the purpose of each syllabus is expressed either differs from, or is similar to, the others.
- Is there any particular set of aims you have encountered that you particularly dislike? Why?
- Is there any particular set of aims you have encountered that you particularly like? Why?
- Does any consensus emerge across the various documents? Are we in a position to identify a common national perception of the nature of RE that transcends local differences? Or are we dealing still with incompatible diversity?

Local government and SACREs

As RE's place in the curriculum is subject to local democratic procedures, and local involvement (including in aided schools), the role of LEAs, and their ability to provide support, are central to RE's position. Local government reviews and elections, and initiatives such as the creation of the grant-maintained (GM) sector (1993) and Education Action Zones (1998) have also affected RE's position.

> Detailed arrangements for the provision of religious education and
> collective worship are properly a matter of local responsibility . . .
> Nevertheless the Government seeks to encourage improved standards and
> secure comparable opportunities for all pupils in non-denominational
> schools.
>
> (DFE 1994a, para. 6)

Since 1988 every LEA has been required to have a SACRE to advise it on aspects of RE and collective worship, and to recommend a review of the LEA syllabus when necessary (DFE 1994a, paras 90–2). The SACRE also receives inspection reports on schools in the LEA area. A SACRE is comprised of four (or five) groups representing similar interests to the ASC, but not necessarily through the same people. Details of the make-up of both SACREs and ASCs are set out in Figure 1.1. SACREs have kept RE on the agendas of Local Education Committees, and some have been forums for interfaith dialogue, and on occasions confrontation. There is now a National Association of SACREs (NASACRE) which has also had some influence in the 1990s. The effects of the existence of SACREs on RE's place in the curriculum have been far-reaching, double edged and controversial. The quality of their activities can support and improve RE, and the position and training of RE teachers. The quality of the relationship between SACRE, schools and teachers is vital, and as an RE teacher you would be well advised to find out more about the SACRE in your local area.

Figure 1.1 Composition of Standing Advisory Councils and Agreed Syllabus Conferences

The following summary of the constitution of SACREs and ASCs post-1993 is summarised from the DFE Circular 1/94, *Religious Education and Collective Worship* (DFE 1994a, paras 103, 105). A SACRE may also include co-opted members who are not members of any of the five groups. There is no provision for an ASC to include co-opted members. A SACRE and an ASC are each comprised of four or five groups or committees representing, respectively:

- Christian denominations and other religions and religious denominations, the number of whose representatives shall, 'so far as consistent with the efficient discharge of the committee's functions, reflect broadly the proportionate strength of that denomination or religion in the area' (paras 111, 112);
- the Church of England;
- such associations representing teachers as, in the opinion of the authority, ought to be represented, having regard for the circumstances of the area;
- the local Education Authority;
- relevant grant-maintained schools.

Central government

> The government also attaches great importance to the role of religious education and collective worship in helping to promote among pupils a clear set of personal values and beliefs. They have a role in promoting respect for and an understanding of those with different beliefs or religious practices from their own, based on rigorous study of the different faiths. This country has a long tradition of religious freedom which should be preserved.
>
> (DFE 1994a, para. 9)

Although RE is organised locally it is national legislation which keeps it there. The Education Reform Act 1988, and subsequent legislation in 1992 and 1993, created an atmosphere of conflict and confusion for RE which is discussed later in the chapter. Wider government policy also affects RE: local government review and reorganisation, educational emphases on school effectiveness, the National Curriculum, management, quality assurance, standards, literacy, numeracy, citizenship and values, etc. The formation of national bodies such as SCAA (now QCA), OFSTED and the TTA has also had various effects on RE standards, and debates about its nature and aims, and key personnel in these organisations, have helped to keep RE on the agenda in wider curriculum developments. The New Labour government of 1997 has not yet made any direct changes in legislation controlling RE, but if RE had been under the control of the Secretary of State, as other subjects are, it might have become an optional part of the reduced primary curriculum in 1998. Its local position protected its very existence. Central government policy and advice and the central organisation of funds to LEAs and subjects have affected the place of RE, and public perceptions of its aims and purpose.

RE associations and professional groups

Although RE in maintained (and aided) schools is designed and implemented locally, the national view of RE is influenced by suggestions (and objections) from teacher associations, teacher trainers, higher education groups, RE associations and charitable trusts. Research projects and curriculum development materials are used by teachers as they experiment with different methods of teaching and learning in RE. It is in this way (through the works of teachers and other educators) that RE in the classroom began to leave behind the religious education legislation of 1944. In some LEAs, where support for RE has been slow to emerge, these commercially produced materials have often been a vehicle for change. Some charitable trusts (for example, Saltley) have entered into informal partnership with SACREs through school RE competitions, or through support for RE training and research (e.g. All Saints Trust, St Gabriel's Trust, the Farmington Institute and the Keswick Hall Trust). The actions of RE associations and professional groups have kept the debate open on RE's place in the curriculum; sometimes they have appeared to be in direct conflict with central (and local) government and advice, but more often they have acted as mediators, filtering the advice to support the teacher in the classroom, and other RE educators.

Religions and religious denominations

The opinions, beliefs and values of members of religious groups and denominations have a direct effect on RE (and indirectly on other subjects) and on RE's position in both local and national legislation and policy. Members of all six major religions (and others) represented in Great Britain have been involved in national working groups, local SACREs and ASCs, and all regularly work in schools. RE's place in the curriculum is endlessly influenced by religion, and by religions, and by public attitudes to both. One challenge facing teachers of the future is how to keep RE relevant to those participants (teachers and pupils) who are not members of the vocal minorities who influence national policy and local syllabuses (Rudge 1998a).

These are some of the current realities facing RE and its teachers. Where they came from is the topic of discussion in the next section of the chapter.

RE: AGENDAS AND OWNERSHIP

The previous section dealt with the givens of the place of RE in the curriculum. The current realities of RE's status will continue unless there is a change in the law. They are the factors that will most immediately affect you as a teacher as you plan your RE, and some of their implications are covered in later chapters of this book. They are necessarily bound up with religious and social history, and the actions, beliefs and opinions of key personnel and groups. (Cf. Copley 1997, Cox and Cairns 1989, Parsons 1993, 1994, for detailed accounts.) You need to consider the following related issues as you develop your rationale for teaching and learning, since RE continues to develop, and you are now part of it.

The 1988 legislation on RE and collective worship arguably showed that RE had been 'there and back again' (Parsons 1994, p.164). Though the subject in the classroom had changed beyond all recognition from the Religious Instruction of 1944, the legislators and their advisers seemed determined to recreate the past. A range of reasons for the continuation of RE's local position have been given:

- a lack of central government interest;
- a fear of change and controversial legislative procedures;
- an appreciation of good practice in local curriculum development;
- the idea that RE really does affect religious belief and commitment, and that pupils in any local area should not be affected too much by the religious beliefs and values of others (Cox and Cairns 1989, p. 25).

The national government in the early 1990s made attempts to influence decisions about RE's content and pedagogy, both through legislation and through advice. Alterations to the composition of SACREs and ASCs (Figure 1.1) were intended to bring local pressure to bear on syllabus development and implementation. Local ASCs, whilst recognising the national picture, were expected to recommend a local form of RE which kept local communities happy, and which would ensure the protection of the majority religion(s). The debates about the role and intentions of the Model Syllabuses published by SCAA (Baumfield *et al.* 1995; Wintersgill 1995) illustrated further central pressures on the local nature of RE, and highlighted the concerns of some about the relative benefits of thematic or systematic teaching in RE.

How had this uneasy situation evolved? The speed and the complexity of change in RE over fifty years, highlighted earlier in this chapter, had given rise to a range of controversial issues. Here we can deal in detail with only three: the nature of the educational enterprise and its aims; the place of Christianity and other religions in RE, and the question of the ownership of the RE curriculum.

RE: nature and aims

Views of the nature and aims of education immediately affect approaches to RE, just as views of religion affect models of the subject. These views of education can be roughly described in three types.

RE as induction into community and culture

First there is a view of education, and therefore of RE, as nurture into communities of culture, beliefs and values. The main aim of RE in this setting is to nurture both the pupil and the wider society into a particular faith, and even into a particular denomination. The 1944 Act sought, implicitly, to nurture children into Christianity, though not into any specific Christian denomination. Contemporary debate now focuses on whether any form of proselytism, regardless of its being illegal in maintained county schools, can ever be genuinely effective. A counter-argument views all education as a type of nurture or indoctrination, and claims that RE teachers are inevitably engaged in nurturing the faiths of pupils in the class since they are certainly not aiming to destroy them. Teachers can also be seen as bolstering interest in religious perspectives on life in an increasingly secular world. Of all the approaches to RE, teachers (of all subject backgrounds, primary and secondary) feel most nervous about nurture. It has problems of relevance and credibility in the classroom, and appears to fly in the face of equal opportunities and anti-racist policies. Many RE teachers with a strong commitment to a religion recognise the need for objectivity and distance in the way they handle material and plan lessons; all teachers of all backgrounds, religious or not, should be prepared to do the same.

RE as the liberal study of religion

The second model of education may be described as liberal, and even utilitarian, education in which the teacher tries to become the mediator of controversial material and opinions by adopting a distanced neutral stance, and developing in pupils the skill and ability to use knowledge and understanding to make well informed judgements. This leads to an approach to RE which may be termed 'studies of religion(s)'. Its commitment to religion itself and an attitude of openness makes it the approach with which most RE teachers feel most comfortable. It is essentially focused on 'out there' and not 'in here', and on 'them', not 'me'. One of its main aims is to promote respect for religion, and for the human right to belong to different religions. The problem, of course, lies in the practical classroom reality. There is no such thing as the neutral teacher, although we all aim for neutrality at times. The selection of material and methods of teaching immediately betray interests and preferences. Dialogue and body language in the classroom reveal prejudices and even well informed likes and dislikes. Pupils can become experts in the minutiae of religious practice, and yet ignorant of the wider value of encountering beliefs. 'What is religion?' and 'What or who constitutes religions?' are basic questions that are rarely addressed (Jackson 1997). This approach may account for the success of AT1, 'Learning about Religion', as set out in the SCAA Model Syllabuses in RE, as well as explaining the less influential role of AT 2, 'Learning from Religion' (OFSTED 1997).

RE as an agent of humanisation

The third model primarily views education as humanising concern. It addresses the 'whole' person, and is concerned with issues of justice as well as respect, and with empowerment as well as community. The aims of RE in such an education are concerned with how we educate pupils to grow and develop spiritually through reference to, and the expression of, religion in general rather than any one religion in particular. Knowledge of religion is the instrument, not the goal (Grimmitt 1987), and an RE of this kind has to take full account of secular world views (Bolton, in Copley 1998, p. 21). It also has to consider the uncomfortable fact that theologies and religious philosophies may be constraining as well as emancipating, illiberal as well as liberal (Wright 1998b). It is essentially a reflective approach to RE based on rigorous and affective study, but it also implies a critique of religion and religions. Once again, the pitfalls lie in the translation of theory into practice. With only 5 per cent of curriculum time, perceived pressures of assessment and recording and a large number of classes and pupils to deal with each week, many secondary RE teachers find themselves appreciating the theory, and avoiding it in practice. Others find the notion of a critical stance in RE inherently unsettling.

   In reality pupils in both primary and secondary schools will receive their RE from a range of professionals who combine aspects of all three approaches and their related rationales. You may find yourself using all three in your classroom at different times. The current truce in RE between the advocates of the different approaches is exemplified by the twin idea of *learning about* and *learning from* religion(s). This phrase, explored fully by Grimmitt, now appears in shorthand form in many Agreed Syllabuses and in the SCAA models as attainment targets (Grimmitt 1987). The way it is now used is superficially helpful, but open to question and incomplete in itself.

The place of Christianity, and of other religions, in the curriculum

The second issue highlighted at the beginning of this section concerned the place of different religions in RE. Christianity, defined by the 1988 Conservative government as the 'predominant' religion in Great Britain, became both a defender of RE against the prospect of its disappearance under the National Curriculum and the villain of the piece, used as a stick with which to beat RE teachers for promoting relativity and confusing the pupils. The last decade has been dominated by debates about content: which religions, when, and how much? The debates became so entrenched that a point was reached where the draft Model Syllabuses attempted to attach a percentage of time to each religion over the whole curriculum. Fortunately this self-defeating idea was abandoned, but not before its divisive effects had been felt in the media coverage of RE at the time, and in SACRE meetings around Britain. The politics and theologies which presented a view of religions as separate and different raised questions about the meaning of the word *integrity* as applied to religions in the context of RE. A religious education which somehow blurred the edges of religions and allowed pupils to consider the commonality of some religious beliefs was viewed by some as the reckless promoter of religious syncretism.

Critics of multifaith RE who presented it in public debate as an 'incoherent mish-mash', creating contamination between faiths, and a 'mess of secular pottage' were challenged by John Hull, Professor of Religious Education at Birmingham University (1991, p. 9). He argued that those who opposed multifaith RE chose to present themselves and their beliefs as requiring separateness and space in order to avoid contamination and maintain their individual holiness. Hull proposed an alternative way of considering the holiness and integrity of faiths.

> In myself, I am not particularly holy, and perhaps in yourself you are not wonderfully holy, but the ground between us is holy. The boundary which separates shall become the holy ground, the common ground, the mutuality of response and responsibility which makes us truly human.
>
> (Hull 1991, p. 38)

Transferring this radical approach into the classroom means that the RE teacher chooses material and methods which present religious beliefs and traditions with integrity. Pupils are encouraged to respond to them with similar integrity. A great deal has been written and said about the integrity of faiths in the RE classroom, little about the integrity of RE teachers and, more important, their pupils. Whose RE is it anyway?

Ownership of RE's purpose and agenda

The last issue is about ownership of RE's purpose and agenda. It is linked with the question about the position of religions in RE, and it is contentious and complicated. Is RE 'owned' by professional educators, by the religious communities or by politicians and their advisers? Is shared ownership feasible in the future? It has certainly been difficult in the past. Religious groups play an important role in defending and developing RE, but there are times when teachers feel as if religion is trying to own RE, and to control their professional freedoms. The compilation and publication of the SCAA National Faith Working Group reports intended to inform and accompany the Model Syllabuses was a courageous and innovative move, already tried with some success by some LEAs (e.g. the 1994 Lancashire Agreed Syllabus). These reports have been used by ASCs around England and Wales to resolve questions about what should be taught about each faith, and when, in terms of planning across the Key Stages. Although educators were involved in their compilation, these reports are effectively a blueprint for the content of RE *as approved by faith communities*.

The essence of these three related issues for RE lies in our collective and individual views of religion. Religion can be defined in various ways, and sometimes religions do not appreciate being defined by education. However, religions affect all of us, they are part of the common heritage of humanity, and if the nature of education is to be concerned with human development, religion is a matter both for educational concern and for educational enhancement. Of course, this raises the question 'What is religion?'

Ninian Smart (1973) argued that it can be answered in two stages. His method has been widely influential in developing the Study of Religions approach to RE. First, you can describe religions using categories drawn largely from anthropology and sociology which may then be applied to any one religion or to all. Second, you can describe religion as a way of answering *religious* or *ultimate* questions faced by individuals and by humanity as a whole. These questions are about life, death, meaning, purpose and value, and they are central to the notion of RE as an agent of humanisation. Education should be concerned with *being, having* and with *meaning* rather than mere *information* (cf. Elliot, in Rudduck 1995, p. 65).

If RE has anything to do with addressing the issues of the nature of religion and of existence then it has to address both parts of Smart's answer, not just the first. It must consequently seek to find more answers, and recognise that it is not the only subject that does so. RE does not own religion in the curriculum, and the religions certainly do not own RE.

RE: CULTIVATING HUMANITY

In 1998, ten years after RE's legal re-creation, the real process of RE development is going on, as always, elsewhere. In classrooms during every school day, pupils are both receiving and contributing to their religious education. Debates about ownership and agendas for RE no doubt will continue, and will cause still more division, compromise and change. This section of the chapter is looking at the future, on the assumption that the future is already with us. As you start your RE teaching you will discover the reality of the *nowness* of RE. Beliefs and values, religious or not, permeate every classroom community: RE is not happening in isolation.

The wider purposes of current legislation cannot be ignored when considering RE's future place in the curriculum: schools are expected to contribute to the spiritual, moral, social and cultural (SMSC) development of pupils. For example, if spiritual development has to do with the acquisition and application of spiritual wisdom, regardless of age and intellect, then RE certainly has a wealth of material and experiences to contribute wisdom (Rudge 1998b; Elliott, in Rudduck 1995, p. 67). The present interest in citizenship and values is a direct result of the SMSC debates, and RE's contribution to these cross-curricular issues is valued and recognised by some, though denigrated by others (Teece 1998). Analysing and measuring that contribution is not easy, or even appropriate, but schools and RE departments have been pressed to address them fully through inspection and advice. How does RE make a difference to the development of personal identity?

Internationally, RE in the UK is regarded with a mixture of curiosity, incredulity and admiration. Its positive achievements, especially as a major contributor to the field of multicultural education and interfaith dialogue are well known. To those looking in from the outside the fact that RE is still here is astonishing. Historical precedent, tangled legislation, pressure groups and professional commitment certainly protect its position, but that does not necessarily explain why religious components of state schooling persist in Britain. Elsewhere it is either handled at a distance through denominational schooling, by visitors to schools providing voluntary supplementary education to pupils from specific communities, or by complete banishment from state classrooms. Perhaps RE is there in the curriculum to inoculate the population against the worst excesses of religion? What would the British curriculum, and British society, look like without RE? Where, and how, would religion be encountered? Can you learn from religion without a structured form of learning about it?

Establishing a rationale for RE is important, and as we have seen there is more than one rationale. To do so for any subject requires making some idealistic claims, and those listed at the beginning of this chapter may appear to you to be daunting, or even impossible, in the light of what you have subsequently read. However, ideals are important, and though reality only rarely lives up to them, what has been described as the 'dumbing down' of the RE of future generations is not the answer (Bigger 1998). Religious literacy, religious knowledge, religious spirituality, religious understanding, religious dialogue, religious reflection – all are part of the RE curriculum. RE's place in the whole curriculum is to provide a school-based education through religion that, however limited, will contribute to any person's continuing and developing humanity.

Your role as the teacher should never be underestimated in RE's curriculum development. You are facing one of the central challenges of education, that of co-creation of learning with pupils, and the particular brand of RE you create will be unique (Wright 1993, p. 106). Whatever the syllabus you are using, you will select material as a stimulus to learning and your pupils will respond to it. Clear aims, manageable objectives and rational principles create memorable and sensitising RE. *What* you present to pupils, *how* you jointly use it and *why* you are doing so are the key principles of planning.

It seems possible that the curriculum of the future may try to reinvent a liberal education with a cutting edge, one that cultivates humanity (Nussbaum 1997): it may seek to provide an opportunity for an education in the emotions as well as the intellect, and a focus on critical reasoning; it may be an education that is concerned with social justice, seeking to empower teachers, and emancipate learners; more than that, it may be an education which places people, not subjects, at its heart.

> The essence of emancipation, as I conceive it, is the intellectual, moral and spiritual autonomy which we recognise when we eschew paternalism and the rule of authority and hold ourselves obliged to appeal to judgement. Emancipation rests not merely on the assertion of the right of the person to exercise intellectual, moral and spiritual judgement, but upon the passionate belief that the virtue of humanity is diminished in man when judgement is overruled by authority.
>
> (Lawrence Stenhouse, quoted in Rudduck 1995, p. 6)

Teachers of RE, including new ones, are an important part of this reinvention. You may like to look at Bolton's aims for RE teachers, which encapsulate the real possibilities for the future, challenging us to resist, to enable, to empower and to develop (Copley 1998, p. 21). We need to agree to differ about the detail of RE, and to focus our attention on the heart of the matter, namely the classroom relationship between teacher and pupils and the encounter they share with religious, and other, world views. We can then ensure that RE's place in the curriculum becomes essential for future generations. As we reinforce a religious education for *being and becoming*, whilst acknowledging the curriculum for *knowing and having*, teachers and pupils together will continue to lead the way across the sacred and secular ground of RE.

Task 1.4 RE and values

The extract below is from a draft of *Guidance for Schools: The Promotion of Pupils' Spiritual, Moral, Social and Cultural Development* (QCA 1997, p. 35). The values that underpin the document were compiled by the National Forum for Values in Education and the Community between 1996 and 1997. Note the overlapping period between two different national governments.

Society
We value truth, freedom, justice, human rights, the rule of law and collective effort for the common good. In particular we value families as sources of love and support for all their members, and as a basis of a society in which people care for others.

On the basis of these values we should
- understand and carry out our responsibilities as citizens;
- refuse to support values or actions that may be harmful to individuals and communities;
- support families in raising children and caring for dependants;
- support the institution of marriage;
- recognise that the love and commitment required for a secure and happy childhood can also be found in families of different kinds;
- help people to know about the law and legal processes;
- respect the rule of law and encourage others to do so;
- respect religious and cultural diversity;
- promote opportunities for all;
- support those who cannot, by themselves, sustain a dignified lifestyle;
- promote participation in the democratic process by all sectors of the community;
- contribute to, as well as benefit fairly from, economic and cultural resources;
- make truth, integrity, honesty and goodwill priorities in public and private life.

Which material and appropriate teaching styles would you select for an RE unit of six hours in Year 9 in order to promote these values in the context of the SMSC development of pupils? Should RE 'promote' them? What problems and contradictions do they present? Are they helpful to teachers and pupils? In other words, what is your rationale for the unit's design?

SUMMARY AND KEY POINTS

The place of RE in the curriculum is dependent upon legislation, official organisations, communities and people. RE is both compulsory yet optional and local yet national. The realities facing RE in the 1990s can appear complicated and daunting; they have arisen through the relationship between religion(s) and education, and through the speed of social, economic and cultural change in the last fifty years. The issues for RE which have emerged since 1944 are concerned with the position and appropriate aims of RE in a changing educational system, the place of Christianity and other principal religions in RE, and questions about the ownership and agendas of the RE curriculum. As a teacher you should be aware of the need to consider and reconsider your own rationale for RE, and your professional contribution to its place in the curriculum. RE is concerned with learning about religion, learning from religion and learning *through* religion. The encounter between teachers, pupils and world views is the key to effective and affective RE in a whole curriculum which seems to be moving again towards an education for *being and becoming*, and the cultivation of humanity.

FURTHER READING

Copley, T. (1997) *Teaching Religion: Fifty Years of Religious Education in England and Wales*, Exeter: University of Exeter Press. A useful, very readable and informative review of the period in question, using a range of historical evidence, including source material from politicians.

Copley, T. (ed.) (1998) *RE Futures: A Reader in Religious Education*, Derby: PCfRE/St Gabriel's Trust. A report on a series of seminars between 1995 and 1997 convened by the then chairperson of PCfRE, Jeremy Taylor. Thought-provoking and designed to raise questions by teachers and other educators.

Cox, E. and Cairns, J.M. (1989) *Reforming Religious Education: The Religious Clauses of the 1988 Education Reform Act*, London: Kogan Page. Important source of interpretations of the Act immediately after its appearance from educators and others representing different religious, and other, world views. An interesting source now, as its predictions are as fascinating, with hindsight, as its analyses of the period between 1944 and 1988.

Department for Education (1994) *Religious Education and Collective Worship*, Circular 1/94, London: HMSO. If you really want to understand the complexities of Conservative policy on RE and worship, you will have to read the whole thing. This is the key document of the last decade.

Hull, J. (1998) *Utopian Whispers*, Derby: CEM. A collection of editorials from the *British Journal of Religious Education* focusing particularly on government legislation and the politics of religious education.

Parsons, G. (ed.) (1993) *The Growth of Religious Diversity: Britain from 1945* I, *Traditions*, London: Open University/Routledge.

Parsons, G. (ed.) (1994) *The Growth of Religious Diversity: Britain from 1945* II, *Issues*, London: Open University/Routledge.
Written as course material for OU course A231, these two volumes contain accounts and analyses of the social, religious and cultural changes in Britain during the last fifty years. Excellent background reading to the development of RE, and detailed information about religions in Britain today.

2 Religious Education in State and Faith Community Schools

Fred Hughes

This chapter aims to introduce you to the broad context in which RE takes place, in particular the system of schooling in England and Wales. It first describes the dual system of partnership between the state and a variety of faith communities in terms of the provision of schooling, focusing especially on the various types of school and their historical background. It goes on to outline the current legal requirements for RE and collective worship, as well as the current school inspection arrangements in these two areas of the curriculum. The next major section considers some of the available approaches to RE, particularly the relation between 'open' and 'confessional' RE in the context of state and faith community schools. The final part of the chapter explores the relationship between education, nurture and indoctrination against the background of the dual system.

OBJECTIVES

By the end of this chapter you should:
- understand some of the differences between religious education in state and faith community schools;
- have clarified your understanding of the concepts 'education', 'indoctrination' and 'nurture';
- have formed a professional opinion regarding the state schooling/faith schooling debate.

THE DUAL SYSTEM: STATE AND FAITH COMMUNITY SCHOOLS

In England and Wales the context of RE is dominated by the dual system of partnership between the state and various faith communities, in which both work
together to provide primary and secondary education for all children. We begin by
looking at the various types of school you are likely to encounter in your career. We
must take a little time with this, since at present the situation is undergoing considerable change. After that we will unpack some of the historical background of contemporary schooling as it relates to RE.

Types of contemporary schools

There is a diverse range of different types of contemporary schools. Though the situation is fluid, with changes frequently being implemented, much of the basic terminology arises from the Education Act of 1944 (HMSO 1944).

The main division is between *maintained* schools funded mostly through public
funds, for example local and central taxation, and *independent* schools, which are
mostly financed privately, for example through fees and scholarships. Over 90 per
cent of school-age children in Britain attend maintained schools.

Schools in the maintained sector may be divided into five major groups:

- county/community schools;
- grant-maintained schools;
- City Technology Colleges;
- voluntary controlled schools;
- voluntary aided schools.

County schools are in the main established and operated by Local Education Authorities (many of them County Councils, hence the name). Most *grant-maintained*
schools are former county schools that opted out of the control of the LEA in order
to achieve a greater measure of autonomy and self- government, and which receive
most of their funding direct from central government. The relatively few *City Technology Colleges* are specialist schools set up to foster excellence in certain areas of the
curriculum.

There are various types of *voluntary* school. These are schools founded by a charitable organisation, frequently but not exclusively a church in the form of a Dioce-
san Board of Education. Here funding and control are shared in a partnership
between public and private charitable funds: as a rule of thumb the local authority
pays for the day-to-day upkeep of the schools, including staff wages, while the charity contributes to more basic costs such as capital building projects. Most of these,
especially in the primary sector, are *voluntary controlled* schools, where much of
the control in the partnership passes from the charity to the LEA. In the case of
voluntary aided schools the founding body retains most of the control but receives
financial aid from public funds. In voluntary aided schools the foundation body has

a majority on the governing body, but such is not the case with voluntary controlled schools.

Most of these voluntary schools are Christian church schools of either Church of England (Anglican) or Roman Catholic foundation, though a few involve other denominations such as Methodists. The most significant non-Christian voluntary schools were founded and are now run by the Jewish community. A recent and highly significant innovation by the New Labour government has been the extension of voluntary status to what were previously private schools rooted in religious traditions other than Christianity and Judaism.

The foundation bodies of voluntary schools retain a high level of control over their admission policies. Because the Church of England is the established national church, it has been committed to providing schools for the whole community rather than simply for its church community alone. Where Church of England schools are oversubscribed, links with the church may be a factor in admission policy, but many Church of England schools operate an open admission policy, opening their gates to all pupils in the local community whose parents want them to attend. This has led to the odd situation of a number of Anglican schools in which the pupil community is predominantly Muslim. Roman Catholic and Jewish schools, by contrast, have tended to see their role in terms of service to their specific religious communities. These schools have generally tended not to be for everyone in the local community. It is not always so, but generally a key aim has been to provide an appropriate Roman Catholic or Jewish education in a religious community school for every child from families that belong to that particular religious community.

The picture, however, is being further complicated by the School Standards and Framework Act (HMSO 1998), which required changes in these various types of school. From September 1999 county schools became *community* schools while voluntary aided and voluntary controlled schools retained their status. However, voluntary and community schools have the option of changing category from September 2000. Grant-maintained schools have the option of becoming voluntary or *foundation* schools.

Though these changes are taking place in 1999–2000 it is likely that the old titles will remain in use, at least in popular parlance, for some time to come. It is for this reason that both the old and the new systems have been described here. A summary of a rather complex situation is provided in Figure 2.1.

The historical background

A short historical overview can help readers understand how the present situation has developed. The first schools in Britain were not county schools maintained by the state. Rather they were founded and maintained by the churches and are traditionally known as *independent* schools because they were founded independently of government organisations. They have sometimes been closely associated with cathedrals. Examples are King's School, Canterbury, established in or about 598, and St Peter's School, York, established in or about 625.

The church continued to be the main provider of schools until the twentieth

Figure 2.1 Changes in school designations from 1999/2000

Type of school up to August 1999	Changes in 1999 and 2000
County school	Community school
Voluntary aided school	Voluntary aided school
Voluntary controlled school	Voluntary controlled school (likely)
	Voluntary aided school (possible)
Grant-maintained school	Voluntary aided school (likely)
(if formerly voluntary aided)	Voluntary controlled school (possible)
	Foundation school (possible)
Grant-maintained school	Voluntary controlled school (likely)
(if formerly voluntary controlled)	Voluntary aided school (possible)
	Foundation school (possible)
Grant-maintained school	Foundation school (likely)
(if formerly county)	Community school (possible)
City Technology College	City Technology College

century, but the foundations of the present dual system of public education, grounded in partnership between church and state, were laid in the nineteenth century. Though the independent schools established by the churches became equated historically with a class-bound educated elite, the churches increasingly poured funds into schools for children from working-class families. Indeed, the notion of education for all regardless of ability to pay was a vision that originated in the Church of England. It was these schools that the government in the previous century saw fit to contribute to financially. The first government grant for schools was in 1833. It was a grant to the National Society for Promoting the Education of the Poor in the Principles of the Established Church and to the British and Foreign Schools Society, mostly a Nonconformist Protestant movement. The first government grant for Roman Catholic schools was made in 1847.

The state only became a direct provider of schools following the Education Act of 1870. This Act allowed the establishment of *Board* schools, later to become county schools, alongside the flourishing voluntary church schools. The Education Act 1902 allowed voluntary schools to be supported from the rates.

The Hadow Report of 1926 recommended that separate senior schools should be provided for all pupils, thus introducing the distinction between primary and secondary education that remains today. Previously pupils attended a single *elementary* school before finishing school or moving on to Higher Education. The Church of England found it difficult to fund enough separate senior (secondary) schools. This was one matter which the Education Act 1944 sought to address, making the state the major post-war provider of new secondary schools. The dual system continued throughout the twentieth century but in the main with the state sector increasing and the voluntary sector diminished.

The long involvement of the church in education partly explains the continuing involvement of the churches, for example their membership of Standing Advisory Councils for Religious Education and Agreed Syllabus Conferences. Also the long-standing involvement of the churches in the provision of education partly explains the continuing place of RE and collective worship in schools, and the next section indicates the current legal position.

THE LEGAL FRAMEWORK

The legal requirements for RE

County/community schools

The position in the new community schools (county schools prior to September 1999) is as follows.

- The Education Act 1944 required Religious Instruction (RI) to be provided for all registered pupils at maintained schools. The Education Reform Act 1988 adopted the term *Religious Education* rather than RI, reflecting what had become common usage in most schools.
- RE must be provided for all registered pupils, though parents have a legal right to withdraw their children from it should they choose to do so.
- Every LEA must adopt an Agreed Syllabus for RE which is to be followed by all community schools in the area administered by the authority.
- The Agreed Syllabus must 'reflect the fact that the religious traditions of Great Britain are in the main christian whilst taking account of the teaching and practices of the other principal religions represented in Great Britain' (HMSO 1988, Section 8.3).
- The RE delivered through the Agreed Syllabus 'shall not include any catechism or formulary which is distinctive of any particular religious denomination' (HMSO 1944, Section 26; HMSO 1988, Section 8.2).

Voluntary controlled and aided schools

RE in voluntary controlled schools should follow the local Agreed Syllabus, but parents can request it to be in accordance with the school's trust deed or previous school practice. RE in voluntary aided schools is in accordance with the trust deeds or previous practice in the school, though if they wish parents can ask for RE to be in accordance with the local Agreed Syllabus. Parents' requests for the RE given to their children to be other than the norm for the school must be granted if the governors think it reasonable.

RE in voluntary schools often has a distinctive character, reflecting their specific religious foundation. There is often an emphasis on giving RE good resources, both in terms of curriculum time and in terms of funding for the purchase of learning materials.

The content of RE will tend to follow closely the school's specific religious foundation, Christian, Islamic, Jewish, etc. In church schools, for example, the content of RE is mostly Christian, often linked with the church calendar, based on festivals such as Advent, Christmas, Easter and Whitsun. Often there are strong links between RE and collective worship. The voluntary school will probably be highly committed to both RE and worship and see them both as contributing to the same aims, so there may be no desire to keep the two separate from one another.

Many voluntary schools maintain strong links with their local faith community and place of worship. This can mean that the local clergy or religious leaders are frequently in school, to lead collective worship and sometimes to teach RE. Some clergy are on governing bodies and may spend time in school working informally with staff and pupils, and sometimes parents. Some voluntary schools take pupils to the local place of worship in connection with RE or for special school services, for example a service of Christmas carols, a leavers' service or a harvest festival. Some church schools provide opportunities for pupils and teachers to receive holy communion in school.

Many voluntary schools try to provide a distinctive ethos, partly through making the symbols of their faith visible in the school entrance, in the hall or in classrooms. Most voluntary schools are open in their encouragement of religious faith and commitment, though many are sensitive to suggestions of indoctrination or unfair persuasion. This ethos and acceptance of nurture with integrity can provide a context in which RE can be distinctive in the ways indicated.

Whilst most voluntary schools will tend in the main to draw pupils from their own faith communities, many Anglican schools are aware of a mission to serve the local community and recognise that many of their pupils belong to other faith traditions. In this situation, the importance of respect and tolerance is normally stressed without playing down the specific commitment of the school's foundation. Here RE lessons are likely to be multifaith in content.

Taken together, these features can give RE in voluntary schools a somewhat different style from that in schools without a religious foundation. This is not, of course, to suggest that those schools never take pupils to places of worship, never have visiting clergy and tend to provide relatively little curriculum time and meagre resources for RE. It is partly, but not entirely, a matter of degree.

Grant-maintained/community schools

Grant-maintained schools were established following the Education Reform Act 1988. They could follow the Agreed Syllabus of the Local Authority area in which the school is situated, but could also chose to adopt an Agreed Syllabus from a different area. The changes brought about by the new legislation reduce the options for choice. Grant-maintained schools that revert to voluntary status will need to step into line with the practice of such schools, outlined above. Grant-maintained schools which elect to become community schools will be able to use only the Agreed Syllabus of the local authority, though they will be allowed some years in which to make any necessary changes.

City Technology Colleges

Most City Technology Colleges follow the same track as grant-maintained schools in terms of Agreed Syllabuses available to them. However, some, sponsored by the Church of England, have voluntary status as regards their RE provision.

Independent schools

Independent schools do not have to follow any Local Authority Agreed Syllabus for RE. Some independent schools have collaborated in the production of a religious education syllabus, then used them in a number of these schools (Central Subject Panel for Religious Studies 1994).

The legal requirements for collective worship

The complex question of collective worship is investigated in Chapter 11. Here you are offered merely a brief summary to ensure that your initial orientation is correct.

The Education Act 1944 required the school day in every county and voluntary school to begin with collective worship, involving all registered pupils unless withdrawal had been requested by their parents. All pupils in each school had to be assembled together for the purpose unless the school premises made it impracticable to do so.

The Education Reform Act 1988 continued to require collective worship to be daily but it removed the requirement for the worship to be at the start of each day and for all pupils in each school to be gathered together. This means that the worship can now take place at the start of a day or later, and that there can be a single act of worship for all pupils or worship in different groups formed by age or for teaching or some other school activity.

The 1944 Act did not stipulate that the worship had to be Christian, though at the time this was assumed, as it was for RE too. However, the 1988 Act was more explicit about the nature of the worship in county schools: collective worship in county schools 'shall be wholly or mainly of a Christian character' (HMSO 1988, Section 7.1). Such worship will be of Christian character if 'it reflects the broad traditions of Christian belief, without being distinctive of any particular denomination' (7.2). However, not every act of worship need be wholly or mainly of a Christian character 'provided that, taking any school term as a whole, most such acts which do take place do comply' (7.3). Section 12 of the legislation established a procedure through which county schools can obtain a 'determination' that daily worship for specified pupils need not be Christian collective worship. This is applicable in cases where the family background of pupils makes Christian worship inappropriate.

Collective worship in voluntary schools can be in the tradition of the religion or denomination which founded the school.

The legal requirements for school inspection

All maintained schools (community, voluntary, foundation) are inspected by the Office for Standards in Education (OFSTED). An impending OFSTED inspection will dominate the life of your school, and you will have to ensure that you are properly prepared for it. Like any inspection, it can be a strenuous process.

The legal basis for it came mainly from the Education (Schools) Act 1992 and the School Inspections Act 1996 (HMSO 1992, 1996). When community schools are inspected, RE is inspected along with all other subjects in the curriculum. Among aspects included in the inspection are the quality of the teaching, the achievements and progress of the pupils, and the extent to which the RE meets the requirements of the relevant Agreed Syllabus. Collective worship is also inspected: for example, the degree to which it meets legal requirements and contributes to pupils' spiritual and moral development.

Voluntary schools are inspected under Section 10 of the 1996 Act, but Section 23 deals with the inspection of aspects of the school which are conducted in accordance with the school's trust deed. In voluntary aided schools this includes RE, collective worship, the ethos of the school and the contribution these make to the spiritual and moral education of pupils. In voluntary controlled schools this includes worship but not usually RE. With inspections carried out under Section 23 the governors are responsible for appointing the inspector. Otherwise OFSTED oversees the appointment of inspection teams. The reason for the different arrangements has to do with the special nature of voluntary schools, in which the modern distinction between education and religious nurture is not always sharply drawn, hence the need for inspectors with specialist expertise and training.

APPROACHES TO RE

RE is not the same wherever it is found. It varies. Some of the variety is indicated by the qualifying words which are often attached to the words 'Religious Education'. There are 'confessional RE', 'experiential RE', 'interpretative RE', 'multifaith RE', 'open RE', to name just a few (Hammond *et al.* 1990; Jackson 1997). These descriptions do not identify entirely separate understandings of RE. Rather, some overlap or intersect, as we shall see. The variety has arisen for various reasons. It is partly because schools have different ideas about what they are trying to do. It is prompted partly by trends and developments in society, which influence education, including religious education. Another reason is that teachers search for RE that pupils find interesting and relevant.

Task 2.1 Analysing approaches to RE

Find two or three RE tasks given to pupils – for example, by observing a lesson, examining a textbook or a pupil's RE book. Write your reaction to these tasks in terms of how demanding, interesting and appropriate they were for the pupil(s) concerned. What were the intended learning outcomes of the tasks?

RE in the state sector

The different types of RE are sometimes controversial. One influential document, published in 1971, described the view of RE held by the Roman Catholic church and some Jews, Muslims and Protestants as 'confessional' or 'dogmatic' because they saw the role of RE as to inculcate and perpetuate their religious beliefs. A more 'undogmatic' approach they regarded as 'the educational approach' (Schools Council 1971). In general this 'open' or 'educational' approach is linked with RE in the 'state sector', that is, in county, community and foundation schools.

Open RE

The British Humanist Association has promoted 'open' RE for some time (BHA 1975). At its best 'open' RE recognises that religious matters are controversial in society. It seeks to respect the variety of backgrounds from which pupils come. It wants to help them as they reflect on their own beliefs and values. This kind of RE does not prescribe the conclusions pupils should come to through their search. It is more 'open' than that.

Open RE is preferred by some partly on the grounds that it properly reflects the varied and controversial nature of the religions in British society. They are conscious that during the twentieth century there was a decline in church attendance and in the extent of the power and influence of the churches in British life. They do not think that a rounded or whole education can omit learning about and from religions, but neither do they believe that RE should seek to secure commitment to Christianity or any other particular religion. This view accepts that RE should follow trends in society. Britain became more multifaith in the 1970s largely because many immigrants practise a religion other than Christianity. This was soon seen as a good reason for pupils studying several different religions in school.

Also, because society as a whole is unsure about where the truth lies in matters of religion, its RE should reflect that openness or uncertainty. This open RE has to include the exploration of several religions. To restrict the content to one religion would be to limit openness, if not to avoid it. Though the legislation for England does not stipulate the religions to be studied in community schools, it has been widely accepted that six religions should be included, namely Buddhism, Christianity, Hinduism, Islam, Judaism and Sikhism (SCAA 1994a, b).

Another reason why some people wish to foster 'open' RE is that they think it gives the pupils appropriate dignity as human beings and particularly as vulnerable young people. This view emphasises that RE must be open, so that all pupils are free to respond as they wish. The pupils come from a variety of backgrounds – some religious, some not, and with varying intensity. Some are trying to find their own way, which sometimes means facing the tricky question of how much to depart from the views held by family members. Being sensitive to the position of pupils means providing an 'open' RE, one in which there will be no assumptions about the conclusions pupils will come to, if any.

To many people this kind of RE is very appropriate for community schools. If you wish to teach this kind of RE you need not be personally practising a particular religion, though if you do have a commitment in one particular religion you are not disqualified provided you accept the value of teaching several religions in a fair, accurate and balanced way.

Open RE should not be mistaken for a 'neutral' kind of RE. It is certainly not neutral with regard to all values. The open approach values the recognition of variety in religion. It also values the dignity of pupils, with the opportunities and responsibilities they have as they review and develop their own convictions. When we remember that those who favour this approach know the kind of RE of which they do not approve (the closed kind, as they see it), we realise that the approach is far from neutral. It values and promotes openness. It believes that RE is valuable for pupils but does not want it to commend any particular religious position, except perhaps the openness at its root.

Its proponents may prefer an open society to one that is committed to a particular religion. Its proponents sometimes regard some traditions as contradicting their ideals – for example, the existence of an established church (the Church of England), the presence of bishops in the House of Lords and the tradition of having a Christian coronation service.

Open RE and the teacher

If you are a trainee RE teacher or are considering applying for a place, your own experience of RE when you were a pupil may still be influencing your views. Perhaps you remember a teacher you would like to emulate. Maybe one or more of your teachers had characteristics you would like to avoid in your own work!

All aspiring RE teachers have to decide whether they will see their RE as promoting openness regarding such matters rather than as commending Britain's long-standing Christian traditions. Seen like this, RE can be said to have a political dimension. It is partly about the way pupils are influenced by their RE and therefore about the kind of society being developed. Intending RE teachers need to consider whether the vision of open RE and an open society is a vision they support. Similarly, some intending RE teachers are active in a religion that operates schools and they may well wish to consider whether they support those schools enough to teach there given the opportunity.

The limits of open RE

However, a liking for open RE does not involve thinking there are no limits, as if 'anything goes'. For example, those who value open RE are unlikely to be content with a racist response from pupils. Nor does their openness mean they are happy to accept underachievement or poor-quality teaching. Teachers can't be that open!

It is important to consider whether this 'open' kind of RE is the only valid kind of RE for the wide variety of schools in Britain. Different kinds of schools provide different contexts for religious education. A liberal democracy must recognise that some parents wish their children to be educated in accordance with their religious beliefs – the parents' beliefs, that is. Some faith communities wish to operate schools in which the curriculum is based on Christian values and principles, or Islamic or Jewish ones. To prevent this would be to impose another kind of education instead, perhaps one that the government of the day prefers. That would be a partisan decision. It would be the end of the dual system which has been supported in England and Wales at least since 1870. It could be said that this would be to deny some people

Task 2.2 Exploring 'open' RE

Explore your own attitudes towards 'open' RE by making a list of the strengths and weaknesses of that particular approach to teaching the subject. Is there any 'bottom line' at which the teacher must 'close' the lesson, e.g. the use by pupils of racist or other remarks that lack tolerance and sensitivity? What criteria can you use for recognising the need to draw a line under 'open' discussion?

Find an RE syllabus, either an Agreed Syllabus or a syllabus for a particular school. Write a paragraph indicating how 'open' the syllabus is. Does it contain bias, either explicitly or implicitly? Think how you might respond if your RE teaching had to follow the syllabus concerned. Think about any changes you would like to make to the syllabus.

Observe an RE lesson with a view to unpacking its level of 'openness'. How is the agenda controlled? What limits, either explicit or implicit, are imposed on classroom interaction by either teacher, pupils or resource material? What ideologies, positive or negative, can you discern at work in the flow of the lesson?

their right – their right to educate their children in accordance with their religious beliefs.

Experiential RE

Before coming to RE in faith community schools, I want to make some comments about 'experiential' RE. This can be a helpful bridge between the situation in 'state' schools and that in faith community schools.

At one time, experiential RE referred to RE that involved using drama and role-play or gave pupils the experience of visiting places of worship or of meeting people who practised various religions. This recognised that RE is about more than learning and remembering 'facts' about religions, connected for example with religious ceremonies and festivals, or sacred books and buildings. Encountering religions could also involve attitudes, the emotions, the imagination and the will. This is sometimes called the affective dimension. It did not ignore use of the mind and rational capacities but recognised also that human learning is much broader than that.

The understanding of 'experiential' RE in the 1990s took on a different slant. The shift was highlighted by the publication of the influential text edited by John Hammond, David Hay and a group of colleagues entitled *New Methods in RE teaching: An Experiential Approach*, and other texts soon followed (Hammond *et al.* 1990; Beesley 1990). The key idea was that pupils can engage in activities that offer them a variety of experiences which can heighten their appreciation of the religious dimension. In particular these activities involve the imagination and invite personal reflection. This approach has been criticised for many reasons (Cooling 1991; Thatcher 1991; Thompson 1991) but experiential activities are now used by many RE teachers, with varying degrees of frequency. Such activities are sometimes used in faith community schools, perhaps partly because they at least acknowledge that religious education should be more than learning 'about' religions. It should also include some personal learning 'from' religion (SCAA 1994a, b).

RE in faith community schools

Generalising is always risky and it is when considering RE in faith community schools! An earlier section mentioned some of the differences often found between Church of England and Roman Catholic schools. Roman Catholic schools usually want their RE teachers to be Catholics. Church of England schools normally want their teachers to have some sympathy with the aims of the school but they do not usually expect their RE teachers to be Anglicans, though they can be, of course! Though there are differences between Catholic and Church of England schools, there are also similarities in what they are attempting to provide and achieve, so the rest of this section explores them together.

What then is the nature of RE in faith community schools, how can it be justified and how 'open' is it? Most faith community schools in Britain have a Christian foundation. Some are linked with particular denominations, mostly the Church of England or the Roman Catholic church, but a few are linked with the Methodist church. In addition, there are faith community schools with a Jewish or Muslim foundation.

The aims of faith community schooling

Generally, the educational aims of such schools are related in some way to their foundation documents or their long-standing traditions. The beliefs of these religions each form a distinctive world view. The main beliefs are about God, the origin of the created world, human nature and the way people can relate to God and each other, and human destiny. Those who consciously promote faith community schools have in mind schools where the particular (religious) world view influences the curriculum and ethos, the view of spiritual and moral development, and the way those involved relate to each other. Sometimes the intention is that the world view should influence the whole life of the school.

These basic aims inevitably affect the nature of the RE provided in faith community schools, RE which is often called 'confessional', particularly by those opposed to it. First, the RE syllabus may emphasise the beliefs, history and practices of the faith community concerned. Second, one of the aims may well be to encourage or secure some kind of faith commitment as understood in the faith community involved. Third, some of the leaders in the particular faith community may have more direct involvement in the RE than they normally would in schools without a religious foundation. Fourth, the position of RE teachers may be different from that of teachers in schools without a religious foundation. They may be expected to uphold and promote the beliefs of the faith community and they may want to do so.

Perhaps one of the differences can be illustrated like this. Teachers in schools without a religious foundation are often encouraged to distance themselves somewhat from the beliefs and practices of every religion taught. This is the preference for saying 'Christians believe . . .' or 'Muslim practice is . . .'. This is thought to be more open and less inclusive than saying 'We believe.' Plainly in a multifaith course no teacher can repeatedly say 'We believe . . .' or 'I believe . . .' with reference to the key beliefs of each of several religions as they are explored. Religious beliefs cannot be swapped that easily! But, in a faith community school, teachers may feel quite justified in speaking more inclusively, by saying, for example, 'In our school . . .' or 'The church our school belongs to believes . . .' or 'We encourage . . .' or 'We try . . .' or 'What we are doing in this festival is . . .'

Issues in faith community schooling

There are a number of difficult questions that should be considered by those involved in a faith community school. If you are thinking of teaching in such a school you should continue to think through your views on these questions. One question is the extent to which encouragement to religious commitment is justified. This is a pertinent question for several reasons. One is the controversial nature of religious beliefs and questions or the uncertainty about how religious truth claims can be verified. Another question that arises from this is the point at which encouragement amounts to persuasion that is indoctrination, which I take to mean the attempt to secure allegiance to a particular religious stance without those concerned understanding why they give such allegiance or without doing so voluntarily.

Third, there is a practical or pragmatic reason why it is important to be clear about the justification for RE that is partly intended to lead to religious commitment. That is the question whether indoctrination works. If the faith community believes that coming to the particular religious commitment expected is necessary in terms of eternal welfare, it may tend to gear the whole style of the RE towards that result. If one is destined for heaven rather than hell, as a consequence of religious indoctrination, the lack of awareness of alternative religious beliefs and the absence of freedom may appear justified. But the point here is that, even in terms of the intended outcome, attempting indoctrination may be counterproductive. That is, quite apart from securing the genuine commitment intended, the attempted indoctrination may produce more opposition and unbelief than would result from a less restricted approach – a more open approach.

This may well come down to a question of theology or doctrine. If the faith community believes that mere conformity, insincere participation, leads to salvation, then its proponents may well say that it follows that anything that keeps the young people within the faith community is better than allowing them to wander astray into some other set of fundamental beliefs. However, those involved in the work of faith community schools are usually not content to manipulate pupils into mere conformity. They do not want to be seen as supporting hypocrisy, that is, approving of pretending to believe what at heart one does not. To acknowledge that genuine faith has to be given voluntarily, and has to be based on understanding and conviction, is to open up the whole question of appropriate methods in RE in a faith community school.

This key question comes into sharp focus when those in faith community schools face the question of what approach to adopt towards pupils who begin to show they are no longer convinced of the truths held by the faith community, if indeed they ever were. In this context the RE, in my view, has to take a somewhat open approach. That does not mean the staff and governors renouncing their commitment to the religious stance of the school. It does not mean the RE teachers having to pretend the school is other than it is − a faith community school, with all the implications that carries. But it does mean showing the doubting pupils that their search is valid, that they are right to admit the questions they are asking, and that they are still valued by and still can belong and contribute to the community of that school. When RE teachers in faith community schools adopt this approach, far from betraying their calling, they are following it with great integrity.

This discussion demonstrates some of the differences between education and indoctrination. Faith community schools have good reason to offer education, including religious education, rather than indoctrination in the sense of closing the pupils' minds so they encounter only the stance held by the faith community school.

This discussion also shows how complex is the matter of RE in faith community schools. That does not mean that in contrast the nature and role of religious education in state schools are simple and easy! It does mean that those involved in faith community schools need to think about the nature of nurture. The next section explores this, with particular reference to Christian nurture, since the majority of faith community schools in Britain are related to the Christian faith and the education provided often includes elements of Christian nurture.

EDUCATION, NURTURE AND INDOCTRINATION

It is possible to contrast nurture with some concepts of education and with indoctrination. The concepts are complex. A popular concept of education in the West since the Enlightenment is that it involves primarily the development of reason. In this concept the rational capacities are highly regarded, even supreme. One of the features of this view is that each individual develops their powers of critical analysis. The task is not to foster acceptance of a particular set of beliefs or traditions, but to develop the independence that comes from a well developed mind.

Indoctrination contrasts with this enterprise. The goal of indoctrination is to close the mind. The aim of those intent on indoctrination is to impose perspectives and values on pupils without any concern that they understand why they should accept them, without giving them the opportunity to consider alternative points of view, and without providing them with the possibility of freely given assent. Indoctrination, whether into a religious or a secular viewpoint, does not want to risk pupils coming to alternative conclusions, is not concerned about individual, voluntary consent, and rather seeks conformity, and resists divergence.

Nurture as an educational activity

Responsible nurture is more balanced than either of these extremes. It is not merely training the mind; still less is it closing the mind. It acknowledges the place of rationality but does not raise it above all other human capacities. It recognises the value of community, and mutual interdependence and the legitimacy of tradition. Where young people are involved, it desires to help them appreciate and identify with the culture and values of the society in which they grow up. Nurture has the additional dimension of wanting those brought up in a faith community to understand the beliefs and practices and to value them. To have a sense of one's origins and to have a sense of belonging can be a great blessing. To have an independent mind, to efficiently, critically analyse every position considered and never find one's own can be a lonely business.

It may be that the concept of nurture needs to be rehabilitated. In some circles it isn't quite politically correct or professionally correct to speak well of nurture, but as Brenda Watson wrote, 'deliberate nurture is generally part of what responsible parents and adults do' (1987, p. 9). Yet nurture should not involve indoctrination, not least because having a closed mind is inconsistent with making a conscious choice as a response of faith arising from understanding.

I have argued before (Hughes 1986) that RE can function as Christian nurture, even in schools without a religious foundation and even if that is not one of its specific goals. Christian beliefs and practices can be respectfully explored in RE. Pupils with a Christian background can find that RE helps their understanding of Christianity to grow and their self-awareness to develop. Much depends on the teachers. If practising a faith is permitted and respected by the RE teachers, then RE need not be threatening, even if several religions are explored. But if the teachers want the RE to point Christian pupils out of their faith perspective, they can use RE in a way that is inimical to Christian nurture. In my view, professional RE teachers ought not to use RE for that purpose.

Just as we can reflect on the kind of RE we support, so we can consider what kind of nurture we support. Brenda Watson puts this well when she suggests that

> nurture can be the cradle of education, when it is conducted in a way which enables children as they grow to question and reflect upon how they are being brought up. It can, however, be simply another word for conditioning.
>
> (1987, p. 9)

Task 2.3 Evaluating religious nurture

For individual reflection and/or group discussion:

- What is your understanding of religious nurture?
- Is it justifiable in state schools? Why?
- Is it justifiable in religious schools? Why?
- What reactions to religious nurture have you encountered? In school? In wider society?
- How might RE teachers and courses help pupils with their religious faith?
- How might RE help those who have no faith?

So the general aim of nurture-through-education is to guide people to and in discipleship of some kind within the context of a faith community. But it is not to be achieved at any price, nor is it to use any or every tactic or method, because some would be morally and theologically unacceptable.

Nurture and faith development

The insights of faith development theory can inform our understanding of religious nurture. James Fowler's key view of faith is to see it as a universal phenomenon, the way in which people make meaning in life (1981). In his model of faith development Stage Three occurs mainly in the age range 11–18. These young people want to go with the crowd and conform. What or who they are is shaped to a large extent by their relationships and roles. At this stage the group I belong to and what others think of me is very important to me.

The desire young people usually have to belong to a group can be an asset in any church activities for young people, including church-supported schools. However, the nature of Stage Four in Fowler's terms, from approximately age 17 onwards, and the transition to it, can be very instructive for our understanding of those involved. At this stage beliefs and commitments perhaps previously rather unexamined are now questioned and reviewed. Each wants to become their own person. They want to make their own choices and commitments instead of being shaped so much by the group. This is a key matter in terms of understanding the position of some young people in, e.g., Christian schools. Some young people make the transition to Stage Four and they embrace, or embrace again, a Christian position but more consciously, and after more enquiry and reflection, than before. Some make the transition in a relatively short period of time. A year or two is quite short in relation to a lifetime. Others take a decade or more. But some take much longer and some never reaffirm the Christian faith that was commended to them in their youth. These people need special consideration, but not these only, because those who continue their faith can also be helped or hindered.

What then does nurture mean in this transition period, which is sometimes long and painful? How do teachers in faith community schools approach young people in this period? These are relevant questions in relation to work with young people who will affirm or reaffirm a religious position and with those who don't, since at the time the leaders and teachers don't know which young people will discover or continue to have a faith and which will not! When young people in a faith community school begin seriously to question the beliefs on which the school is based it is not necessarily a sign of obstinacy or rebellion. It can be a healthy search for clarity and understanding. I have already indicated that I think the various faith communities, including Christian schools, should make room for people who come to doubt some of the basic beliefs of the faith community involved.

The theological foundations of educational nurture

This position can often be given theological support. This is important, because it means that encouraging pupils to actively explore their community traditions may have far deeper roots than the Western liberal tradition. There is not space here to consider the theological foundations of education-as-nurture across all the major faith traditions. However, the issue is an important one in faith community schools, and needs to be explored in greater depth. Consequently I offer here, as an example, a sketch of a theology of nurture-as-education from my own Christian tradition.

A Christian understanding of the nature of Christian faith itself is deeply related to the nature of each human person. In essence this is the question of the nature of a theology of Christian faith and faith development. Such a theology has the following main features. Repentance is a matter of the conscience and will and heart. Belief in Christ is an inner, personal conviction which carries important consequences in terms of the way Christians seek to live their lives. To be genuine such responses have to be voluntary. The implication is that the nature of Christian faith itself prevents people from imposing or compelling it in others. Nobody can command or force another person to have Christian faith. Certainly a Christian response and commitment can be encouraged and nurtured, but never can they be successfully forced. Attempts to require and impose Christian allegiance, of which sadly there are some significant historical examples, are ill founded theologically. Coercion is illegitimate in the Christian scheme of things.

Allied to this is a Christian understanding of the human person. God gives human beings many opportunities and awesome responsibilities, but clearly God does not compel every human being to have Christian faith. Presumably God could have done so, but that universe would have been different from the one we inhabit! For example, faith, love and human nature would be different. But imagining some other hypothetical world is not much help to us in relation to the present topic. In the present world, maybe it is a mystery why God gives humans the dignity of responding positively or negatively to Christian truth claims. It is something to do with the nature of the human person. In Christian belief all people are made in the image of God, but the context given has not ensured obedience, or prevented fallenness.

The point here with regard to Christian nurture is that there are good theological reasons for not making it so tight that there is no scope for a voluntary response of faith or rejection. This is true of all faith-based schools. Pressure to express beliefs beyond what someone feels at heart they currently can may be harmful to their personal search for answers to the most fundamental questions of meaning and truth which human beings face. There is a place for enthusiasm and encouragement to religious commitment in faith community schools, but there is also a need for wisdom and sensitivity, so that unfair and harmful pressure is avoided.

Task 2.4 Investigating the effectiveness of RE

On a large sheet of paper brainstorm all the factors you can think of that stifle the effectiveness of RE. Use different-coloured markers to cluster similar ideas together. Now rank your clusters in order of their relative influence on the quality of RE teaching. How might these factors be addressed? Repeat the exercise, this time addressing the issue of the factors that enhance the effectiveness of RE.

SUMMARY AND KEY POINTS

RE in state schools has to be somewhat open in order for it to be acceptable to the range of pupils and parents involved. But this openness is not neutrality. For example, it recognises the value of both learning about religions and learning from religion. As far as we can tell, RE will continue to be part of the curriculum of most schools and many of them will continue to need RE teachers who support RE that helps pupils explore several religions whilst permitting but not requiring adherence to any.

Religious education in faith community schools should be permitted in a liberal democracy. The RE in such schools is likely to pay particular attention to the religion to which the school is related, even in some sense a preference for that religion. Religious nurture in faith communities, including any schools they operate, can be undertaken with integrity. There are good reasons for not indoctrinating pupils in the sense of securing conformity without understanding or willing assent. This means making the RE somewhat open but without discounting the relevance and influence of the faith on which the school is based.

Being a schoolteacher is always a demanding task, and teaching RE in a state or faith community school is no exception. But helping pupils explore the fascinating life-and-death issues involved in religions can be an important and fulfilling occupation. State and faith community schools often have somewhat different approaches to RE and collective worship, but the rationale for RE teaching and worship in both sectors continues to be debated. This means there is a need for teachers who will reflect on practice and contribute to the ongoing debates. This challenge is enough to stretch the abilities of anyone!

FURTHER READING

Astley, J. (1994) *The Philosophy of Christian Religious Education*, Birmingham, Alabama: Religious Education Press. Astley subjects Christian RE to rigorous philosophical scrutiny and comes up with a clear justification of the value and importance of a distinctively Christian approach to education.

Chadwick, P. (1997) *Shifting Alliances: Church and State in English Education*, London: Cassell. A masterly survey of the historical development of the partnership between the established Church of England and state education provision in general, and provision for RE and collective worship in particular.

Copley, T. (1997) *Teaching Religion: Fifty Years of Religious Education in England and Wales*, Exeter: University of Exeter Press. This book traces the developments in RE from 1944 to 1994. It contains sometimes fascinating insights into the thinking of many religious educators and politicians active in the period concerned. It is a detailed and interesting account, likely to increase the understanding of anyone not familiar with the course of RE since the Second World War.

Duncan, G. and Lankshear, D.W. (1995) *Church Schools. A Guide for Governors*, London: National Society. Although not intended for teachers, this short survey is an indispensable introduction to the range of issues currently facing faith community schools.

Hammond J., Hay D., Moxon, J., Netto, B., Raban, K., Straugheir, G. and Williams, C. (1990) *New Methods in RE Teaching: An Experiential Approach*, Harlow: Oliver & Boyd. A highly influential, controversial and practical book. It constitutes perhaps the most innovative approach to 'open' RE in the 1990s. One reason for its significance is its concern to balance openness with awareness of the importance of pupils' own religious and spiritual development.

Part II

Teaching and learning

3 Developing Programmes of Study

Jo Backus

This chapter focuses on the process of curriculum planning and on the development of your programmes of study and lesson plans. Your school placements will give you important experience in developing these programmes and plans. The gradual evolution of your stock of programmes of study will constitute a crucial aspect of your professional development.

The purpose of this chapter is to guide you through a model of four basic stages in the process of planning to teach: initial preparation, writing your programmes of study, constructing lesson plans and course evaluation. Alongside this model you must expect to encounter alternative approaches to the preparation process, both in college and on your school placements. You should not be surprised by such diversity: in teaching there is no one 'right' way of doing things. Part of your professional responsibility as a teacher is to be willing to adopt and adapt your own personal approach to the process of planning to teach. What follows, then, is an introduction to one possible way of proceeding.

OBJECTIVES

By the end of this chapter, you should be able to:

- give an explanation of the terms 'aims', 'objectives', 'progression', 'differentiation' and 'assessment' in relation to the delivery of RE;
- construct programmes of study;
- produce effective lesson plans;
- describe and justify your own personal approach to preparing to teach.

FOUR STAGES IN TEACHING PREPARATION

Different terms can be used to indicate the core of the planning process. 'Programmes of study' is the term that is used in National Curriculum documents, and many RE Agreed Syllabuses are adopting similar nomenclature. However, you will find that many RE departments continue to use the more traditional language of 'schemes of work'.

In government Circular 4/98 the Department for Education and Employment set out standards for planning and effective delivery of the curriculum (DfEE 1998a). All courses in Initial Teacher Education (ITE) must conform to these standards although they may be differently enumerated within each PGCE course. You will find it helpful to consult the standards when engaged in planning.

Three curriculum documents are important for the planning and delivery of effective RE in the classroom. The first is the Agreed Syllabus, which details the major curriculum plan for RE county schools for all Key Stages. Unlike subjects in the National Curriculum which have a single syllabus, RE possesses a range of syllabuses developed at local level. These syllabuses constitute the legal documents for the subject. They contain comprehensive accounts of the aims and objectives of RE matched to national legal requirements, and also indicate methodologies and content for effective subject delivery. The planned programmes of study that you will find in RE departments, as well as a teacher's individual lesson plans, must by law draw on the relevant Agreed Syllabus for their rationale and content. A crucial task when you first arrive at your practice school will be to identify which particular Agreed Syllabus the RE department is legally bound to follow.

The second key curriculum document is the school's internal programme of study. This adapts the general Agreed Syllabus plan into individual units of work which run for a given length of time, and provides a narrower window on the learning opportunities for pupils as well as an overview of content and resources. Finally there are the individual lesson plans, which itemise the learning opportunities, outcomes, content and resources for the period of one lesson.

The programme of study sets out the learning opportunities and objectives for pupils, which may be covered over a period of time. It may be a term, half a term or a more limited number of weeks. Developing programmes of study is an ongoing activity. It is one which gives opportunity for reflection on the learning that pupils have acquired as well as allowing creative changes in the curriculum. For example, the partial failure of a lesson may lead you to refine the match between programme content and pupil needs. This flexibility means that account can be taken of new developments and fresh insights into the delivery of the topic. In your teaching practice you will be given programmes of study that have been developed by the RE department. During your practice you will be given the opportunity to reflect on the construction of these programmes as well as a chance to write your own for the specific lessons you are delivering.

Four Key Stages go into the development of programmes of study. These are:

1   initial preparation;
2   writing a programme of study;

3   lesson planning;
4   course evaluation.

STAGE ONE: INITIAL PREPARATION

Before writing a programme of study you will need to prepare the ground so that what you plan is well matched to the needs and abilities of the pupils. You will also need to ensure that your programme is coherent in respect of your pupils' prior learning: the technical term used to refer to the coherent development of the learning progress within and across programmes of study is *progression*.

Preparation will normally involve paying attention to the following:

- an audit of the pupils in order to identify prior learning experiences;
- a review of the requirements of the Agreed Syllabus;
- a consideration of the process of teaching.

Each of these items will now be unpacked in greater detail so as to give a clearer picture of what is involved in this aspect of the planning process.

Auditing the pupils

This aspect of planning involves the acquisition of an educational profile of the pupils in the class or year group under consideration. Three important elements should be considered here: (1) academic ability, (2) faith background and (3) social context.

Identifying the academic ability and special educational needs of pupils

Recognition of each pupil's age, aptitude and ability will give you important clues in the task of identifying the content and methodologies which will suit the pupils in question. Considering the special educational needs (SEN) provision for pupils who have special learning difficulties will ensure that resources and methodology are sufficiently flexible to aid the learning of all the pupils in the class. You will find SEN provision explored in more detail below in Chapter 7. Such an audit need not involve you in too much extra effort: observation of the class, together with an interview with their RE teacher and, where relevant, SEN staff, will set you off on the right track.

Consideration of pupils' backgrounds, religious traditions and world views

Pupils will always bring to their learning a set of assumptions and beliefs which are predicated on a particular faith or world view. This is so equally for atheists, agnostics and religious believers. Though the pupils' beliefs may lack coherence and focus they will nevertheless play a significant role in the expectations and preconceptions that are brought to the classroom. It is important here to ask how this background will affect the learning process. For example, in some cases pupils may already have an affiliation to the particular religion being studied. In such a case their experience and knowledge may well be utilised to enhance the understanding of other members of the class. Further, materials chosen from a textbook on a religious tradition will need to be broad enough to reflect what these pupils already know about their faith.

Assessment of the impact on learning of the social context of the school

This can often be a vital resource for planning. The social context of the school reflects on the nature and range of pupils' academic ability and on the range of their faith backgrounds. If, for example, the school has a large Hindu community in its area planning visits to local temples will give opportunities for dialogue between the classroom professional and members of the faith community in question which can enhance the learning of the pupils.

Task 3.1 Constructing and implementing a class audit

Work with your fellow students and/or your school-based mentor to construct a proforma which will aid the process of auditing a class you are preparing to teach. Ensure that an appropriate balance is drawn between, on the one hand, gathering together sufficient data and, on the other, allowing the audit to become a burdensome task that distracts from its primary purpose of supporting your planning. The proforma ought to cover the following areas:

- the educational strengths, weaknesses, potential and (if appropriate) special educational needs of each pupil;
- a profile of the faith traditions and world-view stances of the class;
- the social and cultural factors in the school's catchment area that have a bearing on your planning.

Trial the pro-forma, analyse its strengths and weaknesses, and produce a revised version to take with you into your first teaching post.

Interpreting the agreed syllabus

In order to plan the curriculum, you will need to consult the Agreed Syllabus for RE currently in use in your school. While in college you may also find yourself working with the Model Syllabuses published by SCAA with the intention of guiding Agreed Syllabus Conferences (ASCs) in the task of drawing up a local syllabus (SCAA 1994a, b). Such syllabuses lay out what might be called the 'big picture' of subject content and delivery. It is vital to recognise your legal responsibility to follow the Agreed Syllabus in your programmes of study and teaching. In interpreting a syllabus three key areas should be considered: (1) the aims, objectives and attainment targets for learning in RE; (2) the material content of the syllabus, that is, the prescribed subject knowledge; (3) the levels of attainment that pupils are expected to reach during their learning.

Task 3.2 Analysing Agreed Syllabuses

Choose two Agreed Syllabuses for RE.
  Consider how these documents define what pupils are expected to learn in their RE and how the content is chosen for a Key Stage of your choice.
  Analyse the similarities and differences between the two documents in terms of the following:

- aims and objectives;
- learning opportunities;
- levels of attainment;
- content.

Discuss with a colleague whether you consider these to be simply a matter of practical concern, or whether there are theoretical and methodological differences to be explored.

Aims, objectives and attainment targets of learning in RE

For convenience we will draw here on ideas and examples drawn from the Model Syllabuses. They were drawn up in consultation with representatives of the various faith communities represented. Controversially they elect to present religions as discrete entities, thereby emphasising the importance to pupils acquiring a coherent understanding of individual religions, rather than focusing on the value of recognising common traits and themes across different traditions.

The prescribed subject knowledge

The Model Syllabuses outline programmes of study for each key stage in terms of specific lesson content. In the parallel situation of the Agreed Syllabus such prescribed content must be used as the legal basis of the actual schemes of work that are drawn up and used in the RE department. In following the guidance and instructions of your Agreed Syllabus you should ensure that your schemes of work are tailored to the specific needs of your pupils, and build on your own personal strengths.

  The choice of module content is always a creative balancing act between giving pupils an opportunity to further their learning in Christianity with giving them an

Figure 3.1 The aims of RE according to the SCAA Model Syllabuses

Though the SCAA Model Syllabuses have not been without their critics, they do on the whole reflect a broad consensus about the subject's educational rationale and purpose. RE should help pupils to develop their:

- knowledge and understanding of Christianity and the other principal religions represented in Great Britain;
- understanding of the influence of beliefs, values and traditions on individuals, communities, societies and cultures;
- ability to make reasoned and informed judgements about religious and moral issues, with reference to the teachings of the principal religions represented in Great Britain;
- spiritual, moral, cultural and social insight by:
  (a) developing awareness of the fundamental questions of life raised by human experiences, and of how religious teachings can relate to them;
  (b) responding to such questions with reference to the teaching and practices of religions, and to their own understanding and experience;
  (c) reflecting on their own beliefs, values and experience in the light of their study;
- a positive attitude towards other people, respecting their right to hold different beliefs from their own, and towards living in a society of diverse religions.

(SCAA 1994a, p. 2)

opportunity to increase their knowledge and understanding of other major world faiths. Monitoring these learning opportunities across the Key Stages is an important part of achieving breadth and balance in curriculum content. Although the Model Syllabus recommends that attention should be paid to giving pupils a coherent picture of religions as they progress through the Key Stages, it has to be balanced by the need to give pupils wider understanding of the context of religions.

Levels of attainment

Most major curriculum documents connected with RE provide specific levels of attainment that pupils ought to be achieving at each Key Stage. These are indicative and provide among other items the opportunity for teachers to consider the standards pupils are reaching at the end of the relevant Key Stages. They also aid the writing of levels of response mark schemes for key assignments that pupils may undertake. The syllabus may also give advice on the learning opportunities which could be used to enable pupils to demonstrate their development towards the indicated levels of attainment. A worked example of this can be found in Figure 3.2.

Figure 3.2 Levels of attainment in RE

Most Agreed Syllabuses outline the levels that pupils should be achieving at the end of each Key Stage in their RE. The Somerset Agreed Syllabus describes 'the range of performance that pupils working at a particular level should characteristically demonstrate', and suggests that 'in deciding on a pupil's level of attainment at the end of a Key Stage, teachers should judge which description best fits the pupil's performance' (Somerset SACRE 1998, p. 55).

In what follows part of a school's internal marking scheme has been set out. It is a description of the criteria for the award of an internal school A grade at Key Stage 4. This grade should be the equivalent of the Somerset Agreed Syllabus level 8. By referring to such grade descriptors while marking the teacher is able to assign grades that are more accurate than a mere 'first impression' response might have been, and which allow the pupil to be assessed against objective standards recognised by the syllabus.

In order to achieve an A grade at Key Stage 4 pupils' work should demonstrate the acquisition of the range of skills and abilities listed under the following headings.

Learning about religions
- Evaluate differing perspectives derived from religious and secular traditions, as well as their own views.
- Identify and evaluate sources.
- Present material with sophistication.

Learning from religion and human experience
- Reflect on what has been learnt and apply it to their own views on the subject.
- Develop sensitivity towards religious believers and beliefs.

Concepts
- Show a sophisticated use of technical terms.

Skills
- Address a wide range of appropriate issues.
- Provide evidence of clear thinking.
- Show awareness of the strength and weakness of contrasting positions.

Exploring the learning process

As well as focusing on an audit of the pupils, and the Agreed Syllabus, you will also have to make decisions regarding the process of learning at the preparatory stage. You will need to take account of at least six factors that come into play at this point in the process of preparing to teach: (1) selection of teaching methods; (2) progression between your programme of study and previous work the pupils have undertaken; (3) differentiation in order to match the learning to pupil progression and preferences

for learning; (4) integration of resources and information and communications technology (ICT) to enhance the learning process; (5) cross-curricular opportunities; (6)
assessment.

Teaching methods

Effective learning will depend on effective teaching. Research has shown that frequently whole-class approaches to teaching are adopted with a format of teacher
talks, question-and-answer and written assignments. This can be a very self-contained
format, enabling teachers to get through a content-heavy curriculum. However, a
criticism of this particular diet is that it is unable to engage the pupils as fully as one
might expect.

It follows that using a range of teaching methods is an important part of your
work as a teacher. Research has shown that as pupils learn in different ways they need
to be aided in their learning by teaching methods which suit their individual learning preferences. As Kincaid suggests:

> when the task is to impart knowledge and understanding it is quite in
> order, although not always appropriate, for the teacher to adopt a
> presentation style of teaching in which he or she either talks to the whole
> class or makes use of audio-visual techniques to get across a certain body
> of information. When the task is to help students develop the skills of
> investigating an issue, of finding information, selecting and sorting out
> what is or what is not relevant, and drawing conclusions from the
> information available, a presentational style is no longer useful. In these
> sorts of tasks students need to be active rather than passive, doing things
> rather than having things done to them or for them
>
> (1991, p. 42)

Progression

Ensuring progression in pupils' learning is a vital part of the planning process.
Having accurate records of pupils' achievement in previous parts of their course
and throughout previous Key Stages can be very helpful here. A question you
need to ask yourself when considering this aspect of planning is 'How will the
work outlined in the programme of study build upon and refine the learning of
the pupils?' The Model Syllabus states that progression is connected with the
knowledge and understanding that pupils should acquire through their work in
school.

An important feature of progression is cognitive development: the knowledge and
understanding that pupils will acquire during their learning, especially their linguistic competence, conceptual understanding and thinking skills. The development of
pupils' religious literacy will include their progressive understanding of technical
terms and the ways in which these operate in religions discourse.

The progression of pupils' learning in RE is normally in terms of two broad
attainment targets: 'learning about religions' and 'learning from religion'. Both nor-

Task 3.3 Exploring teaching methods

On a sheet of A4 draw up a chart indicating the raft of basic teaching methods available to you in the classroom. You will need to base it on your personal experience of being taught, on your observations in schools and on conversations with colleagues in college. You may find it useful to refine your chart in the light of charts produced by your fellow students.

Select a lesson plan. It may be either one you have produced yourself or a plan of a lesson you have observed being taught. Now rewrite the plan three times. Each new version should make use of a different selection of teaching methods. This activity is designed to make you more aware of the way in which the same learning outcomes can be achieved using a range of different teaching methods and learning styles.

Critically review your revised lesson plans with some of your colleagues. Ask yourself the following:

● What are the individual strengths and weaknesses of each lesson plan?
● What implications for learning are contained in each plan?
● How well do the learning objectives and teaching methods match up?
● What criteria are you using to evaluate the plans?
● Are there any specific methods that most attract you?
● Which methods are you likely to find most difficult to implement?

mally carry equal weight and are meant to enable an open, philosophical approach to the subject matter as well as taking account of the spiritual, moral, cultural and social development of the pupils. Progression also involves the development of key skills and attitudes: investigation, interpretation, analysis, reflection, empathy, imagination, evaluation, critical argument, association, identification, expression, spiritual awareness, moral insight, etc.

Differentiation

You will already be aware that pupils learn at different rates and in different ways. This is true both within a scheme of work and between schemes of work. What will suit one pupil in the way knowledge is managed may not suit another. This aspect of planning deals with the crucial question of differentiation, by which we mean the deliberate construction of learning to take account of the strengths and weaknesses of individual pupils. All key curriculum documents place emphasis on this aspect of planning to remind teachers of the need to cater for all levels of ability in their encounter with pupils. It is a hotly debated subject among RE

Figure 3.3 'Learning from' and 'learning about' religions

> The Somerset Agreed Syllabus adopts the two basic attainment targets iden-
> tified by the Model Syllabuses: 'learning from religion' and 'learning about
> religion'.
>
> *Attainment Target 1, Learning from religion and human experience.* This
> includes the ability to:
>
> - identify, name, describe and give accounts in order to build a coherent
>   picture of each religion;
> - explain the meaning of religious language, stories and symbolism;
> - explain similarities and differences between, and within religions.
>
> *Attainment Target 2, Learning about religion.* This includes the ability to:
>
> - give an informed and considered response to religious and moral
>   issues;
> - reflect on what might be learnt from religions in the light of one's own
>   beliefs and experience;
> - identify and respond to questions of meaning.
>
> (Somerset SACRE 1998, p. 9)

professionals but, broadly speaking, there are a number of ways in which it can
be achieved.

A clear indication that your lesson plan or programme of study has been
constructed with differentiation in mind will be the presence of phrases such as 'By
the end of the lesson all pupils will be able to . . .', 'Most pupils will be able to . . .',
'Some pupils will be able to . . .'. Such phrases will be augmented by the concepts,
attitudes and skills that you feel pupils should demonstrate.

Consultation with the departmental staff to check whether what you have
planned will need modification to fit the needs of all learners in the group is important. Decisions on how to differentiate learning can be difficult to make. On some
occasions it will be appropriate to provide specific resources for some pupils to aid
their learning, i.e. matched to specific difficulties they have. On the other hand, the
whole class may benefit from the use of so-called 'writing frames' which give pupils
indications of what to include in their work. Utilising a variety of assessment tasks
will aid the process of differentiation, and can be matched to the preferences the
pupils have in their learning.

In many cases it is helpful to design specific assignments for pupils which bring
together all the learning possibilities specified in the programme of study, and which
are meant to enable teachers to check whether their aims and objectives have been
achieved. They also give a specific opportunity to check the standards the pupils are
achieving at that time.

Figure 3.4 'Outcome' and 'task': two basic models of differentiation

Many teachers find differentiation a difficult process to come to terms with, especially when faced with the challenge of simply producing lesson plans of reasonable quality. It is important that from the start differentiation becomes central to the planning process. The failure of a lesson is often due to lack of differentiation: giving pupils inappropriate undifferentiated work which is either too easy or too difficult is a recipe for disaster. A good start to taking account of differentiation is to work with each of the following two basic models.

Differentiation by outcome
Here pupils are set the same task to achieve, but the variety of levels they work at will show their differing abilities. Such tasks need to be very well constructed, and pupils need to be given clear support and guidance, if you are to ensure that all pupils regardless of ability can access the task sufficiently well. 'Discuss the importance of prayer and pilgrimage for Muslims' is a question that could be answered, at an appropriate level, both by a lower-ability Year 7 pupil and by an A Level candidate. Here the learning process will be differentiated by the different outcomes.

Differentiation by task
By far the more difficult method of differentiation, though often the more effective, is differentiation by task. Here the teacher sets different pupils contrasting tasks on the basis of their ability. It may be done by offering the class a choice of questions, or grouping pupils into ability groups, with each group working on specially designed activities, or even by producing individual tasks for specific pupils. Essentially this method identifies different tasks for pupils of differing ability. Pupils may be given the opportunity to opt for a particular task which they feel able to achieve, but then encouraged to attempt more difficult tasks as they progress.

Resources and ICT

Consideration of resources and ICT are both vitally important in lesson planning. You need to avoid the trap of first writing your programmes of study and lesson plans and only then asking the question of how your teaching can be supported by resources and ICT. This 'supplementary approach' to lesson planning frequently leads to lessons that are disjointed and poorly resourced. Your use of resources and ICT should involve an 'integral approach' in which you begin the planning process with a broad range of resources already in front of you. Being able to refer to resources as you plan both stimulates the imagination and tends to produce an integral learning package. There is no space here to investigate these crucial issues further: to do this you should consult Chapter 13 on resources and Chapter 14 on ICT.

Cross-curricular opportunities

Opportunities for exciting and interesting work for pupils can be achieved through working with other departments in the school on thematic projects, e.g. a historical survey of a town for pupils in Year 9 can be augmented and enhanced through an RE study of the religious buildings and communities that the town has maintained over time; or a Year 10 module on the topic of creation can be enhanced through joint work between RE and Science departments.

Assessment

Finally you will need to consider the place of assessment in your programmes of study. You will need to make sure that each programme includes a clear and practical indication of how you intend to assess the learning of your pupils, in terms of both their formative development and their summative achievement. You will also need to ensure that the programme of study has built into it a means of self-assessment. You need to be aware of the strengths and weaknesses of the programme just as much as you need to be aware of your pupils' progress. Only by developing a critical understanding of the strengths and weaknesses of your planning and delivery can you hope to refine and develop it for future use. As a professional teacher you must develop ways of ensuring that your evaluation of a series of lessons is not based merely on your own subjective impressions. If you fail to do so you could find yourself falling into the trap of confusing good behaviour and enthusiasm on the part of your pupils with quality learning. Entertainment and education do not necessarily go together. The broad topic of assessment is outlined in greater depth below in Chapter 6.

STAGE TWO: WRITING A SCHEME OF WORK

One of the major weaknesses in the planning of inexperienced teachers is the desire to move too quickly to the second basic stage of preparation, that of actually writing the programme of study. It is important not to forget the importance of working through the initial stage of preparation. Once you are ready to write your programme you should bear in mind the following issues.

Selecting the format of the scheme of work

It will be clear at an early stage of your PGCE that there is no one universally accepted form that your programmes of study should take. The model(s) used in your schools may be very different from the one presented to you in college. As a professional teacher it is important to make a balanced judgement in reaching a decision regarding the form your own schemes of work will take. A sample format is outlined in Figure 3.5.

Figure 3.5 Sample 'programme of study' pro-forma

Practical details			
Class		Day/Dates	
Year		Time	
Teaching room		Number of lessons	

Aims and objectives	
Scheme aim	
Scheme objectives	1 2 3
Agreed Syllabus link	

The context of teaching and learning	
Ability range	
SEN pupils	
Faith backgrounds	
Social context	

The process of teaching and learning	
Progression	
Differentiation	
Resources	
Teaching methods	
Cross-curricular link	

Figure 3.5 Continued

The lesson sequence		
Lesson 1	Aim	
	Outline	
Lesson 2	Aim	
	Outline	
Lesson 3	Aim	
[etc.]	Outline . . .	

Assessment		
Pupil assessment	Assignments	
	Grade criteria	
	Methods	
	Recording	
Course assessment	Process	
	Criteria	
	Recording	

Balancing detail and time

Teaching is always rooted in a series of constraints. You are never likely to find yourself in an ideal context. As a professional you must learn to make appropriate compromises. In terms of writing a programme of study it is important to pay sufficient attention to detail if the scheme is to have any value. However, you must also guard against the danger of finding yourself devoting too much time and effort to the programme to the detriment of other important responsibilities. In the model programme presented in Figure 3.5, for example, each section may contain merely a brief bullet-pointed reference to the key issues involved. Planning should be integrated with your teaching and function to aid and support it. Over-pedantic planning that bites into the limited amount of time available to you will be detrimental to good classroom practice.

Utilising information technology

You will find it useful to establish a standard pro-forma which you simply fill in every time you come to plan a scheme of work. Sensible use of word-processing technology is important here: by drawing up a pro-forma file, and then simply copying it and completing a duplicate form for each scheme of work, you will save yourself an enormous amount of work, both because you are not writing out the pro-forma each time and because many of the details will be repeated from scheme to scheme. It is important to impose basic routine and structure on your planning at an early stage.

Relating the scheme to the Agreed Syllabus

As a professional teacher it is not sufficient to do the right thing: it is also important to be *seen* to do the right thing! Your scheme of work must conform to the requirements of your Agreed Syllabus. The fact that it does needs to be made transparent. An OFSTED inspector should not need to spend an evening cross-referencing between your scheme and the Agreed Syllabus in order to be assured that your scheme is a legal one! The connections should be immediately obvious. One way of doing this is to insert in brackets references to the appropriate sections of the Agreed Syllabus in the actual text of your programme of study.

Revising the format of your scheme

You should always remember that learning to teach is an ongoing process, and that consequently the format of your scheme of work is likely to develop over the years.

STAGE THREE: LESSON PLANNING

The lesson plan provides you with a detailed description of the heart of the teaching process: the individual lesson. Your teaching file should contain the programme of study developed for each course you teach, and each scheme should be immediately followed by the individual lesson plans, arranged in chronological sequence.

It is important for your plan to achieve a balance between concrete practical issues and broader theoretical concerns. A lesson plan with clearly articulated learning outcomes is useless if it fails to remind the teacher to make sure that vital resources are present in the classroom. Similarly a lesson plan that addresses all the immediate practical aspects of teaching whilst failing to be rooted in a clearly educational rationale is unlikely to support the learning process in any depth.

The content and structure of the lesson plan need to be clear and focused. As with schemes of work, you will encounter a diversity of approaches to lesson planning during your PGCE year and beyond. Teachers use a variety of formats to write up their lesson plans, and the college will normally supply a selection of formats. An example is provided in Figure 3.6, and the following ideas and suggestions are broadly based on that example. Never forget, however, that it is your professional responsibility to create, own and develop your personal way of doing things.

Figure 3.6 Sample 'lesson plan' pro-forma

Lesson plan: Green Street School Religious Education Department

Lesson topic			
Teacher		Room	
Class		Time	
Key Stage		Lesson sequence	

Lesson aim	
Attainment targets	1
	2
	3
Agreed Syllabus links	

Learning sequence			
Stage	Time	Activity	Teaching method
1			
2			
3			
4 [etc.]			

Resources	
	1
	2
	3

Teaching checklist	Key concepts
	Key skills
	Key attitudes

Homework	Task
	Due in by

Lesson evaluation and notes	

Administrative information

The plan is important not only as a preparation document and means of recording your teaching: you will need to use it as a reference point and guide in the classroom as you actually implement the plan. Consequently you should include in your lesson plan a range of basic administrative detail: lesson topic; name, year group and Key Stage of the class; the date, location and duration of the lesson; the position of the lesson in the sequence of lessons set out in your scheme of work.

Aims and attainment targets

It is vitally important that there is a clear match between the lesson plan and the overall programme of study. Without this it is almost impossible to offer your pupils focused and progressive teaching. It means you must consider how the lesson delivers the chosen aspect of learning taken from the programme. Further, there should also be consideration of what is to be taught, teaching and learning resources, differentiation and assessment of the learning objectives.

The lesson aim, which sets out the basic focus and purpose of the lesson in a single basic statement, must relate to the Agreed Syllabus for RE and flow directly from the programme of study.

The various lesson objectives, sometimes referred to as *learning outcomes* or *attainment targets*, serve to state clearly the specific learning that you want pupils to undertake during that lesson. Teachers use a variety of phrases to aid clarity when presenting objectives. One such phrase you will get to know well is 'By the end of the lesson pupils will be able to . . .'. This is developed by adding useful terms which indicate skills or knowledge components such as 'state', 'describe', 'identify', 'demonstrate an understanding of'. It is easy to allow such phrases to become mere rhetoric. However, a skilful lesson planner will ensure that the plans serve to support teaching by reminding the teacher to focus on the essentials of the learning process.

Writing clear and well focused learning objectives can help you to see whether you have delivered what you set out to do, as well as enabling you to use them in the process of monitoring and assessing pupils' learning. The list of objectives should be limited to a realistic number. It will normally amount to three or four chosen items. A quick check on the process is to ask yourself the question 'If I describe the objectives to the pupils, will they understand what they are supposed to do and what is expected of them?'

Finally, as has already been mentioned, it is imperative to show clearly the relation of your lesson plan to the legal requirements of the Agreed Syllabus. If you find it difficult, then making sure that there is a section in your planning pro-forma devoted to describing the nature of the link may help the process of disciplined planning.

The learning sequence

Each lesson you teach will need to progress through a clear learning sequence. A good lesson plan will immediately draw attention to the progression inherent in the lesson. You may find it helpful to think of the lesson in terms of a series of numbered 'building blocks', each with its own time allocation, specified activity and teaching methodology.

It is important to establish the routines for pupils in the classroom, and to that end you should use the process of lesson planning to focus and reflect on the issue. The learning sequence should also make clear the managerial aspects of the classroom situation. Ideally you will begin your teaching career by following the established routines already put in place by the pupils' regular teacher. This is especially so if the routines already in place are clearly articulated and effectively implemented: you should try to avoid the misapprehension that the good teacher is always reinventing the wheel. Although there will be similarities for all teachers, there will be interesting differences, and, in establishing your own, you may want to discuss them with the teachers in school.

As you become more skilled and confident in the classroom the need to articulate your lesson routines in your lesson plans will begin to fade. However, until you have achieved such a level of experience it is probably best to heed the advice that lesson routines should be clearly articulated in considerable detail. The lesson routines to be included in your plan should include: entry into the classroom; bringing pupils to attention; taking the register; issuing and collecting homework; dismissal procedures.

Resources

It is important when planning your lesson to consider the resources you will be using. This is essential for the smooth delivery of a lesson. It is important as you set out on your teaching career to list clearly all the resources needed for the lesson. The hustle and bustle of classroom culture are such that it becomes easy to forget key pieces of equipment. The collapse of a lesson because the student teacher has failed to bring the relevant set of worksheets and is forced to abandon the class and head back to the staff room to get them is surprisingly common. Don't be afraid to list everything you need: door keys, chalk, attendance register, etc.

Teaching checklists

Once you are sucked into the dynamics of classroom teaching it is extremely easy simply to forget the aims and objectives you set for the lesson. In view of this you may like to follow the lead of many students who have found it helpful to include in their plan, often in 'bulletpoint' style, an at-a-glance checklist of the key concepts, skills and attitudes that you wish their pupils to engage with during the lesson.

Homework

Failure to set homework is a classic trap many trainee teachers fall into. It can be very tempting to 'forget' to set homework, not merely because it leaves you with less marking but also because it can be a way of courting pupil approval of you as a teacher. You must avoid any such trap at all costs. Professional responsibility is paramount, and only by taking the learning process seriously yourself will you ever be able to convince a class that RE is intrinsically important. Hence the value of adding a section to your pro-forma that will remind you exactly what homework needs to be set.

Evaluation

It is important that, as soon as possible after the lesson, you note down a brief evaluation of the strengths and weaknesses of the lesson, together with any necessary administrative notes. Such evaluation will form an important part of the detailed assessment process that, by placing the lesson under scrutiny, will allow your skill as a teacher to be enhanced. This is explored in greater depth in the next major section of this chapter.

Implementing lesson plans

The lesson plan is a plan, not a straitjacket, for learning. When they are beginning their career most teachers do follow their lesson plans closely, but in time they learn to develop the skill and confidence to adapt that which is taught in response to pupil reactions. This may mean moving the lesson in a different direction from that anticipated in response to issues that arise in the classroom. A good rule of thumb for the beginning teacher is to stick to the lesson plan as closely as possible, but be aware that there is no need to panic if you find yourself deviating from it.

You should address technical items that may aid or hinder the delivery of the lesson. It is useful to have a seating plan or other aid to help you remember pupils' names, aiding interaction between you and the pupils. It could be included in your teaching file as a supplement to the basic lesson plan.

STAGE FOUR: COURSE EVALUATION

It is important to think of the planning process not simply as a journey from A to B but as an ongoing cyclical process. The sequence 'preparation – developing programmes of study – creating lesson plans – course evaluation' ought to bring you full circle. The evaluation process should be formative, feeding in new information that forms the basis of the next round of lesson preparation.

Principles of evaluation

Lesson evaluation gives you an opportunity to reflect on the extent and manner in which the aims and objectives of the lesson have been met and why. Although these should be your own comments, initially you may want to enlist the aid of your tutor who observed the lesson to aid your analysis. As you gain confidence and your relations with your pupils mature you will find that allowing them to evaluate your lessons can be one of the most important sources of information about the lessons.

A framework for evaluation

Figure 3.7 suggests a framework for the personal evaluation of your lessons and schemes of work. Each of the criteria is based on good practice and derives in the main from the DfEE Circular 4/98. Although you will not wish to comment on all the evaluation items mentioned below after every lesson, you may wish to comment on a selection agreed between yourself and your tutor which reflects your development and progress.

SUMMARY AND KEY POINTS

The process of preparing to teach is not a simple skill to be mastered. Rather it stands at the heart of the teaching process. As a professional teacher you must learn to accept responsibility for the methods and content of your planning and preparation, within the framework required by the Agreed Syllabus. This chapter sought to stimulate reflection on this responsibility by suggesting one possible model of the planning process: preparation, developing schemes of work, creating lesson plans, course evaluation. It also introduced you to some key educational concepts which you need to take on board if your planning is to include effective aims, objectives, continuity and progression.

Figure 3.7 A framework for programme evaluation

Communicating with children. To what extent does your teaching:

- establish appropriate relationships with pupils?
- use of their names to facilitate a good learning environment?
- set clear and consistent lesson routines and expectations of behaviour?
- reflect concern for both the individual and collective needs of pupils?

Planning and evaluating. To what extent does your teaching:

- set clear lesson objectives?
- have a sound structure for the lesson?
- establish high standards and expectations of learning?

Teaching and class management. To what extent does your teaching:

- match teaching methods and content against aims and objectives?
- monitor pupils' progress and intervene to aid their learning?
- establish a purposeful learning environment?
- maintain appropriate levels of discipline?
- utilise a variety of teaching and learning strategies?
- deliver a lesson with good pace and direction?
- give pupils clear instructions so that they know what is expected of their learning?
- involve designing and selecting appropriate resources?
- consolidate learning by the use of recap and other similar methods?
- celebrate pupils' work and achievement through, e.g., displays of their work?
- demonstrate awareness of pupils' individual needs and prior learning?

Monitoring, assessing, recording and reporting. To what extent does your teaching:

- assess your teaching and learning effectiveness?
- make use of feedback to pupils to enhance their learning?
- use level descriptions or examination criteria for assessment?
- reflect a range of assessment techniques?

Developing and maintaining specialist skills. To what extent does your teaching:

- demonstrate a secure knowledge of your subject?
- cope with subject-specific questions?

FURTHER READING

Department for Education and Employment (1998) *Teaching: Higher Status, Higher Standards*, Circular 4/98 London: HMSO. This contains the government's standards for all trainee teachers in all subject areas. You should familiarise yourself with the sections dealing with RE and ICT.

Kincaid, M. (1991) *How to Improve Learning in RE*, London: Hodder & Stoughton. A very useful text offering theoretical and practical advice and suggestions on how to improve the delivery of RE in the classroom. Topics covered include learning theory, the place of RE in the curriculum, assessment and the evaluation of learning.

Kyriacon, C. (1998) *Essential Teaching Skills*, London: Stanley Thornes. A clear, practical guide to the teaching skills you will need as a trainee teacher. Areas covered range from planning and preparation to reflecting on and evaluating your practice.

Parker-Jenkins, M. (1995) *Children of Islam: A Teacher's Guide to Meeting the Needs of Muslim Pupils*, London: Trentham Books. As suggested in this chapter it is important to consider the framework of thinking children bring with them to the classroom. This scholarly work offers you an opportunity to consider the way in which religion and culture inform Muslim children's world views. By implication it poses questions about provision for all children in the classroom.

SCAA (1994a) *Model Syllabuses: Model 1, Living Faiths Today*, London: School Curriculum and Assessment Authority.

SCAA (1994b) *Model Syllabuses: Model 2, Questions and Teachings*, London: School Curriculum and Assessment Authority. These documents are a response to Sir Ron Dearing's request for Model Syllabuses in RE. In the process of developing them both faith communities and teachers were consulted. The Model Syllabuses are increasingly being used in the development of Agreed Syllabuses for Local Authorities.

Somerset SACRE (1998) *Awareness, Mystery And Value: The Somerset Agreed Syllabus for Religious Education*, Somerset: Somerset SACRE. This is a good example of contemporary design in Agreed Syllabuses for RE. You will, however, need to familiarise yourself thoroughly with the particular Agreed Syllabus you are responsible for teaching.

4 Pupil Learning

Trevor Cooling

This chapter reviews the way thinking has changed since the 1950s as to what pupils should be learning in RE. In particular it focuses on the sorts of attitudes that you should be concerned to promote and suggests that openness to learning from people who are different from oneself is a central aim of education in modern multifaith societies. This requires you to develop teaching strategies which overcome the negative perception of religion prevalent in modern youth culture. There is an ongoing debate in the literature on RE about how the subject matter studied in RE should be used to achieve this goal. Two recent curriculum development projects are reviewed to support the notion that the key skills required of pupils are the ability to listen carefully to the believer's perspective and the ability to apply what is heard to the pupils' own world of experience. A particular emphasis is given to the value of planning lessons based on understanding religious concepts, rather than just passing on information about the religions.

OBJECTIVES

By the end of this chapter, you should be able to:

*   describe the main changes that have taken place in the philosophy of RE in recent years;
*   comment on the attitudes and skills that RE should promote;
*   understand the rationale of two recent curriculum development projects;
*   evaluate the importance of concepts in RE;
*   apply your thinking to the design of effective learning strategies.

THE CHANGING NATURE OF RE

Anyone wishing to understand RE might be advised to start by looking at the changes that have taken place in the philosophy of school dinners (a much neglected topic on most PGCE courses!). In the 1950s and 1960s the philosophy was that schools knew what children needed and they were all expected to eat it. After all, it was good for them! Etched on my memory is a picture of awe-inspiring dinner ladies serving up slabs of (often yellowing) liver, adorned with anaemic cabbage and lumpy mashed potatoes swimming in watery gravy. The typical dessert was a sea of tapioca ('frog spawn' in kid-speak), with a rudimentary blob of jam in the centre. All, I was assured, most nourishing.

Things began to change in the 1970s, largely because dealers in pig swill were doing so well. So dawned the age of the school cafeteria, with its philosophy that pupil choice should determine what was served in the canteen. No longer did schools feel it was appropriate to *tell* pupils what they *ought* to eat. It was a matter of personal choice. The school set the menu, the pupils chose. And so we moved into the era of beefburgers, beans and chips. Schools were to be the precursors of McDonald's.

Unrestrained pupil choice soon led to anxieties among school catering professionals. Maybe pupils were not always choosing what was in their own best interest? So we moved to the current philosophy of healthy eating, where schools seek to guide pupils to ensure that the choices they make are good for them. The future health of the nation requires us to abandon the notion of unrestrained choice.

The history of RE provides a remarkable parallel to these changes. In the 1950s and 1960s it was widely assumed that the purpose of the subject was to induct pupils into the religious heritage of the nation, namely Christianity. The largely unquestioned assumption was that it was both good for them and good for the country. The approach was what we now call 'confessional RE'. Two things led to the widespread abandonment of this philosophy. First, teachers became aware of the dangers of indoctrination. Second, the nation as a whole began to wake up to the significant presence of people from other religions in its ranks as well as in the wider world. Teachers were also aware that the diet of Bible study, characteristic of the confessional approach, was resulting in the educational equivalent of overflowing swill bins. Pupils were turned off. So, in the late 1970s, RE teachers increasingly adopted the approach of 'phenomenological RE', more popularly called 'multifaith RE', which emphasised the importance of pupils learning about a number of religions and choosing for themselves. The approach championed the academic, objective and respectful study of religion. It was widely assumed that this phenomenological study would automatically be more interesting to the pupils, as it offered them a wider choice than the confessional Christian approach.

A significant number of RE textbooks currently in use in schools adopt this phenomenological approach. They often organise the content under themes which are supposed to be common to all the religions, such as 'sacred books' or 'rites of passage'. The assumption is that by emphasising what is common between the religions, pupils learn to respect people from a variety of different religious traditions. The aspiration is that pupils will learn tolerance, become less prejudiced and realise the importance of making their own, autonomous choices in life through the study of a number of religions.

For a number of reasons, there is growing dissatisfaction with the phenomenological approach. Two in particular are relevant to the theme of our chapter. First, the emphasis on pupils making their own choices in the matter of religion ignored the question of whether all the choices that could be made were equally acceptable. For example, does the teacher mind if the pupil decides to become a satanist? Clearly there is a need for pupils to learn to make *discerning* choices, not simply *just* to choose. Second, there is a big question as to how relevant the amassing of knowledge about a variety of religions is to modern teenagers. The phenomenological approach was modelled on the university subject called 'Religious Studies'. People who take this subject at university are fascinated by information about the world's religions. However, it is a big assumption to think that 14-year-olds will also feel that way. And are we *really* sure that learning information about the religions will lead to less prejudice and more tolerance?

When the philosophy of the canteen moved from pupil choice as an end in itself to educating pupil choices, it was not a return to the idea that the school simply told the pupils what was good for them. So too, when the philosophy of RE moved beyond the phenomenological approach, it did not abandon the idea that learning about a number of religions was important in favour of telling pupils what to believe. It did, however, pay much more attention to looking at the contribution that learning about the religions made to the personal development of the pupils, in terms of the attitudes it generated and the relevance of the content to pupils in their own life experience.

Task 4.1 Identifying approaches to RE teaching

Find a number of different RE textbooks. Decide which of the following is the main approach adopted by each textbook:

- the confessional approach, where the intention is to transmit the ideas of one religion to the pupils in the hope that they will come to believe them;
- a non-confessional approach to teaching one religion which aims that pupils should understand the religion but doesn't seek to gain the pupils' acceptance of it;
- a multifaith approach where the emphasis is largely on pupils acquiring information about the religions;
- a multifaith approach which requires the pupils to make judgements and which seeks to educate those judgements by encouraging pupils to reflect on them.

Discuss the strengths and weaknesses of the four approaches, as developed in the textbooks, with your mentor or another student.

RE AND THE PERSONAL DEVELOPMENT OF PUPILS

Promoting personal development through RE leads, I suggest, to the identification of two key issues: the *culture of our pupils* and the *future of plural societies*. These issues are addressed in turn.

The culture of our pupils

For a number of years I taught RE in a boys' grammar school. After a period of time I started to claim that I was in charge of the Special Needs work. What I meant was that I was working with able and articulate young people who seemed to find it impossible to undertake an intelligent study of religion. Many of them just couldn't see the point. In my current job I work with lots of RE teachers. I keep hearing the same message from them, and it is not just academically able boys that have the problem.

Perhaps one of the most important insights to come from that loosely defined movement called postmodernism is that we are all, to some extent, products of our culture. Our pupils are shaped by the media, the norms of their peer group and the cultural air they breathe. One thing is very clear: religion is not a significant element in this cultural climate. Two researchers working in the field have this to say:

> What appears to be taking place is this. As young people leave the world
> of childhood, they are absorbed incrementally into the world of
> adulthood. Today much of this is characterised by the secular rather than
> the religious . . . In this sense to be irreligious is to be normal.
>
> (Kay and Francis 1996, p. 144)

Secularity is therefore the air our pupils breathe. Like fish which simply assume the water in which they swim, many of them will unconsciously assume the norms of a secular approach. What does that mean for you as an RE teacher? I suggest there are two possible consequences, depending on the way secularity is understood.

First, secularity can express itself in *antagonism* and *anger* towards religion. This is the atheistic response, which sees religion as responsible for many of the evils in the world and regards it as an intellectual impostor, holding to untenable beliefs as a source of illusory comfort. Those who opt for religion are regarded as inadequate escapists, unable to cope with the realities of a godless world. Underlying this view is the influence of a philosophy commonly called *scientism*, the belief that 'real' knowledge is found in the realm of science and mathematics. Religion, with its incredible views on the supernatural, is held to be in direct conflict with it. Research suggests that scientism may be a widespread philosophy in modern youth culture (Kay and Francis 1996).

Second, secularity can express itself simply in *apathy* about religion. The influence of the philosophy of relativism, the idea that truth is a personal matter, has undermined commitment to the big philosophies of life. Not only religion has suffered, so have other all-embracing causes, including political philosophies such as Marxism. There really doesn't seem much point in campaigning for what, after all, is only a personal hobby horse. The point of life is to get on with enjoying it. An article in the *British Journal of Religious Education* described the majority of modern young people as belonging to the 'I am nothing' grouping (Rudge 1998a). You will find this concept explored in greater detail above in Chapter 1. Labelling oneself in terms of a big cause, especially a religious one, is simply not 'cool'. The phenomenological study of major world religions is not going to seem awfully attractive if this is the major philosophy of your culture!

However, it is not the whole picture. Commentators on the culture of modern youth also report a spiritual hunger which, although it may be repressed by the pragmatic materialism of Western consumerism, is still a motivating force. The work of David Hay has been particularly influential in this regard (1990a). In extensive surveys he found convincing evidence that many people have deep spiritual experiences which have enormous personal significance and meaning, but which are rarely talked about with other people. The reason is an implicit secular censorship which makes people think that owning up to having had such experiences will make them appear abnormal. The truth is that they are in fact 'normal', but it is the conspiracy of silence that makes them appear abnormal. You will find further discussion of Hay's work in greater detail in Chapter 10.

The future of plural societies

The debates about the role of RE in promoting personal development have been influenced by concern about the future of religiously plural societies. The spectacle of Catholic, Orthodox and Muslim ethnically cleansing each other in the former Yugoslavia, of Catholic and Protestant murdering each other in Northern Ireland and of Muslim and Hindu at each other's throats in India has created much nervousness about the fragility of such societies.

This concern was heightened by the clash that took place between conservative Christians and the RE profession in the debates that surrounded the place of RE and collective worship in the 1988 Education Reform Act (Jackson 1992; Robson 1996). The Christian lobby worked hard to secure a predominant position for Christianity in the curriculum. The RE profession resisted, wishing to defend the multi-faith approach.

The details of this complex debate are not our concern now. What is important is that the attention of influential writers on RE was focused on a particular type of religious attitude, namely that which seeks to defend its position against that of others, sees other people from different religious traditions as a threat and adopts various strategies to diminish the influence of the perceived opponents. In a highly influential editorial in the *BJRE*, Professor John Hull (1992) described this as 'religionism'. It operates on the basis of a 'name and shame' philosophy. You name people according to their religious affiliation and then seek to shame them if their affiliation is different from your own. Hull described the attitude of mind as follows:

> We are better than they. We are orthodox; they are infidel. We are
> believers; they are unbelievers. We are right; they are wrong . . . The
> identity which is fostered by religionism depends upon rejection and
> exclusion.
>
> (1992, p. 70)

Hull went on to suggest that one of the functions of RE should be to promote
more open and healthy, less defensive attitudes. A similar argument was put forward
by Professor John Hick in the RE journal *Resource* when he suggested that Christians should stop thinking of Christianity as the only true religion and adopt what
he calls 'religious pluralism', the view that the different world religions are simply different ways of conceiving of God and that they are therefore all 'true' (Hick 1997).

Task 4.2 Exploring the religious attitudes of pupils

Observe a discussion lesson with a class of older pupils (Year 9 or
above), and record the key contributions made by the pupils.

- Note down any examples of phrases used which seem to illustrate
  attitudes influenced by secularism or religionism.
- Are there any contributions which give evidence that pupils may
  have had spiritual experiences which are important to them?
- If possible compare your findings with other students': do they con-
  cur with the national research you have read about in this chapter?
- Together decide how RE teaching needs to respond, if at all, to the
  changing cultural climate that your pupils inhabit.

The shift from a cafeteria of religions

What, then, is the implication of these two issues for pupil learning in RE lessons?
In many people's minds it is that we can no longer be satisfied with pupils simply
making their own choices on the basis of information supplied in the classroom, but
rather that we, as their teachers, have to make sure that their choices are 'sound' and
their attitudes 'healthy'. I now examine two influential views as to what this will
entail.

First, David Hay (1990b) has argued that RE should constitute 'de-indoctrina-
tion'. What he means is that teachers have to combat the negative effects of secular-
isation by adopting methods which affirm and encourage the deep spiritual
experiences that are latent in most human beings (Hammond *et al.* 1990). Only in
this way, he believes, will RE seem relevant. Pupils are not going to learn anything
from religion if they reject it outright as a waste of time. So one of the tasks of RE
is to undo the antagonism and apathy towards religion that is engendered by secular
Western culture. In that way religion will become relevant to the pupils, so that,
instead of simply opting for the prevailing secular 'beefburger and chips' rejection of

religion that is the norm of their culture, they will adopt a healthier attitude more sympathetic towards religious belief.

Second, John Hull argues that RE must oppose religionism. I was once at an RE conference where a teacher said, 'I always tell my pupils there are no right or wrong answers in RE.' Her motivation for saying this was that she wanted to move away from the situation where her pupils viewed religion as a phenomenon in which people had to believe that they were right and everyone else was wrong. Her idea was to combat the popular view of religion as involving tribal loyalties which brought one into conflict with those from other tribes.

It seems hard to object to any of this. Why shouldn't an RE teacher want to engender more sympathy for her subject content by challenging the anger and apathy generated by secular attitudes? Why shouldn't we oppose narrow and vindictive attitudes which cause disharmony in society? Any sound approach to promoting citizenship must surely do that. The problem comes when we remember why the confessional approach was rejected as a model for RE. It is widely accepted that it is inappropriate in a plural society for schools to tell pupils what religious beliefs they ought or ought not to hold. But if we, as teachers, set out to combat a secular approach, surely that in itself is a form of confessionalism? It will hardly be acceptable to those who believe that secularism is right. And there are some very influential and intelligent secularists around, for example Professor Richard Dawkins. Furthermore, if we promote the idea that all religions are equal, will that not be deeply offensive to many religious communities? For example, most Muslim parents are not going to be happy with their children being told that Islam is only one among a number of true religions. So how do we avoid confessionalism if we are to persuade our pupils of the relevance of religion and of the evils of prejudice?

To answer this I suggest we have to distinguish between the imposition of a particular view and the encouraging of a more open approach. Popular secularism is harmful because it causes pupils to reject the possibility of a religious approach to life *without thinking seriously about it as an alternative view*. This form of secularism has made them blind and deaf to other voices. It closes down the possibility of meaningful conversation between religious people and non-religious people. Likewise a religionist approach manifests a similar problem, because it drives us back into our own tribe. Both these are clearly unacceptable in a plural society, because they lead to conflict and rejection of others and stop pupils benefiting from contact with other people from whom they may have much to learn. The health of a plural society depends on people being prepared to listen to each other, on their being willing to work together for the common good and on the ability to make concessions to other people out of respect for their aspirations, way of life and deeply held beliefs. Neither popular secularism nor religionism encourages this sort of 'conversational' approach (Jackson 1997). So the RE teacher can legitimately resist them in the pursuit of an educational approach which promotes responsible citizenship.

Wanting to encourage pupils to be reflective and open is very different from telling them what they *ought* to believe. Promoting a reflective approach helps pupils to become more critically aware of the culture that has shaped them and helps them to see the possibilities of learning something valid from other people. The shared characteristic of both popular secularism and religionism is the inability to comprehend the possibility or legitimacy of another point of view and the inability to reflect critically on one's own position. However, to tell pupils that a secular approach is wrong *per se* or to tell them that they must believe that all religions are true is to move beyond what is legitimate. The difference can perhaps be illustrated by returning to the statement of the teacher at the RE conference. Instead of telling pupils that there are no right and wrong answers in RE, which is in effect to tell them that they ought to adopt relativism, I suggest we should explain that there is no agreement as to what the right or wrong answers are in religion. This is simply to ensure that they are aware that the existence of pluralism is a matter of fact that has to be accommodated in some way. It is not to tell them how they should respond to that fact.

LEARNING FROM RELIGION

The phrase *learning from* religion was coined to capture the aspiration that pupils should not just acquire information but should learn something about themselves, in other words that their study has outcomes in their own life and thinking. The function, then, of RE is to encourage a more reflective approach to religious matters so as to create the context in which this can happen. The question then becomes how, practically, can we use religion to achieve these goals? There are basically two extremes in approaching this question (with my apologies to Vikings and, particularly, to missionaries – for whom I have the greatest respect – for the parody).

The RE teacher as Viking

I once heard a lecture where it was said that the job of the RE teacher is to ransack the world's religions in order to find material that can be used to promote the personal development of the pupils. By this the speaker meant that RE teachers should not be too concerned about teaching religion from the point of view of the believer, but rather that they should look for gems that could be plucked out of their context in the religion and used for some other purpose. An extreme and facetious example would be using the New Testament story of Jesus feeding the five thousand to teach the importance of picking up litter (because Jesus's disciples picked up twelve baskets in the story). This has nothing to do with the significance the story has for Christians. It rips it out of its Christian context to use it for another purpose, supporting the school's litter education programme.

The RE teacher as missionary

In stark contrast, this position views the religious content as sacrosanct, to be conveyed in a predigested form to unquestioning and passive recipients. The expectation is that just learning the religious material will have a salutary effect on pupil personal development. It is therefore assumed that the systematic learning of religious information automatically produces the required outcomes. Certainly the confessional approach *as taught in some schools* would have been a classic example of this. (I hasten to add that there can be excellent examples of confessional teaching.) Less obvious perhaps is that the phenomenological approach fell into exactly the same error. It too assumed that information about religion taught to pupils would automatically have moral effects, in particular that it would make them more tolerant. Recent research suggests that this may not be correct (Malone 1998).

Andrew Wright has suggested that the greatest danger of this position is that we represent religions as providing packaged, simplistic answers to the great intellectual and spiritual challenges faced in life by human beings (Wright 1993). The trouble with this approach is that it makes the religious life seem to consist of simplistic answers to complex and challenging questions. Wright argues that if we are going to produce pupils who have learnt to be theologically literate, we must introduce them to the *ambiguity* of the religious life. By this he means the awareness that faith does not necessarily offer straightforward answers.

Neither of these approaches constitutes an adequate model for the way in which religion may be used in RE so that our pupils learn from it. The first fails to do justice to the fact that each of the religions should be taught in a way that respects its integrity and is recognisable to a member of the faith community. To do otherwise is to fail to equip pupils with an important skill for life in a plural society, namely to be able to listen carefully to someone else so as to see as clearly as possible the way things look from their perspective. This is essential if the blinding effects of both religionism and secularism are to be overcome. At the same time we have seen that *just* reflecting the believer's perspective may well mean that the religious content will remain largely irrelevant to the pupil. If our pupils are to learn from religion they must be taught it in a way which overcomes its seeming irrelevance. Otherwise it will be drowned out by the secular voices in our pupils' culture. How can these aspirations be achieved? In the next section we shall examine two approaches which seek to do this.

APPROACHES TO LEARNING FROM RELIGION

Ethnography and the Warwick RE Project

The Warwick RE Project (WREP) derives from the work of a team in the Institute of Education at Warwick University headed by Professor Robert Jackson (Jackson 1997). A premise of their work is that understanding the faith of another person means entering, as far as possible, into their way of life. The responsibility of the RE teacher is to ensure that the way a religion is represented to the pupils through textbooks and in other ways is not distorted. They recommend ethnography as an ideal methodology. By this they mean the direct study of individuals in the context of their own family and community life with a view to observing, and to a degree experiencing, what life is like for them. This 'conversational' approach, as Jackson calls it, will lead to the undermining of stereotypes and greater empathy for the life and aspirations of other people. Ideally the Warwick team would like pupils themselves to become field ethnographers, but they recognise the practical limitations. So it has published a series of textbooks, under the general title Interpreting Religions, which draw on their own extensive ethnographic research among young people from a variety of religious communities in England (e.g. Robson 1995; Mercier 1996; Wayne 1996). In one book, for example, we meet Kamran, a thirteen year old Muslim who lives in a terraced house in Birmingham, and learn about his daily life, beliefs and attitudes (Mercier 1996). Ethnography, the Warwick team believe, will undermine secularism and religionism by bringing the pupil in the classroom into conversation with the young person in the faith community.

The Warwick team do not assume that creating this conversation is an easy task. They recognise the huge gap that exists between the secular culture of most pupils and the religious world of the young people in the textbooks. They see two separate tasks as being necessary. First, the pupils need to be sensitised to their own culture and the assumptions it generates. If they aren't so sensitised, the assumptions inevitably distort their perceptions of the life of the young person in the faith community. Second, our pupils need to become aware of what Jackson calls the *grammar* of the young person's faith, by which he means the complex of practices, relationships and beliefs which constitutes the life lived by that person. In this approach, the pupil is encouraged to move to and fro, from their own perspective to that of the young person in the book, as a means of understanding where both they and the young person in the book are coming from. This is described as *building bridges* and depends on the teacher being able to identify concepts which are familiar to the pupil and concepts that are central to the faith of the young person and to bring them into line with each other. Thereby pupils see the relevance of the faith world to their own, often predominantly secular, world by examining concepts in the two worlds which relate to each other. For example, pupils are encouraged to think about the books which have had a good influence on their own lives when studying Muslim attitudes to the Qur'an (Mercier 1996, p. 25).

A final question is how pupils can learn something about themselves from the study of someone else's faith? The Warwick Project has coined the term *edification* to answer it. This is explained as follows:

> Engagement with another's way of life has the potential to make an impact on one's own thinking and attitudes. The WREP approach encourages students to do more than reconstruct the religious lives of others. It also encourages them to relate the material studied to issues which are of concern to themselves.
>
> (Robson 1995, p. 4)

> What might appear to be entirely different and 'other' at first glance can end linking with one's own experience in such a way that new perspectives are created or unquestioned presuppositions are challenged.
>
> (Jackson 1997, p. 130)

The Warwick team think that an encounter with someone else's life of faith should have an impact on one's own life. They regard one of the purposes of RE as being to capitalise on the opportunities for edification by planning specific learning activities which encourage it.

Theology and the Stapleford Project

Another project which takes a similar approach to the Warwick material is the Stapleford Project, based at the Stapleford Centre in Nottingham. It is close to my own heart, as I have been involved in developing it for the last ten years (Cooling 1994a, 1997). The big difference from the Warwick approach is the emphasis placed on the role of theological concepts in giving access to the faith of another person. It is this that is seen as the key rather than ethnography. As with the Warwick Project, the theoretical background of the approach has been translated into practical form in a textbook for use in RE lessons (Wright 1995a).

Figure 4.1 'Concept cracking': a worked example

As a practical classroom tool the 'concept cracking' approach has been broken down into four specific steps, which can be remembered using the acronym USER (**Unpack, Select, Engage, Relate**). It can be illustrated using the story from the New Testament where Jesus turns the traders out of the Temple in Jerusalem (Mark 11:15–17).

1   *Unpack the concepts*
Before teaching any topic it is important to be aware of the different theological concepts that underpin it and are important to the understanding of its meaning and significance. If, as teachers, we are not clear about the ideas we are covering, our pupils certainly will not be. In the case of this story, the key concepts include anger, injustice, holiness, Jesus as God's son and judgement.

2   *Select one or two concepts as the focus for the lesson*
It is very important to focus your lesson on one or two key concepts that you are seeking to teach. Otherwise your pupils will become confused. Let us tackle the concept of righteous anger in this example, to get across the idea when anger is justified and when it is not.

3   *Engage with the pupil's world of experience*
This is perhaps the hardest and yet the most important stage in the process. The key is to find parallels in the pupil's world with the concept of righteous anger. One possibility would be to ask pupils to give examples of occasions when they have been angry. The purpose of the activity is not so much to pass judgement on the particular instances as to establish the idea in pupil's minds that there are right and wrong forms of anger and to begin the process of searching for criteria to distinguish them. This will build a bridge between the pupil's world and the religious concept.

Figure 4.1 Continued

---

4   *Relate to the religious concepts*

At this point introduce the story from the New Testament. An effective way of doing so is to use the painting called 'Christ driving the traders from the Temple' by El Greco (cf. M. Cooling 1988 for full details of how to do this) and to ask the pupils to comment on how Jesus's behaviour is portrayed in the painting. In particular they will notice there are two groups of people, those who are the object of his anger and those who are being affirmed. A role-play could then be used in which pupils take on the role of members of the two groups and debate Jesus's behaviour. Finally there will need to be a whole-class discussion in which the question of why Jesus thought his anger was justified is discussed. It should draw out themes like the importance of resisting injustice and exploitation, the holiness of the Temple and Jesus's special relationship with God which made his anger uniquely justifiable, as far as the Gospel writer is concerned. Pupils should be encouraged to express their own views, perhaps through the medium of a diary entry by someone who was present in the Temple, as to whether or not Jesus's anger was justified.

There are two important points to note from this example:

- Steps 1 and 2 represent important preliminary work which must be done by us as teachers to clarify our own understanding of the topic. This is very important as a way of giving the lesson a clear focus. However, the actual teaching will often begin with step 3 in order to ensure that the lesson seems relevant to the pupils. Most lessons will have to begin with an activity that is designed to build a bridge between the pupil's world and the religious topic.
- This process accommodates both the concerns we have been discussing about pupil learning in RE. Considerable effort is expended on ensuring that the pupils overcome their initial negativity to Jesus's behaviour, so that they understand, as far as possible, the Gospel writer's perspective. So there is emphasis on the importance of listening as a skill in learning about religion. However, considerable effort is also expended on ensuring that the pupils learn something of personal relevance from the story. In this case they will have reflected upon the difference between justified and unjustified anger in their own lives.

A major premise of the project is that the alienation which most people experience when encountering religion is because the concepts which enable one to make sense of a religion are largely absent from the secular culture. It advocates the process of 'concept cracking' as a means of unpacking and exploring religious and theological concepts in the classroom. For example, seeing a picture of Muslims prostrate in prayer can, unfortunately, be a source of great hilarity to many Western teenagers. The difficulty is that they have no experience of the concept of submission to a higher being, which is being expressed through the body language of the Muslim worshipper. It is simply not part of a Western liberal view of life which emphasises rights and autonomy rather than duties and submission. So teaching about Islamic prayer will remain a lost cause unless some way of allowing our pupils to get their minds round the idea of submission can be found. They may well end up with a page full of pictures and labels illustrating prayer positions at the end of a lesson on Muslim prayer, but unless they have some feel for their meaning and significance for Muslims they might just as well have hieroglyphics on the page. So a key task for the teacher in teaching any religious topic is to identify the theological concepts which are integral to understanding the meaning and significance of that topic. Otherwise we could be teaching nothing but meaningless information.

Of course it is one thing to identify a key theological concept, it is quite another to teach it to teenagers. A lesson on the concept of submission hardly seems likely to grab the attention. However, like the Warwick approach, the Stapleford team argue that theological concepts have their parallels in the concepts that are part of the everyday experience of teenagers in modern Britain. An important part of our job as RE teachers is to look for ways of translating religious concepts into forms that make sense in our pupils' world of experience. For example, with Muslim prayer a key preliminary to understanding is to have been made aware of the importance of body language in human communication. There can be great fun to be had in a lesson exploring how, in our everyday lives, we use our bodies to say things. An interesting homework is to ask pupils to spot some of the more unusual things people say in this way! This can then be followed by a lesson where Muslim prayer positions are examined with this question in mind: 'What are these people saying which is an unusual thing for people to say in Western society?' This could be followed by pupils working out ways in which they would express homage through their own bodies. Can they conceive of situations when it might happen? Older pupils might like to consider these words from the marriage service: 'with my body I thee worship', or

---

Task 4.3 Lesson planning using the 'concept cracking' framework

Select a topic from the RE scheme or work being used in your practice school. Now prepare to teach this topic conceptually by:

- brainstorming the various concepts that underpin the topic (Unpack);
- deciding what is the key concept which it is necessary for your pupils to grasp if they are to understand this topic (Select);
- identifying parallels for that concept in their own world of experience (Engage);
- developing bridges which can be used to enable the pupils to see the relationship between the key religious concept and the concept from their own world of experience (Engage and relate);
- considering how the students may be able to apply what they have learnt from their study of the religious concept in their own world of experience (Relate).

'with my body I honour you' in its modern form. The important general point to note is that these learning activities are designed to convey a feeling of what the concept of submission means for the believer.

This approach is designed to overcome the alienation that many pupils feel towards religion. It certainly contributes to the process of *learning from* religion, by enabling them to listen to the believer with more empathy and thereby developing a key skill which will eliminate the negative effects of secularism and religionism. However, it needs to go beyond simply enhancing their understanding of religion if it is to contribute to developing the pupils' understanding of themselves. Here is where the emphasis on concepts as the focus gives a particular edge. Initially it is very hard to see how looking at Islamic prayer positions can help a Western teenager who rarely, if ever, prays, let alone participates in corporate rituals of prayer. But once we focus the attention on the concept of submission expressed through the body, it opens up consideration of a wealth of parallel experiences. Do they ever consider submitting to anyone? What would make them willingly do it? Has our society got it right in seeing submission in a negative light? And so on. The following quotation from a primary school RE specialist sums up the point:

> It is not the religion *per se* from which the child is learning, but rather from some of the key concepts, feelings, experiences, values and truth claims upheld and engendered by that religion, its faith and its communities.
>
> (Albans 1998, p. 4)

IMPLICATIONS FOR THE CLASSROOM

In closing, I will just make a few comments on the implications of what I have been saying for the classroom.

Designing learning activities

One of the most alarming features of research into the teaching of RE in secondary schools is the revelation that the learning activities that pupils are given are often very ineffective (OFSTED 1997). There are two major problems. First, it appears that many of the learning activities set do not move much beyond the level of information recall. Second, activities that pupils will already have done in their primary schools are reappearing in the secondary school RE programme. The 1997 OFSTED report describes its findings as follows:

> Many activities set at Key Stage 3 were widely used at Key Stage 2 and were quite unsuitable for most secondary school pupils. Pupils in years 4 and 7 were asked to make advent calendars. Pupils' work in years 3, 6, 8 and 9 included a cartoon account of the six days of creation, usually followed by a picture of God sleeping in a bed on the seventh day. The

only difference in outcome from both the tasks was in the quality of the art work . . . There were too many instances of filling in missing words.

(OFSTED 1997, p. 29)

The effect on pupil learning will be devastating. If pupils are already switched off religion, being given tasks to do which they carried out in primary school can only reinforce the idea that religion is trivial and irrelevant, just kids' stuff. To overcome this perception the learning activities we set must be worthwhile and demanding. This means that we must plan activities which require the pupils to use the information they are learning in a way that enhances their understanding of the concepts that are the focus of the lesson. So, in our Islamic prayer example, exploring the way humans communicate through body language and then discussing how it relates to Islamic prayer will generate much greater understanding than simply asking pupils to draw and label the prayer positions. It will also open up opportunities for pupils to apply what they learn in their own lives. A key question to ask when designing learning activities is 'What sort of conversation between pupils will this activity generate?' If the answer is: trivial conversation, it is a fair bet that the activity is trivial.

Figure 4.2 Examples of tasks designed to develop religious literacy

Examples of activities – applicable to a number of religions – that get beyond simply regurgitating information on a topic, but which require the pupils to use that information to express their understanding, are:

- Pupils work in pairs. Each one of the pair has to design three questions on the topics they have studied. The first is a factual recall question, the second is a question which probes significance and the third requires an application in a new situation. The pupils write answers to each other's questions and discuss their answers.
- Pupils imagine that an event or story they have learnt about is to be made into a video. They have the job of writing the back cover blurb in no more than 100 words. The task is to highlight the most significant points to capture the potential viewer's attention.
- Pupils are asked to plan a new festival to celebrate an aspect of the topic they have studied. They must explain the symbolism and significance of their suggestions, justifying them from their studies.

A further key question focuses on the need to ask ourselves what exactly is the purpose of each learning activity we set. Possible purposes could be to:

- acquire new information;
- engage the pupils' interest and help them see parallels in their own lives;
- explore the meaning and significance of the information;
- stimulate the application of the ideas in the pupils' own lives (edification).

If we know exactly what we want to achieve, we can design our activities accordingly and are more likely to offer a range of different types of activity which will help to maintain the interest level of our lessons. If we don't ask ourselves what the purpose of our learning activities is, the likelihood is that they will end up focusing on accumulating information.

Task 4.4 Evaluating learning activities

Collect a range of examples of learning activities from your own teaching, from your observation of others' teaching and from books and other sources. For each decide:

● What was the intended purpose of the activity?
● Did it help the pupil interact with the religious material so that their understanding was enhanced?
● How could it be improved either to achieve its intended purpose or to achieve a different purpose?

Asking the right questions

Asking questions is a very important teaching skill. As with designing learning activities, the key is to have thought through the purpose of asking a question. If we don't we almost inevitably drift into asking questions which require no more than information recall. Consider the following questions:

● How would this person react if . . .?
● What would it mean if . . .?
● Can you think of a situation when . . .?

You will find that questions such as these are needed alongside those which elicit information-based responses. Planning the questions you may use is a very important, but much neglected, part of lesson planning.

Using a variety of languages

One of the difficulties with teaching religion is that it is easy to trivialise it by using straightforward descriptive language alone. The mystery and ambiguity, the trust and devotion, the paradox of truth, the vividness of spiritual experience that lie at the heart of most religion can vaporise as we seek to describe it. To be true to the nature of religion, we must use a variety of modes of expression which allow pupils to capture a glimpse of the indescribable. Story, poetry, art, music, drama and other art forms are integral to the nature of our subject (M. Cooling 1996).

SUMMARY AND KEY POINTS

Recent thinking on RE has emphasised the importance of pupils learning from religion as well as learning about it. Putting it another way, RE should contribute to the personal development of our pupils as well as increase their knowledge of the religions. This means that we, as teachers, have to develop strategies which move beyond the transmission of information about the religions to enabling the pupils to apply insights from what they learn to their own lives. In doing this there are two major obstacles for us to overcome, popular secularism and religionism. The key skills to be developed are that of being able to hear a person who may have very different views from our own and then being able to apply what we have heard in our own lives. Ethnography and a focus on theological concepts are suggested as two ways of achieving these goals.

FURTHER READING

Cooling, T. (1994a) *Concept Cracking: Exploring Christian Beliefs in School*, Nottingham: Stapleford Project Books. This is a short, practical guide to teaching theological concepts in RE, based mainly on Christianity. It was published at the same time as the Model Syllabuses of the SCAA and reflects the thinking behind Model 2. The booklet is out of print but is available on the Stapleford Centre's web site at www.stapleford-centre.org. It should be read alongside Chris Wright's classroom text (1995a).

Cooling, T. (1994b) *A Christian Vision for State Education*, London: SPCK. This is a substantial work which reviews some of the major debates on the nature and purpose of RE which are influencing current thinking about the curriculum. As the title suggests, the book is written from a Christian perspective, but its philosophy is relevant to teachers of all commitments.

Jackson, R. (1997) *Religious Education: An Interpretive Approach*, London: Hodder & Stoughton. This seminal book describes in detail the ethnographic approach developed by the Warwick RE Project. It deals with the theoretical issues that surround modern RE teaching as well as describing the practical responses made by the Warwick team in the development of materials for the classroom. The book should be read alongside the pupil textbooks in the series Interpreting Religion (Robson 1995; Mercier 1996; Wayne 1996).

Qualifications and Curriculum Authority (1998a) *Exemplification of Standards in Religious Education: Key Stages 1 to 4*, London: QCA. This highly practical book gives examples of learning activities in RE and illustrates the objectives that they are designed to achieve in both learning about and learning from religion.

Wright, A. (1993) *Religious Education in the Secondary School: Prospects for Religious Literacy*, London: David Fulton. This is a book that should be read by every RE teacher. It is a masterly sketch of the debates about RE. Wright puts forward an invigorating view of the subject based on the promotion of religious literacy.

Part III

Classroom issues

5 The Role of Language in Religious Education

Ann-Marie Brandom

Language is that which we use to communicate to others our needs, ideas, desires, values, stories, opinions or beliefs, and as such language is open to interpretation. Language is dependent on its context, on the emphasis given to the particular words used, or even the body language which may accompany such words in translation. The meaning of such communication does not become clear without, again, the use of language to identify, explain and expound what is meant. Thus all language requires dialogue for clarification of meaning or purpose. Religious language is no exception.

The term 'language' is used in this context to refer to that which is both symbolically communicated and that which is spoken of in the religious world. It is fundamental to this chapter that such 'religious language' is understood in two ways: (1) as language which is reflective of the specific community from which it derives its authority and (2) as language that is common to all religions. Having said that, it must be made clear that it is only through dialogue that we have the opportunity to discover the 'truth', the 'validity' or the 'meaning' of that which is being communicated in religious terms. It is to this end that the aim of this chapter is to: (1) encourage the definition and use of subject-specific terminology; (2) invite reflection on current trends in the classroom in the light of the necessity of using religious language; and (3) propose some practical exercises which can be tried in the classroom.

OBJECTIVES

By the end of this chapter you should be able to:

- identify subject-specific religious language;
- develop your own glossary of terms relevant in teaching each world faith and the philosophy of religion;

> - make such language relevant and challenging to the appropriate Key Stage you are teaching;
> - devise activities whereby religious language is used by the pupils in an accurate, informed and reflective manner;
> - identify which model of RE you wish to use in the classroom to promote effective religious dialogue.

RELIGIOUS LANGUAGE

The importance of religious language in RE

Many of you reading this now can easily recall an instance where a misinterpretation of language, either verbal or non-verbal, has led to an embarrassing and unnecessary incidence of confusion. All of us can recall such situations, and the RE classroom is no exception. Just as ambiguity exists over everyday language so it exists with religious language. Knowledge, understanding, ideas, beliefs, opinions and thoughts about religion need to be aired by your pupils using the appropriate religious language in order for clarity of understanding to take place. The role of language in the RE classroom requires time and scrutiny on behalf of the teacher in order to ensure that confusion is averted and the students use appropriate religious language in an informed and balanced manner.

The attention you pay to the use of religious language in the classroom can enhance the quality of each lesson you teach: it can inform the knowledge and understanding of the topics being studied for all levels of ability; it can enhance the calibre of discussion of each topic, both inside and outside the classroom; and it can facilitate a more structured approach to the ultimate questions in life, inherent within the nature of our subject. Only by giving appropriate attention to religious language can you hope to enable students to come to grips with and appreciate the complexities of religion in a positive way.

Just as you have been bombarded by a whole new vocabulary since you started your PGCE course and have begun to assimilate it as you go about your work in college and school, so the same principle applies to the subject of RE for the pupils you will be teaching. The religious language specific to RE requires skilled interpretation if our students are to learn effectively.

The notion of religious language is one which, whether your undergraduate studies were in Religious Studies or Theology, you have already spent at least three years coming to grips with. The fact that you now have to enter a classroom where words such as 'reincarnation', 'forgiveness', 'spirituality', 'love', 'guru', 'sin', and 'divine' brings you face to face with challenges that are at the very heart of the task facing you as an RE teacher. One of the principles of hermeneutics is interpretation. In RE you must anticipate the different understandings students will bring with them when they come to examine religious concepts. Such anticipation will better enable you to help them to use such language with greater understanding and insight.

Religious language and the learning process

How do you do this practically in your planning? You must first examine the material you are about to teach and identify the key religious concept to be studied. You will need to become aware of how religious concepts are interpreted within specific religious traditions, as well as the common perceptions of them beyond the tradition that 'owns' them. This reflection on language will allow you to develop a pattern of teaching in which your pupils are:

- presented with core subject material, language and concepts;
- invited to give initial reactions to the information;
- introduced to the variety of ways in which those both within and outside the faith community understand the language;
- encouraged to revisit the material in the light of this information and given the opportunity to reconsider their initial interpretations.

CASE STUDY

The Christian concept of 'miracle'

The issue of 'miracles' occurs in many instances in world faiths. Let us take the instance of miracles in Christianity. The word 'miracle' has popular connotations, as in the sentence 'It will be a miracle if England ever win the World Cup again (and don't we know it!).' However, the word functions differently in the context of the 'specialist' or 'technical' language of Christian theology. Here 'miracle' clearly means more than an unlikely occurrence. It has to do with the interruption of the natural order of things by the supernatural. It is easy to equate this with mere magic, but the Christian understanding goes deeper. The significance of 'miracles' in the life of Jesus, from a Christian point of view, is that they reveal the nature of Jesus as both God and man, the incarnate Christ. They are a demonstration of the compassion of God and indicative of the establishing of the 'Kingdom of God'.

In your lesson plan you must highlight the concept of 'miracle'. This in turn will demand that you deal with the concepts of the 'Kingdom of God', and the 'incarnation'. In terms of an entire programme of study you will need to extend this into an exploration of the nature of God, and the significance of each miracle in terms of the whole Christian world view. But let's just concentrate on the word 'miracle' for the moment.

Once you have sifted out the central religious concepts involved in studying miracles, and have anticipated the students' reactions and initial understanding of the concept, you can identify how that concept is viewed from within the faith tradition. Miracles are a contentious subject within the Christian community and opinion, basically, may fall into two camps. There are those 'conservative' Christians who accept the miracles as historical events and even choose to believe that miracles still occur today, then there are the 'liberal' Christians who view the miracles as purely symbolic, a metaphor to enable us to understand God better. The contention within Christianity between those who are conservative Christians and those who are liberal Christians is intense, and your pupils will need to be aware of this and be helped to engage with the debate.

You should then plan to examine the external views held on miracles. These will range across a broad spectrum. At one extreme your teaching should refer to modern naturalistic assumptions that miracles simply don't happen, and that therefore Christianity, in its traditional form at least, is rooted in delusion and superstition. In contrast you should also encourage your pupils to be aware of current postmodern suspicion of scientific authority with its greater openness to 'spiritual reality' and refusal to dismiss Christian claims *a priori*.

Once you have introduced the topic and examined the actual core material in its appropriate context, your pupils can be introduced to the variety of positions which it is possible to hold on the subject of miracles. You should encourage them to identify, at a level appropriate to their ability, the key components of each position and explain why these different positions are justifiable ones. The students can then be invited to identify their own position within the range of options on the agenda and justify it. Class discussion on the truth, viability and ambiguity of the contrasting positions will need to explore why positions can differ and the tension existent within the faith community on the issue. The students can be taught how to reflect intelligently on the issue of miracles in a manner that is both sensitive to the deep-rooted importance of miracles in the Christian tradition, yet also critically aware of the controversial nature of the concept. In this way you are training the students to examine the religious context of the miracles, appreciate the diversity of the understanding of miracles from within the faith community, and external conflicts of interpretation. By encouraging such engagement with religious language you will be developing the religious literacy of your pupils.

You must not assume that religious language can be used without explanation. This is one of the keys to ensuring that your use of language is appropriate and it is one of the first things you have to learn. How are you going to make the concept of 'anicca' relevant to your Year 9 pupils? How are you going to teach 'Tahwid' to Year 7 or the concept of 'Brahman' at Key Stage 4? Think about the above worked example. What kind of RE do you want in the classroom? How are you going to achieve it? These are important questions and the use of language will be fundamental to whichever process you choose.

RELIGIOUS LANGUAGE IN THE CLASSROOM

Introducing a vocabulary

In 1994 the Schools Curriculum and Assessment Authority (SCAA) published a set of Model Syllabuses intended to support the work of those responsible for devising RE syllabuses at local level (SCAA 1994a, b). SCAA included with the syllabuses a *Glossary of Terms* (SCAA 1994c). The purpose was twofold: (1) to offer teachers guidance on the meaning of key words as used in each religious tradition; (2) to standardise the spelling of such words. The Model Syllabuses accepted the importance for pupils of developing a working knowledge of key words and technical terms which are in use within each religious tradition.

In the same way it is vital when you are preparing your lessons to identify the religious language you are about to use, to understand what it means yourself, and to take responsibility for ensuring that your pupils do likewise. Do remember, though, that to understand a word you need to do more than learn a dictionary definition: genuine understanding is revealed in a pupil's ability to introduce such language appropriately into a conversation.

Time and effort must be devoted to defining the concept you are about to teach (Chapter 4, above). You must be familiar with the material you are going to use in the classroom and identify the specific religious terminology. At the same time you must recognise the importance of presenting the terminology in a form suitable to the age and ability of your class. Avoid the trap of thinking that critical engagement with subject-specific vocabulary is a task open only to A Level students. All pupils you teach are capable of engaging with religious language provided it is presented at an appropriate level. Even if the concept is a complicated one, it does not mean that the students will not understand it. Their understanding depends upon your ability to break down both the concept and the language for them. Their understanding also depends on your expectations of them. It is a recognised factor in teaching RE that the students will arrive in your classroom with their own world view. They may not have the 'correct' religious language to explain that world view, but it will be there. They will also be sensitive to your expectations of them, hence the need to reinforce what they already know as well as challenge them with what they have yet to come to grips with.

Language and world views

In the first instance then you must be aware of the fact that the students will arrive in your lessons with a particular world view. Your job is to give them language by which they can identify their world view, teach them a deeper awareness of the other existent, coherent world views and the language which accompanies them and then facilitate the dialogue which can ensue from informed viewpoints.

Task 5.1 Identifying the world view of the pupil

Choose a small number of willing candidates from the pupils you teach. It need not necessarily be the whole class. If possible select them from a number of different year groups. (You could usefully carry out the research among your fellow PGCE students if you wish.) On a worksheet ask pupils the five questions listed below. In the initial stage you may want to ensure anonymity. There is no age limit for this activity, although you may need to revise the language to meet the needs of younger pupils.

- Who or what is 'God'?
- What is the purpose of your life?
- According to what principles do you live your life?
- What will happen to you when you die?
- Why is there suffering in the world?

How do the responses fit into the following categories of world view?

- specific confessional (Buddhist, Christian, Hindu, Islamic, Jewish, Sikh, etc.);
- liberal universalist;
- agnostic;
- atheist;
- postmodern non-realist.

By completing this activity pupils and students will be able both to identify with a particular world view and to recognise how their world views relate to others. This in turn will help your task of introducing pupils to an understanding of a range of world views.

Having established that each student has some form of understanding of the ultimate questions of life, you then have to identify how you will actually inform the students of the language they must familiarise themselves with in order to discuss religion even more meaningfully. Once you have identified which concept you need to teach the students it is no good having the same method for teaching them new religious terminology each lesson. Instruction in the lesson on the correct use of words must arise from what you are doing. If you use the same format each time both you and the students will die of boredom. You must, however, ensure that the new vocabulary is written down somewhere for them so they can see how it is spelt and in what context it is used.

Creating a glossary

The simplest thing is to ensure that you write the words on the board for all to see. The words should be there at the beginning of the lesson to allow you and the students to focus on them. Alternatively, write them up as you go along or have them written on the worksheet you give them. You have to decide whether you want the words to have definitions on the board or the sheets or whether you want to teach them the definition as you go along. The students should be encouraged to build up their own glossary of terms in their books and you should provide regular opportunities both in the lessons and in their written work to check the appropriateness of the usage. This will encourage confidence in the use of religious language and the accuracy of such use in lessons, particularly in discussion work. It will also familiarise them with the necessity of accuracy in terminology when there is ambiguity of religious understanding, as well as alert them to the possible ambiguity of religious terminology!

Task 5.2 Exploring approaches to religious language in the classroom

Among the lessons that you observe when you first go into schools choose three or four lessons on different religious topics and through-out each lesson list the subject-specific religious language used by the teacher and/or the pupils. Analyse the words you have listed in the light of the following questions:

- Are the pupils given a definition of specific religious language at any point in the lesson? Is the correct spelling taught?
- Does the teacher assume an understanding of the religious language?
- Can you assess whether the students understand the terminology being used?
- In what way does the teacher ensure that the students understand and use religious language appropriately?
- Is there a list up, either on the board or somewhere in the room, of difficult or new or significant religious words?
- Do the pupils have a glossary of terms in their books?
- Are the pupils encouraged to use the religious language in discussion, either with each other or in groups?

Task 5.3 Preparing to address language issues during your teaching practice

Obtain and familiarise yourself with a copy of the policy on the use of religious language in your RE department if one exists.

Decide on the approach and policy regarding language that you intend to adopt.

Initiate your own personal glossary of key religious terminology.

Obtain for your records a copy of the SCAA *Religious Education Glossary of Terms*, published in conjunction with the Model Syllabuses.

Language at each Key Stage

Once you have recognised the need for such attention to the detail of language, you must be able to identify what material is relevant to each Key Stage. Given that there are so many textbooks written for each stage, it is important to familiarise yourself with the resources available on a particular topic. You will find information on what is available through your teaching practice school, your college, the local RE Centre, the local Advisory Service and specialist bookshops (Chapter 13, below).

Task 5.4 Identifying appropriate language for each Key Stage

Find two or three textbooks written specifically for each secondary Key Stage.

- Identify key religious words in one chapter of each book and examine the language used to explain the religious concept(s) the chapter deals with.
- Compare the chapters from each Key Stage textbook with one another, making special note of the similarities and differences in the layout and the nature of the set tasks.
- Compare the language between Key Stages, looking especially at similarities, differences and evidence of progression.
- Practise drawing up a lesson plan for each year group within each Key Stage, using each of the chapters. What preparation do you have to make in order to ensure the effective delivery of the religious language contained in the chapters?
- Try devising a worksheet for each year group within each Key Stage, using the guidelines you have noted. What preparation do you have to be aware of in order to ensure the effective delivery of religious language teaching?

THE HERMENEUTICS OF RE

It will by now be clear that there are a number of models on offer for the teaching of RE. As a professional RE teacher you will have to decide what your aims are for your classroom, to decide which model of RE you will follow in order to achieve those aims, and then devise your programmes of study accordingly. Each model adopts a particular view of the learning–understanding process, each has its specific hermeneutical programme, and each uses language in a particular manner (Wright 1996a, 1997b, 1998a).

The phenomenological model

In the first instance the phenomenological model, popular in the 1970s and 1980s, and still alive today, requires the teacher and the student to be objective in the study of the topic in hand. Phenomenological RE is concerned with providing pupils with the skill and insight necessary to properly understand and think about religion. Pupils must examine religion by suspending their own judgement in order to appreciate the issues from the believer's point of view. In this way they are taught to gain a form of knowledge of the faith perspective which enables them to identify distinguishing characteristics of the faith, how it is celebrated and how it is unique to the worshipping community. Thus the student will 'learn about' religion (Grimmitt 1973).

It is acknowledged that in order to understand religion it is not enough merely to know the 'facts'. Authentic learning requires giving the pupil the opportunity to learn what it is to 'step into the shoes' of a believer. It is important then to have knowledge and understanding of the factual elements of the feast of Passover in Judaism, but it is also important for a pupil to understand what it must *actually feel like* to be the Jew celebrating Passover. Empathy stands at the heart of phenomeno-logical RE, and without it RE is reduced to mere rote learning.

To teach in this way requires neutrality from both the teacher and the student and is a direct reaction against the 'confessional' aims of RE. Rather than have syllabuses which train students to be good Christians, the phenomenological approach encour-ages students to identify commonalities in both religious language and religious experience. Indoctrination and bias are to be avoided. The underlying view of reli-gion in phenomenology is that of the universality of truth: all religions are equal and should be examined objectively. This is significant because the emergence of the phenomenological approach to RE surfaced at the same time as the new umbrella discipline of 'Religious Studies' won its place in higher education and at the same time as the multifaith and multicultural nature of the UK was finally being recognised.

It is also significant that the phenomenological approach stems from an under-standing of language as a means of identifying or labelling something. This model of language has its roots in empiricism. Empirical knowledge of the world is the result of our sense experience, and of our ability to use language to describe that experi-ence. An extreme form of empiricism is logical positivism, a heavily influential (though now largely discredited) philosophical movement allied to scientism. For the positivist only that which can be verified by the senses, and then labelled through language, can have meaning. Consequently any talk of God is quite literally mean-ingless: since we cannot experience God through any of our five senses, we have no way of verifying whether language describing such experience is true or false, and as a result we treat it as mere nonsense.

Positivism must not be confused with phenomenology, since the phenomenolog-ical concern for empathy and the recognition of the essence of observed phenom-ena is far more sophisticated than positivist approaches to knowledge. Nevertheless the empiricist strain remains influential in the phenomenological study of religion. Study of religion has more to do with describing and empathising with religious cul-ture than asking theological questions about the nature and reality of God. Smart (1973) listed the phenomenological description of religion under six categories: doc-trinal, mythological, ethical, ritual, experiential and social. This structured description allows appreciation of the commonalities of religious viewpoints and life stances. Strictly speaking, the essence of religious phenomena, that which holds them together and allows us to label them 'religious', is their concern for the divine or transcendent realm. Thus when the first major phenomenological RE syllabus, the 1979 Birmingham Agreed Syllabus, included the study of humanism as a quasi-religious life stance it actually departed from strict phenomenological description. This is important, illustrating how easily phenomenological RE can slip into mere empirical description of religious and quasi-religious culture.

It was crucial in RE that the subject matter was approached from the child's horizon. This key insight reflects the legacy of the work of Goldman (1965) and Loukes (1961), and especially their insistence that effective learning must always link up with the experiences of the learner. Ideas, beliefs, opinions and thoughts about religion need to be aired by the students in our RE classrooms, using the appropriate religious language, in order for clarity of understanding to take place. The acquisition of the type of factual information advocated by the phenomeno- logical model is important and necessary, but there is evidence to suggest that the focus on phenomenology as a model for delivering RE does not encourage the acquisition of higher-order thinking skills (Kerry 1980). If this is the case and pupils are not trained with skills to move beyond the level of concrete operational thinking, as defined by Piaget, the ability of the students to deal with the ambi- guity of religion will be severely hampered.

The spiritual model

The emphasis on the 'experience' of the student as the starting point of effective RE, coupled with the awareness that badly taught phenomenological RE descends to the level of mere description, leads us in to the current vogue for the 'spiritual' or 'expe- riential' model of RE. This model was comprehensively introduced to teachers of RE through the work of David Hay (Hay 1985; Hammond *et al.* 1990). Hay argues that the empirical world view so dominant in the phenomenological model was not addressing the actual experience of many people in the world. If God could not be proved to exist, according to the logical positivist, then why was religion not dying out? Why did Hay's research (1982) suggest that 'experiences of the spiritual' were closer to being the norm than the exception to the norm? Religious and spiritual experiences flourish, Hay suggests, but we have lost the language that would enable us to explore and make sense of such experience. Yet the commonality of spiritual or religious experience led Hay to conclude that this experience is what makes us inherently human.

This thesis provided a new rationale for RE and gave the subject new impetus in the mid-1980s, one that flourishes today in many classrooms (cf. Wright 1998b, 1999, for critical accounts). The commonality of spiritual experience provides the perfect communal horizon from which to teach a form of RE that goes beyond mere description and penetrates the experiential heart of religion. The evidence of the public acknowledgement of spiritual experiences provides a ready-made defence of the validity of the subject. Thus RE functions to affirm and nurture spiritual expe- rience and also acts as a framework for understanding them. There is to be no sug- gestion by the teacher that these experiences should lead pupils to adhere to any specific faith system. The purpose of this model of RE is to acknowledge, share and experience the commonality of the phenomena of religious experience. The impor- tance of beginning with the student's horizon remains paramount, as does recogni- tion that each faith system is valid. If emphasis is going to be placed on the validity of the individual's experience of the spiritual there is little validity given to the integrity of worshipping communities. It is this factor which lays the spiritual model open to most criticism (Thatcher 1991; Wright 1996b). Despite criticisms the spirituality model retains centre-stage in many classrooms, a reality reflected in government concern for the spiritual domain (SCAA 1995a).

The problem with this model, particularly in terms of religious language, is the danger of equating religious understanding with 'experience'. This means that feelings or emotions can dictate the religious content being studied. Thus spiritual RE is in constant danger of slipping over into 'emotivism', the philosophical doctrine that what I feel within is what is actually real. Take the example of the Jewish Passover. To understand the message of the Passover is to reflect on the freedom bestowed on the Israelites who were being held as slaves in Egypt. Simply to reflect on the abstract experience of freedom, though, cannot do justice to the Jewish understanding of the Passover, especially when viewed – as it now inevitably must be – in the light of the Holocaust. There is a limitation in dwelling on the experience of freedom, which prevents insight into what it means to be a Jew, to hold certain teachings as sacred and to live by those teachings. The danger in the spiritual model is that it ignores the importance of a coherent religious world view which gives life and substance to an otherwise individualistic, abstract and merely emotive experience. A stress on emotive experience does not allow the question of truth in the religious context to be addressed, because truth here is by definition individual, not linked to an external system of authority.

This model thus builds on the expressive element of the phenomenological model and emphasises what it means for the Jew to celebrate Passover by equating this form of celebration with that which is familiar to the student. The perspective of the individual gives validity to the religious experience. This model can be traced back to Romanticism, a movement which threw off the constraints of a scientific world view to focus on the meaning of what it was to be uniquely human, to think, to feel, to experience. The essence of the spiritual model of RE is to get underneath the outward phenomena of religion and focus on the spiritual experience (Chapter 10, below). Language operates as a means of bringing inner experience to expression. To understand such language one must pass beyond mere words and enter the emotive worlds that are their real source. Consequently lessons in spiritual RE are concerned to encourage pupils to use their imagination and their creativity, hence the importance of creative tasks (Hammond *et al.* 1990).

The critical realist model

The emphases on identifying the external characteristics of religion via phenomenology and then allowing them to develop into an experiential–expressive model of spiritual RE have left the student in the classroom with no formative means of accessing the religious terminology which is the currency of informed debate about religious issues. Grimmitt's own criticisms (1987) about the limitations of the phenomenological model are twofold. In the first place, such a model prevents each world faith being treated in the distinct and unique manner the members of the faith communities demand. The individual religions believe their doctrines or teachings are true, not merely relatively true. In the second place Grimmitt recognises that the phenomenological methodology, far from being neutral itself, is in fact value-laden and therefore not objective (1987, pp. 40 ff.).

Similarly the spiritual model, operating as it does in a postmodern climate which allows all language to be redefined and manipulated as the speaker sees fit, opens the gateway to individualised interpretations of religious terminology without recourse to an external authoritative source for that understanding. Thus pupils in the RE classroom become their own authority on religious terminology and their own interpreter of meaning.

Here we are concerned with a third possibility, moving beyond phenomenology and spirituality. Critical realism is a philosophy concerned to explore the true nature of reality. It accepts that there is a world out there open to investigation, and recognises that human beings are at least partially capable of being able to make sense of it. They do so through a range of interpretative methods, including – but not exclusively – natural science, that use language in a complex manner to achieve increasingly complex descriptions of a complex world.

When RE draws on critical realism it does so because it is concerned for religious truth, and believes that both phenomenology and spirituality, unduly influenced by a fear of confessionalism, have bypassed this crucial issue. It attempts to build on the best traditions of that which has gone before. The student's horizon does need to be the starting point of learning, factual information must be gained if students are going to discuss religion meaningfully, empathetic understanding of a person's faith and spiritual experience is paramount in these discussions, religion is a phenomenon common to all humankind whatever the components of the belief system, whether humanistic or religious.

The difference is that the world view underpinning the critical realist model takes seriously all the claims to 'truth' made by the world religions and secular groups. These truth claims address that grappling with reality that is at the very heart of our existence. Such engagement with the universe leads to the construction of stories and narratives that seeks to retell the story of the way things actually are in the world. Since there is a plurality of secular and religious narratives we have to deal with the ambiguities of this quest for meaning and truth.

Pupils in the RE class are invited to define their current world view and are given appropriate language with which to discuss, debate, question and so understand it better. At the same time they must learn to engage with the narratives of alternative secular and religious traditions. The only way they have of finding their way through this maze of options is to develop the appropriate linguistic skills whereby they can enter into intelligent conversation with adherents of a range of world views. Being religiously educated is all about developing religious literacy. Mere knowledge of religious culture, or mere sensitivity towards spiritual experience, important as both are, simply do not go far enough.

Some would argue that this model is too difficult to present to students. However, at a time when OFSTED is warning secondary school teachers of RE that the tasks being presented to Key Stage 3 students are too repetitive of Key Stage 2 and too straightforward, the time has come to focus on the complexities of religion and not be afraid to take risks in the classroom (OFSTED 1997). We need to capitalise on the growing awareness students who have been taught RE at primary school will have. Yes, the critical realist model chooses to deal with the explicit differences between religions, but students already know about them. They know that tension exists within the Christian church. They know that tension exists between the Sikh community and the Muslim community in Britain. They know that ethnic cleansing still goes on in the world. They deserve an opportunity to be more wisely informed, to be able to understand 'fundamentalism' in all its guises in order to make an informed decision on religious issues. They already have a world view on some of the most important ultimate questions in life. They deserve an opportunity to define their answers and recognise differences and similarities between themselves and others.

In the light of the three different models presented it is important to examine the use of subject-specific language in the types of lessons listed below. It is important to identify what measures are required to teach this type of language effectively. It is also important to note the aims of the various lessons and identify which type of lesson you wish to have and why.

Task 5.5 Language in the RE classroom: practical examples

Examples follow of how language may typically operate in each of the three models of RE. They are based on the delivery of the story of the creation of the world in Genesis 1 as it functions within the Christian community, since that was one of the examples cited by OFSTED of repetitious and unchallenging tasks. The examples are offered not as 'models' of how to teach but rather as snapshots of how the three approaches tend to address specific issues and ignore others. It is important to address each example critically. It may help to ask yourself the following questions for each model:

- What is the subject-specific language that requires definition?
- To what extent do the learning outcomes of each model reflect the understanding(s) of the concept of creation within the Christian faith community?
- Do the learning outcomes take account of conceptions of the story held by those outside the Christian tradition?
- Do the learning outcomes activities address the complexities of the debate within and outside the Christian community, and of Christian/non-Christian dialogue?
- Where does the issue of the truth of the Christian doctrine of creation receive an airing?

The phenomenological model
Learning outcomes:

- familiarisation with the facts of the Genesis story;
- knowledge of what happened on each day;
- understanding of the concept of 'myth';

- identification of the nature of this creation myth in comparison with others already studied;
- recognition of the importance of the story to Jews, Christians and Muslims.

Learning activities:

- reading Genesis 1;
- listing what happened on each day;
- for homework, getting the pupils to divide their page into 8 sections and illustrate what happened on each day;
- in class discussion getting the pupils to identify the similarities with and differences from other creation myths they have studied, thereby reinforcing their understanding of the concept of 'myth' and enabling them to recognise why this story is important to Jews, Christians and Muslims.

The spiritual model
Learning outcomes:

- familiarisation of the pupils with the facts of Genesis;
- knowledge of what happened on each day;
- understanding of the concept 'myth';
- identification of the nature of this creation myth in comparison with others already studied;
- reflection on, and sensitivity towards, the wonder of creation.

Learning activities:

- reading Genesis 1;
- listing what happened on each day;
- for homework, getting pupils to: write their own creation myth; or produce a poem about how wonderful creation is; or draw up a poster for a wall display entitled 'The Mystery of Creation';
- in class discussion asking, 'what kind of world did God create?' 'what kind of world would you create if you were God?'

The critical realist model
Learning outcomes:

- familiarisation of the pupils with the facts of Genesis;
- knowledge of what happened on each day;
- understanding of the nature of the story as it operates within the Christian community;
- acknowledgement of the contention between liberals and conservatives within Christianity regarding the nature of the Genesis story;
- recognition of alternative, possibly negative, non-Christian interpretations of the myth;
- grappling with the truth of the story: what it says about who God is; what it says about the created order; what it says about human beings;

- appreciation of the different viewpoints the students will bring to the lesson.

Learning activities:

- reading Genesis 1;
- listing what happened on each day;
- identifying what the story teaches about God, the created order and human beings;
- recognising the literary genre of the story, i.e. mythical poetry rather than bad science;
- introducing or eliciting the Christian interpretation(s) of the story;
- comparison with alternative non-Christian interpretations;
- exploring class opinions as to the veracity of the myth, and the origins of the universe.

SUMMARY AND KEY POINTS

You may feel that the tasks described in the critical realist model are too academic and do not reflect the expressive range and emotive nature of religion. However, engaging students in such intellectual stimulation can only succeed in bringing the subject to life. Looking from a contrasting perspective, I would argue that a primary reason for many pupils' negative attitude towards RE is indeed the result of a lack of intellectual challenge. Our pupils are bored not because religion itself is inherently boring but because the manner in which we as teachers present it, devoid of conflict, danger and intellectual stimulus, is inherently boring. In adopting the critical realist model you should soon discover that the nature of the informed discussion, which begins to take place in the classroom, spills out into the corridors because the students are debating the nitty-gritty issues of life. They are given the tools to make sense of religion because they are given the language of religious debate to inform their position and enlighten them about other people's viewpoints. It all starts with identifying where they stand on the variety of world views currently held. They bring this agenda with them when they study any religious concept. They are to be given the opportunity to identify the complexities of the world views and rationalise why it is so, then they can debate until their hearts are content and you will have one of the most vibrant subjects in the whole of the school.

This chapter has attempted both to unpack the key issues surrounding the place of language in the RE classroom and to advocate a particular method of teaching whilst acknowledging alternative possibilities. At the end of the day it is your responsibility as a professional teacher to adopt appropriate methods of enabling your pupils to develop their religious literacy.

FURTHER READING

Fisher, R. (1990) *Teaching Children to Think*, Oxford: Blackwell.

Fisher, R. (1998) *Teaching Thinking: Philosophical Enquiry in the Classroom*, London: Cassell. Central to this chapter has been the notion of critical thinking as the process at the centre of RE. In these two important books Fisher explores the place of thinking skills within education. Though Fisher's work is not directly concerned with RE the application of his work to the development of religious literacy is transparent.

Grimmitt, M. (1973) *What Can I do in RE?*, Essex: Mayhew-McCrimmon. This seminal work should not be passed over simply because of its relative age. It outlines the rationale behind phenomenological RE and provides many practical and stimulating examples of the place of language in the RE classroom.

Hammond, J., Hay, D., Moxon, J., Netto, B., Raban, K., Straugheir, G. and Williams, C. (1990) *New Methods in RE Teaching*, Harlow: Oliver & Boyd. Stimulating and accessible, this ever popular book examines the practical means by which to engage with the spiritual-experiential model.

Hay, D. (1985) 'Suspicion of the Spiritual: Teaching Religion in a World of Secular Experience', *British Journal of Religious Education*, 7 : 1, pp.140–7. Hay's influential paper provided the foundation and rationale for the experiential approach to RE.

SCAA (1994c) *Religious Education Glossary of Terms*, London: SCAA. A useful listing of key religious terms. Extremely valuable provided you recognise that the repetition of dictionary definitions and religious literacy are very different things!

Wright, A. (1993) *Religious Education in the Secondary School: Prospects for Religious Literacy*, London: David Fulton. Another seminal work which is suspicious of much current practice in RE and advocates an RE rooted in the development of religious literacy.

6 Assessment in Religious Education

John Rudge

Assessment is a subtle art, not an exact science.

Assessment can be an interesting and challenging aspect of your professional role, provided you are prepared to grapple with it, and don't simply try to find the easiest way round it. It is a complex area. The quotation above reminds us of some of the dangers. One danger is thinking that assessment is an objective exercise, that we can actually 'know that they know'. Another is thinking that the value of your teaching is determined by whether you can test pupils on their ability to recall what you have taught. The culture of testing is deeply ingrained in our schools and in the expectations of our pupils. We need to stand a long way back and take stock of what we really ought to be trying to do.

That assessment is an essential part of teaching and learning should be self-evident. Your professional motivation here should flow from this, not simply from the fact that it features in the standards that OFSTED will be inspecting when they pay a visit to your classroom. The reason it is given such prominence is that successful teaching and learning can go on only if you and your pupils are aware of how they are progressing, what they can do to improve and whether they are getting the most from you as their teacher. All these things depend on finding out how they are getting on and helping them to develop. That is what assessment is for.

The argument in this chapter is that if you keep a broad and open view of what assessment is and grapple with the issues, if you follow a few basic guidelines, and if you are both systematic and flexible in your practical approach to assessment, you will quickly find that it pays dividends for the pupils as learners and for yourself as a teacher.

OBJECTIVES

By the end of this chapter, you should:

- be aware of the key issues surrounding assessment in RE;
- understand some of the principles of assessing pupils which you will need to follow as a teacher;
- be familiar with practical strategies for dealing with assessment during your school experience, and beyond.

ASSESSING, TEACHING AND LEARNING

The first golden rule is that you approach assessment as an essential part of teaching and learning. It is not 'the bit you do after you have taught them and they have learned'. Essential though it is, it is still marshy and treacherous territory, and like all such areas it is easier to walk round it and avoid it than to find a way through it and cross it. Recent years have witnessed an amazing flurry of activity in this area but, now that much of the activity has subsided, the marsh is still waiting to be crossed. We now have a real opportunity, with a few guideposts in place, to rethink how we should tackle this area, so that assessment really does become an essential part of education.

One way of avoiding the challenges of assessment is to take the easy path round the outside, and interpret assessment along the following lines: 'I am the teacher, and you are the pupil. I have the information you need to pass your test and get a good grade, and you haven't! I will give you that information, which you must learn and remember, as best you can, and then I will test you to see if you remember what I have taught you. If you can reproduce the information I have given you, you will get good marks and a high grade. Of course, if you have a good memory, you have a head start over the others, and will quickly rise to the top.'

It doesn't really matter how sophisticated the information provided by the teacher actually is: it may be the names of five religious festivals or a summary of Wittgenstein's philosophical arguments. Learning is reduced to pieces of information which are ingested and deposited, without being digested, processed and recycled. It is a model of teaching and learning in which the pupils are of secondary importance, information is mistaken for knowledge, recall is mistaken for understanding and the prize goes to those with cameras and filing cabinets for memories. Questions about the value of the information, about how pupils might use it to enrich their understanding, and help them to develop as learners and people, are neither addressed nor assessed.

These are vital questions for the RE teacher. At a conference in 1989 on how RE should reflect the whole National Curriculum process of assessment John Elliott warned of the danger of trivialising the subject by conforming to notions of knowing and understanding which take no account of the value implications of such knowledge for the pupils themselves. He suggested – somewhat prophetically, many would say – that RE, and the pupils who study it, would be better served by a process of assessment which reflects 'not so much the extent to which the content of understanding conforms to some predetermined and objective standard, as the quality of the process in which it is constructed' (Rudge 1989). He goes on to argue that knowledge cannot be divorced from the value system in which it is enshrined, nor from the emerging values of the pupils who are learning. This gives the whole notion of assessment a different orientation. It reflects a much wider debate about the purpose of schooling and the measurement of success. As you develop your own understanding of teaching and assessing you might reflect on how far, in your own perception, the potential of RE has been reduced by too much concentration on the surface meaning of 'facts'.

Why do we assess pupils?

Assessment may serve a number of purposes. The popular view, often central in the minds of pupils and their parents, is that we assess them to give them a mark and grade them by their results. That is what exams are for. It is usually called *summative assessment*, but it is not the only, or the main reason, for assessing pupils. As a teacher your main focus should be on *formative assessment*, that is, assessing pupils in order to help them in their learning. We can also, from time to time, use *diagnostic assessment*, that is, assessment designed to find out where pupils are starting from, for example at the beginning of Year 7. This can help teachers plan a course more effectively. Assessment should also have a valuable *evaluative* purpose for the teacher. It helps to establish whether pupils are understanding, enjoying and benefiting from their lessons, and what needs to be done to improve them.

It is only formative assessment which benefits the pupils directly in their learning. It is usually focused on the continuing assessment of pupils' progress in the classroom at regular intervals, and deals with immediate issues they are exploring and their developing understanding of their work. Unlike the other purposes of assessment, it involves feeding back to pupils information, comments, judgements and suggestions which will help them recognise what they have done well, and see how they can improve and progress further. Summative and diagnostic assessments are designed not to help pupils learn but to inform other people – teachers, parents, employers, curriculum planners and policy makers – about what pupils have achieved at a particular point in their development. The pupils do not receive feedback – though they may get an ear-bending from their parents!

The root meaning of *assessment* is derived from a Latin word which carries the sense of *sitting down beside*. That is an important quality for the teacher to reflect on. It leads us to a second golden rule, namely that, in assessing pupils' work, we are trying to encourage and reward positive achievement, however limited, rather than accentuating a sense of non-achievement. Only in that way will you begin to dismantle the culture of failure which can easily dominate the lives of your pupils and put them off schooling altogether.

Difficulties arise when you try to balance the importance you attach to formative and summative assessments. Some believe that results and grades are what matter most; others stress the process of learning as being far more important. You could conclude, as many have done, that the best summative evidence of a pupil's work over two years does not come through an unseen examination at the end, but from evidence collected as a result of formative assessments throughout the course. This view reflects, for example, the debate about how much emphasis in the GCSE should be placed on coursework and how much on the final examination.

It is worth reflecting on how your own PGCE course is assessed formatively. When you write an essay, your tutor gives you feedback. When, as part of the assessment process, you are observed during school experience, you receive comments, criticisms and suggestions from your mentor. You learn from these assessments. They are a means of helping you to make progress. Tutors and mentors are all the time making informed judgements about your progress and feeding them back to you. You are also being asked to evaluate your own progress as part of the assessment process. At the end of the course there is normally no formal examination, and no judgement is made about how you have fared in relation to your fellow students. However, a judgement is made − and sometimes it is a very difficult one for your tutors, mentors and examiners to make − as to whether you have achieved the standards expected of a newly qualified teacher. This decision is based both on your progress during the course and on your attainment by the end of it, and much of the evidence arises from the formative assessments made throughout the course. You might reflect on this when you assess pupils in school, where the pressure always to be putting them in rank order can be very strong. The competitive interpretation of and approach to assessment, treating it as a spur to learning, is highly debatable, both in its intention and in its result.

A third golden rule, therefore, for your purposes, is that assessment is primarily a means of helping pupils learn, and of gathering evidence of their progress. Feedback is the key to this approach.

What are we assessing?

A fourth golden rule of assessment is that you must be clear what achievement you are trying to assess. You may think this is so self-evident that it should not need to be stated. It is, however, lack of clarity about objectives where many of the difficulties about assessment arise. Setting appropriate and focused objectives for learning in your lessons is one of the most important skills you need to acquire. If your objectives are ill-defined or much too demanding (or too easy), you will find the rest of your lesson planning falls apart, and you will be unclear about what you are trying to assess; and if you are unclear, then your pupils will also be unclear.

Merely remembering information is not an adequate goal. Once the principle is established that education is about the pupils, about what is of value to them and about what will contribute to their spiritual, moral, cultural and intellectual development, you have to come up with something better than mere rote memorisation.

This brings us to the heart of the matter, and to some of the key issues surrounding the nature of education itself:

- What is this knowledge we want pupils to have?
- What does knowledge mean, as a quality beyond memorised information?
- How does it help the pupils? Is it the same as understanding?
- How do we hope this understanding will enrich pupils in their own development as persons? By accident, osmosis or design?
- Given that education involves both understanding and evaluation, how are we to assess whether they really have understood and acquired the ability and sensitivity to evaluate?
- How can we know that they know?
- How accurate and reliable is our judgement?

This is not an exercise in academic semantics. We have to begin here if assessment is to be a useful part of teaching and learning. However, the issues are the same right across the curriculum, so you must not feel that you are alone in trying to grapple with these issues, or that RE is in some way an educational oddity.

To clarify the achievements we are concerned with in RE, it may help to reflect on where the subject stands in relation to the kinds of achievements expected across the curriculum as a whole. These may be divided into three broad categories. The first deals with attainments we may describe as practical skills. These would include such things as reading maps, writing legibly and playing a scale on a musical instrument. These are skills of the *can do* type. A second group of attainments is concerned with the development of cognitive abilities, mainly of the *knowing and understanding* kind. These could include such attainments as knowing that the weather profoundly affects people's lives, or understanding the difference between change and progress. A third group of attainments is concerned with the development of *personal qualities, beliefs and values*. These could include such qualities as being sensitive to the living and non-living environment, or being willing to be self-critical about one's own beliefs. A balanced education is going to include all three categories of attainment.

Which category of attainments comes closest to what we understand RE to be about? The answer is likely to lie somewhere in the second and third categories, with some differences of emphasis, depending on your view of RE. It is unlikely that you will find anything in RE that corresponds with the kind of achievements in the first category, important though they are in other areas of the curriculum. Broadly speaking, those who see RE as essentially to do with the objective study of religions will tend to emphasise cognitive abilities, while those who want to see the main purpose of RE as focused on personal development will stress the third group of qualities.

It is important to recognise that the different categories of attainment presuppose different approaches to assessment. With the first category, it is relatively easy, and interpreting assessment as *measuring and testing* is appropriate. It is not appropriate for the other two categories. One of the key issues in the National Curriculum has been the pressure from certain quarters to try to make the overall pattern of assessment conform with this model of measuring and testing. However, it does not fit all, or even most, of the curriculum. We need to broaden our concept of assessment, rather than devalue education to what can be measured and tested. This broader concept of assessment will include a variety of ways of gathering evidence, less precise and more subjective criteria for making judgements, the value of the teacher's own professional awareness, and the views of the pupils themselves about their own development and progress.

If we apply these principles to RE, we still have to find a way through this difficult territory. The most straightforward route would appear to lie in keeping the goals simple, not trying to be too sophisticated. This can be done by seeing RE as concerned primarily, but not exclusively, with two broad attainments which, for the sake of argument, we will refer to as 'understanding' and 'evaluation'. We will consider each of these in turn.

Understanding in RE

For practical purposes, you may find it easier to use *understanding* rather than *knowing*. The point has already been made that knowledge, to have any value, has to refer to something more than memorised information. The information is only of value if it is placed in a context with other information, and organised to give it some coherence. Otherwise it simply remains a trivial pursuit. Once information has been contextualised, it is given meaning by being related to ideas and concepts which provide the basis for understanding. Understanding is shown when information from different contexts is used as an example or illustration to explain an idea or concept. In RE the concern with meaning should be paramount. For example, in studying the five pillars of Islam, it is important that pupils grasp both the context of the practices within Islam and their meaning for Muslims. To do so, they need to relate the practice of the five pillars to the concept of *ibadah*, or service (to Allah). They begin to show understanding of the five pillars when they can explain how the practice of giving *zakah*, for example, reflects the principle of *ibadah*.

Assessing whether pupils have understood something, as distinct from simply remembering what they have been told, involves setting them a task based on a situation, context or example which is unfamiliar to them, so that they have to deploy and apply what they have learned in a new way. This 'unfamiliarity principle' is an essential foundation of good assessment in RE.

Suppose you want to find out what a group of Year 8 pupils have learned from a visit to a synagogue. What they will get out of the visit will depend, of course, on how you have structured the visit as an educational exercise, how you prepared them for the visit and the follow-up work you did in class afterwards, and what you intended the visit to achieve. You could test them by asking them the names of the various things they saw in the synagogue. Or you could ask them, in a general kind of way, to describe their visit. Both those tasks could produce little more than recall of isolated pieces of information. Yet even in their descriptions there is likely to be evidence of some understanding through their choice of what to describe, or how to describe it, or the way they make links between what they have seen and what they have already learned. They may even include personal reflections which go well beyond mere description and show some genuine insight. The problem is that the task is not demanding enough, and does not actually invite some of these responses.

If, on the other hand, following the visit and further work in class, they are given the task of producing a guide to the synagogue, for a group who have not yet made the visit, explaining what makes it a Jewish building, and what they may gain from their visit, we are moving closer to what we mean by understanding. Now they need to select and deploy some of the information they have gathered and apply what they have learned to a new situation. Of course they may remember that the reading desk from which the Jewish scriptures are read is called the Bimah, but such recall of information is not really the object of the exercise. Though interesting, the ability to label religious artefacts is not essential to an authentic understanding of Judaism.

Evaluation in RE

The issues come even more sharply into focus if we include the development of personal qualities, beliefs and values within the scope of our view of assessment. The concept of evaluation is used as shorthand for the assessment of this very subjective element. It is an inadequate but useful concept provided it is used in its root meaning. To evaluate something is to assess its value: in the context of RE it has to do with pupils thinking about the value *for themselves* of what they are learning about the beliefs, values and actions of others. It is a reflective quality.

There are some who object to using assessment in this way. One objection is that it is impossible to assess such a subjective area of the curriculum, however justified the goals may be in educational terms. Therefore we should not even attempt to do so. It has, however, already been argued that we need to broaden our concept of assessment beyond measurement and testing, beyond the elusive quest for total objectivity. Formative assessment, which involves many different ways of finding out how pupils are progressing, and includes as much feedback as possible to the pupils, together with evidence gleaned from pupil self-assessments, is appropriate to these educational goals.

A second objection needs careful thought, especially in RE. Some argue that we should not assess this area because it concerns the personal beliefs, values and attitudes of the pupils. These matters are their concern, not ours. It is no business of ours to enquire into the private lives of the pupils. There are important issues behind this argument, and it is useful to have some ground rules to keep us from the pitfalls. It is not, for example, appropriate to assess matters which pupils may wish to keep to themselves. Pupils should never be pressed to disclose personal or private information, and no assessment or judgement should be made of their willingness or unwillingness to do so. It is also inappropriate to assess whether pupils' own beliefs and values are right or wrong. Whilst discussion of these matters will form part of the ongoing debate of the classroom, they are not issues for assessment. This supports the principle that RE should be open to pupils of any religious persuasion or of none.

On the other hand, pupils' developing beliefs and values are an essential part of the material of RE, and in the classroom the pupils are encouraged to share their ideas with others, and to enter into discussion of often controversial issues. Without this dimension RE has no *existential bite*, and is robbed of its relevance to the pupils. A formative pattern of assessment provides a fitting context in which pupils' development in this area can be encouraged, provided that it is dealt with sensitively by a caring and thoughtful teacher. When it comes to making more formal judgements about the quality of pupils' work, teachers should base their conclusions on the evidence that pupils provide, from what they say or write or show in other ways. Even though they should not make judgements about whether pupils are right or wrong, they can give feedback on the quality and scope of the arguments they use, the range of evidence they put forward to support their viewpoint, and the clarity with which they express their ideas. These are proper matters for assessment, as they are for any educational discourse. We should not be afraid that subjectivity enters into our judgements; the teacher's professional judgement enters into all assessments.

We might therefore envisage a situation where a group of Year 10 pupils has been addressing the issue of vegetarianism. Following discussion, guidance from the teacher, a visit from a local farmer and some work in small groups looking at various aspects of the issue, a task is set in which the pupils are invited to react to a picture of a Jain monk with a brief description of his particular beliefs and practices related to non-violence (which they have not seen before). The unfamiliarity principle is again applied. The teacher will not be making comments about whether the pupils are right or wrong in their own viewpoint. But there will be comments about the clarity with which they have expressed their viewpoint, how far evidence and argument have been used to support the views, what examples or illustrations have been given to elaborate their viewpoint; and because this is an RE topic, the teacher will also comment on the use they made of what they learned about the different religious and moral viewpoints they discussed in class, on how far they show awareness of viewpoints different from their own, and on the insight they show into the religious and moral dimensions of the issue.

You will have noticed how much emphasis has been placed on the 'unfamiliarity principle' in assessing both understanding and evaluation. Indeed, it constitutes our fifth golden rule: base assessment tasks in RE on the unfamiliarity principle, in which pupils are asked to deploy and apply what they have learned to a new situation, context or example.

As a trainee teacher, and subsequently throughout your teaching career, you will need to keep returning to the issues raised in the first part of this chapter, and to rethink how you should approach them in the light of your practical experience. But you will also need to be aware of some of the practical possibilities and constraints of the learning situation.

PRACTICAL CONSIDERATIONS

Assessment and planning

In your own teaching, assessment must play a central and integral role. It begins with your planning. Whatever lesson plan outline you use, it must always include your objectives, what you want the pupils to learn or achieve: 'by the end of the lesson, pupils will understand why the Buddha's enlightenment is important for Buddhists today' or '. . . will be able to evaluate the view that desire is the cause of suffering'. Your objectives, in contrast with your general aim for the lesson, which will be broader, should be assessable. Whatever means you use, you should be able, on the basis of evidence, to make a judgement whether your objectives have been achieved, for yourself and for the pupils.

Task 6.1 Exploring your school's assessment policy

Before you start your practical teaching, familiarise yourself with the assessment policy and practice of your school. To help you do this, you could address these questions:

- What is the school's assessment policy?
- How is it applied to RE?
- How do other RE teachers assess pupils?
- What kinds of tasks are the pupils given to do?
- What sort of comments are put on their work?
- How do the assessments help them formatively?

You could also ask to see GCSE papers and marking schemes. Public examinations are no longer the secret garden they used to be, where some faceless trickster of an examiner would be lurking in the bushes to catch you out with a question which hadn't come up before, and to which only the examiners knew the right answer. You will find questions that vary in difficulty and are set according to prescribed and published criteria. You will see that there are rarely questions with simple right or wrong answers. Most examinations are now marked according to a published scale of 'levels of achievement', available to pupils and teachers alike, so that they know what they are being assessed on. Important principles are enshrined in these public examinations. You can read more about this in Chapter 8 but it is worth absorbing the principles of assessment from the start.

You should also have a look at the Agreed Syllabus, to see if it gives any instructions or guidelines for assessment. Not all do. But most do indicate the achievements we should be expecting of pupils at each Key Stage, often in the form of statements of attainment. Statements of attainment are of paramount importance in developing your awareness of assessment in RE. They may be couched in general terms, but they should guide the planning of your teaching and your overall strategy of assessment. You should have them in mind when you are planning how to develop a unit of work, and writing the objectives for your lessons.

Getting your objectives right and ensuring that you have achieved them is a skill that comes gradually. It is probably best to start with simple, straightforward and uncomplicated objectives for each lesson or unit of work, and to keep them few in number. What you want pupils to understand and evaluate is a good place to start. Every lesson should provide some opportunity for pupils to respond, that is, to say or do something that will help you to see whether you are meeting your objectives. You should carefully evaluate your success in this area, by reflecting on your experience, and identifying the steps you need to take to improve. Rather than concluding that your lesson was 'good' or 'went well' or 'they seemed to enjoy it' (an important criterion, none the less), you need to ask yourself, on the basis of your evidence, whether your objectives were the right ones or could have been more focused; whether the activities you planned were the best ones for your objectives. Did you in practice concentrate too much on one at the expense of the other(s)? Did you try to cram too much information into the lesson at the expense of your objectives?

Tasks

The objectives for each lesson will contribute to the objectives you are trying to achieve over a longer period in a unit of work. As a general rule, there should be at least one formal assessment task in each unit of work. 'Task' is a better concept than 'test'. It implies that the assessment is coherent and is given a context, and does not necessarily involve simply answering unconnected questions. The example given earlier, where pupils prepare a guide to a synagogue, represents this kind of task. As your skills develop, you should be able to make the contexts of the tasks more interesting and varied, at the same time ensuring that the substance of the task is likely to lead to the evidence of their understanding and evaluation that you are looking for. The 'unfamiliarity principle', through which you ask them to apply what they have learned to a new situation, needs to be introduced in each case.

Having set the task, you could break it down further to help them in their response. You could suggest some ideas for going about the task. You could give them an example outline. You could give them some questions to think about. You must check that they all understand what the task is! But you need to be careful that they do not take your example outline as the correct one, and that they do not regard your 'questions to think about' as a test. It is important to remember that we are not to use assessments to catch pupils out. We want them to have every chance to show what they can achieve.

Differentiation

How will your task appear to pupils with different abilities? What about those with particular learning difficulties? What about the very able ones who need stretching? One of the ways of dealing with this issue of differentiation is through the way you teach the class as a whole, and individuals and groups within the class, through the resources you encourage them to use, and the speed at which you expect them to work. The teaching must benefit all the pupils, so that they all feel they are getting something out of it. Another way is to set different tasks, or tasks with different demands or expectations of pupils of different abilities. Another is to have the same process of learning for all the pupils, and to give them the same task, but in such a way that it will produce different levels of outcome depending on the abilities of the pupils.

On the whole, it is this last method of differentiation which is most commonly used in assessment in a subject like RE. In differentiating by outcome, great care has to be taken in making sure that the task is accessible to all, and that it invites responses at different levels. The 'guide to the synagogue' task could be seen as appropriate for this purpose. Some pupils will simply describe what they saw, in a rather unstructured way. Others may offer some explanations. The most able may set their guide in the wider context of their understanding of Judaism and Jewish communities. But you would have to be sure that the task really triggered those different responses by giving some guidance – without giving them a model response. And you would need to think about those pupils in the class who found it difficult to express themselves through written work. Is there an alternative way in which they could offer a valid response?

Task 6.2 Planning for assessment

As you plan to teach a unit of work, prepare the outline of a task you could set the pupils to find out how well they have understood the topic. In your outline task you should try to include:

● an interesting, stimulating or unusual context;
● something that will enable pupils to show both understanding and their ability to evaluate;
● the unfamiliarity principle: approaching the topic from a new angle;
● either some form of differentiation in the task itself or some indica tion of how you think different responses will show different levels of achievement.

You should discuss your outline with your tutor before – and after – trying out the task.

Formal and informal assessment

You need to plan your formal task(s) at the same time as your objectives and activities, to ensure that they are coherent and consistent. Formal tasks will not, however, be the only assessment you carry out during a unit of work. Assessment can take place in any context in any lesson. It can be done formally – for example, through a piece of written work which is marked – or informally – for example, through listening to a group of pupils discussing an issue you have raised, or through talking individually to a pupil. You are not, of course, 'testing' them, but you are listening for evidence of their understanding. A sixth golden rule is that assessment can take place on any occasion when pupils express themselves in any way in relation to the stated objectives. Effective lessons always offer plenty of opportunities for expressing responses.

Listening carefully to pupils talking (assuming the talk is 'on task') will provide a great deal of evidence as to whether your objectives are being met, and whether the pupils are in tune with you. The evidence is not structured but informal. That does not mean that it is merely accidental, even though some evidence can arise quite unintentionally. As your teaching skills develop, you will find that you can pick up all kinds of signals from the pupils that give you evidence about their understanding and evaluative abilities – and about your teaching when they are not on task! You will learn to attune your ears to what is genuinely valuable evidence.

One device you can use to pick up whether the pupils are really with you is to begin a lesson with a quick oral recap round the class of the previous lesson. (Don't be too downhearted: it's probably a week since they last saw you and they may have forgotten your name, let alone anything you taught them.) There is no reason why you should not see whether they remember the name of the piece of furniture with three steps which they saw in the mosque or, come to that, what a *minbar* is. But good recap questions should be brief and get quickly to the heart of the matter, not focus on trivia. The questions should make them think as well as remember – for example, 'What do you think is the most important thing a visitor should know about a mosque?' Recapping is a good way of using assessment diagnostically, and in order to reinforce learning.

Reference has already been made to another means of assessment which may at first seem a contradiction in terms. Self-assessment can play a useful and informative role in RE, especially in relation to some of the more sensitive aspects of the subject. It cannot be the only form of assessment but, used judiciously, it can produce valuable opportunities for feedback and gathering evidence, and provide a stimulus to pupils' thinking. It requires careful management by the teacher and you will need to consult your mentor before venturing into this area of assessment.

Recording

Throughout this chapter the word 'evidence' has been used extensively. It is a key concept in the assessment process. It refers to the information we get from our assessments of pupils' progress. We need to retain some of that information, so that the conclusions we draw when we report to parents at the end of a year or a Key Stage are not just based on our memory, impression or intuition. Recorded evidence is essential for this purpose, and should ideally include information from a variety of assessment contexts.

Your starting point will once again be the school and department's policy on record keeping, and to start with it is best to follow that. Later on, there may be scope for experimenting. The traditional way is to have a 'mark book' and to record marks from formal written assessments during the year. You need to be careful that the process does not become an end in itself, so that you find yourself setting a test every two weeks so that your mark book is neatly filled up and looks impressive.

A better record would involve keeping in mind all the time the broad attainments you are hoping for in the pupils. What you need is good recorded evidence of those attainments. Of course, the results of formally assessed work provide some recorded evidence. But if you can regard a mark book as a flexible tool for recording evidence, you could use it for noting other evidence that might better contribute to an overall view of pupils' achievements. For example, you could keep (or, better still, keep a record of where to find) a pupil's best piece of work reflecting the attainments. Likewise, if you have carried out self-assessments, you could use a simple form to provide further evidence of achievement in more subjective areas. It is also worth leaving space in your book for recording more informal evidence that you may pick up at any time.

Let's suppose that Hussain is a quiet lad who doesn't say much in discussion. One day, in a discussion about marriage, he delivers a carefully worded and well thought out argument drawing attention to some of the advantages of arranged marriages and the disadvantages of 'falling in love', and he presents his arguments with evidence and with passion, and the rest of the class are stunned into silence. Here is probably one of the best bits of evidence you will pick up during the year about Hussain's attainments, but it was unplanned and came out of the blue. You need to note that piece of evidence. If you don't, and all you have got are his test results, by the end of the year you may have forgotten his intervention, or that it was he who spoke out, and you will have missed something important to the overall appraisal of his work. Alternatively, you may have noticed on a number of occasions that Kevin finds it very hard to listen to other pupils' opinions. He always tries to interrupt and not always coherently. That is also an important piece of evidence which can be noted in an appropriate way. Recording this kind of evidence does not imply that you are furiously writing down everything you hear in your mark book. It should be reserved for what is really significant, and experience will guide you in how to discern that.

Reporting

Another skill closely related to the recording of evidence is writing reports. Your mentor will guide you about the school's policy and practice, which can vary widely from school to school. Reporting includes giving a verbal report at parents' evenings. For this you will need to have your recorded evidence to hand. Your school experience should include an opportunity for you to write some reports, under supervision. Report writing is an art. You should ideally aim for a report which is succinct, based clearly on your recorded evidence, positive in tone, and tells the reader something about the pupil's attainment in RE, rather than just about whether they have worked hard and handed in their homework on time.

Levels of achievement

National Curriculum subjects are now making use of what are called *level descriptors* for reporting purposes. The level descriptions are paragraphs of prose setting out the kind of qualities and attainments likely to be shown by pupils of different abilities, arranged on a scale of levels, usually 1 to 8. The descriptions are not intended to set targets for teaching, but are only intended for reporting purposes. The idea is that teachers will look at the evidence they have collected, and then at the level descriptors, to decide which represents the 'best fit' as a description of what a particular pupil has achieved. There is some pressure for RE to move in the same direction, and this is being encouraged in some LEAs. Others make use of a device called 'end of Key Stage statements' (of attainment) which have a somewhat different function. They do set targets in broad and general terms. In this case, reporting would need to be based on how far, according to the evidence, you think pupils have progressed towards the achievements, using such categories as 'working towards' the attainments, 'achieving the targets' and, in a few cases, 'working beyond the targets'.

Standards

One further factor you need to be aware of and thinking about is the concern for identifying and maintaining standards. The examination boards retain sample scripts from previous years representing various levels of achievement, or grades, so that they can compare standards from year to year. There is now a move in this direction to adopt a similar procedure in a more general way, so that schools have some idea of standards from year to year. It can be done in two ways. One is to take note of the guidance contained in published material, such as the QCA's *Exemplification of Standards in RE* or Hertfordshire's *Consistency in Teacher Assessment*, related to their own Agreed Syllabus. The other way, or an additional way, is to establish your own benchmarks in school, retaining some examples of assessed work which in your judgement are representative of particular levels of performance by the pupils in each Key Stage. You would probably need several years to build up and refine these benchmarks, and such standards could never be absolute and definitive. They are simply another tool to help you to be as fair, balanced and consistent in your assessments and expectations as possible. It is another example of a theme which has permeated this chapter, and should influence all your teaching. It is a good cue for a final golden rule: all assessment is based on professional judgement.

Figure 6.1 Seven golden rules of assessment

1	Approach assessment as an essential part of teaching and learning.
2	Encourage and reward positive achievement.
3	Treat assessment primarily as a means of helping pupils to learn and to gather evidence of their progress.
4	Always be clear as to what you are trying to assess.
5	Base assessment task on the unfamiliarity principle.
6	Remember that assessment can take place on any occasion when pupils express themselves in any way in relation to the stated objectives.
7	Base all assessment on professional judgement.

SUMMARY AND KEY POINTS

The material in this chapter covers the basic requirements set out in the standards for Qualified Teacher Status in relation to monitoring, assessment, recording, reporting and accountability, as they might be applied to RE. In addition, the chapter has highlighted some of the principles you need to bear in mind when you are assessing RE. The argument throughout has been that we need to break out of the narrow confines suggested by the processes of 'measuring and testing' into a broader concept of what assessment includes and entails. Seven golden rules have punctuated the chapter, setting out some basic principles you need to keep in mind.

Assessment is an aspect of teaching which should always be part of the ongoing cycle of curriculum development. It is so interwoven with the teaching and learning process that changes and reforms in one area inevitably impinge on the others. The concept of a thinking teacher, rather than that of a classroom operative, is also bound up with the process of development. Although assessment is a complex and difficult area to grapple with, it is well worth becoming part of that process of development from the start.

FURTHER READING

Gipps, C. (1990) *Assessment: A Teacher's Guide to the Issues*, London: Hodder & Stoughton.

Satterley, D. (1989) *Assessment in Schools*, Oxford: Blackwell.

Both these books give a balanced and wide-ranging survey of the issues at a practical level. They explore assessment across the curriculum, and provide a useful starting point for RE teachers who want to develop a wider awareness of the matters raised in this chapter.

Qualifications and Curriculum Authority (1998a) *Exemplification of Standards in Religious Education: Key Stages 1 to 4*, London: QCA. This sets out suggestions for thinking about how RE standards may be illustrated in pupils' work, along the lines being followed in other areas of the curriculum.

Torrance, H. and Prior, J. (1998) *Investigating Formative Assessment*, Buckingham: Open University Press. As the title suggests, this book looks in some depth at the possibilities and problems of formative assessment and provides a careful study of many of the issues that this approach raises.

7 Teaching Children with Special Educational Needs

Jean Harris

For you, the student teacher of RE, special educational needs (SEN) present a challenge which can sometimes be viewed as a minefield. Not only are there legal obligations to be met and observed, a whole new area of jargon and abbreviations to become familiar with, there are also problems that can arise in a classroom situation that will be specific to teaching RE. As a student teacher you will meet a range of pupils whose needs will be many and varied. You will have to be able to identify SEN pupils and have the correct information about them to enable you to fulfil your obligations to them. From a very early stage in your career you will have to use your growing professional acumen to make important judgements in the field. A full working knowledge of procedures, terminology, documentation and relevant colleagues will enhance your performance as well as giving you extra self-confidence. The aim of this chapter is to guide you in taking your first steps in coming to terms with this important dimension of your professional responsibilities.

OBJECTIVES

By the end of this chapter you should be able to:

- identify the key issues surrounding special educational needs in RE;
- understand and use the terminology of special educational needs;
- access documents that detail national and school policies;
- recognise the importance of accurate record keeping;
- develop appropriate strategies for classroom management.

SPECIAL EDUCATIONAL NEEDS: HISTORY AND LEGISLATION

SEN provision and attitudes

There have been many Acts of Parliament and reports this century concerned with the education of young people. Each one has had specific criteria in view and has sought to improve the way in which education is delivered. All the Acts and the many reports are important because each has had a far-reaching effect not only on the way in which children are educated but on how they are viewed by society.

In 1934 Mrs Mary Brownhill stood accused of murdering her 30-year-old son Denis by giving him about a hundred aspirins and then placing a gas tube over his mouth and turning on the gas. She was about to go into hospital and there was no one to look after him. Denis (in the language of the 1930s) was an imbecile who was not capable of looking after himself. Mrs Brownhill had looked after Denis unceasingly, she was a devoted mother. Witnesses at her trial all said that she put the boy first: in all changes of circumstance her first thoughts were of Denis. There were no support systems, no respite homes and no special educational processes that would have assessed Denis and educated him with a view to enabling him to be as independent as possible. Denis was judged by society to be an imbecile and therefore of no value. His life gained importance only when he was dead. The trial judge told the jury that there was no justification for the murder. Mrs Brownhill was found guilty of murder and, despite a strong recommendation to mercy, was sentenced to death. Forty-eight hours later she was granted a reprieve, was eventually granted a free pardon and was in home in time for Christmas. Ten years after Denis Brownhill died, the 1944 Education Act came into being. The Act deemed that some children were ineducable and categorised them as 'severely subnormal'. No provision was made for them in the Act.

The 1944 Act did acknowledge that not all children are the same physically and mentally, and set about defining categories and providing guidance as to how certain children were best educated. Eleven categories were defined:

- blind;
- partially blind;
- deaf;
- partially deaf;
- delicate;
- diabetic;
- educationally subnormal;
- epileptic;
- maladjusted;
- physically handicapped;
- those with speech defects.

The type of school provision was also determined: day or boarding, special or ordinary. Boarding or residential schools had existed before the 1944 Act; after the Act some LEAs purchased property in which to provide residential special education for children who would not thrive in mainstream schools. Children who, in the terminology of the times, were maladjusted and/or educationally subnormal were thought, by some, to benefit from these placements. Some LEAs provided day schools for children who were designated delicate or were physically handicapped. One of the disadvantages of sending a child to a residential special school was that the child was separated from the community to which it would eventually return. Although there was a shift in the way SEN pupils were viewed, they were still categorised. Many SEN pupils were sent to special day schools. In some instances parents were totally opposed to their children attending such schools because of the perceived stigma. Some LEAs provided transport for SEN pupils, and parents were aware that neighbours knew there was something 'different' about their child. It could also cause complications in local peer groups, and the SEN pupil would sometimes be victimised.

The 1959 Mental Health Act allowed parents extra time to appeal against an authority's decision that a child was ineducable. Parents also had the right to a review after one year. Two Acts passed in 1970 also changed the way SEN children were viewed. The Chronically Sick and Disabled Persons Act set out an LEA's responsibilities towards children with acute dyslexia. The Education (Handicapped Children) Act shifted responsibility for mentally handicapped children from the local Health Authority to the LEA. These pieces of legislation were significant: for the first time all children were regarded as educable.

About twenty-five years ago children who had special educational needs were categorised as either Educationally Subnormal (ESN) or Educationally Subnormal Severe (ESNS). The 1970 Education (Handicapped Children) Act helped to redefine the way pupils were perceived and categorised. Changing terminology can take time, as is reflected in some of the textbooks published in the early and mid-1970s, which still made reference to children as 'retarded', 'educationally subnormal' and 'severely subnormal' (e.g. Child 1974, pp. 228–30). These terms eventually changed to Moderate Learning Difficulties (MLD) and Severe Learning Difficulties (SLD). A pupil with MLD will have a level of academic attainment that is significantly under that of her or his peers. A pupil with SLD would, until the 1970 Education (Handicapped Children) Act, have been regarded as ineducable. There are many factors that determine whether a pupil has SLD. Organic or neurological damage, or a biochemical disorder, are among the factors that may cause SLD. Pupils with SLD are usually educated in special schools. The National Curriculum provides the foundation of the curriculum for pupils with SLD. The overall aim of SEN provision is to develop the pupils' skills and attitudes so that they can be, as far as possible, autonomous as adults.

The current legal framework

Changes in terminology reflect a change in approach and attitude to pupils and how their educational needs are best met. Jones and Docking observe that

> Perhaps the sharpest distinction between the old and the new ideologies is
> the view that fundamental to the education of children with special needs

Figure 7.1 Key SEN terminology

- *Assessment* can be applied in two ways: the assessment and recording of the progress of all pupils in a school to ensure that progress is monitored, or the assessment of a child who has been identified as having special educational needs. The two meanings complement each other as procedures for identifying special educational needs often overlap with the more general assessment procedures.
- *Case conference*. A meeting of the professionals, parents and the pupil with special educational needs to review, share and update information leading to decisions about future needs, provision for the needs and progress.
- *Code of practice*. Refers to the standard procedures for the identification and assessment of special educational needs.
- *Educational psychologist*. A professional qualified psychologist who must also be an experienced teacher. The 'Ed Psych' works alongside schools and parents/guardians to offer professional advice on learning or behavioural difficulties.
- *Identification*. A key aspect of the Code of Practice is that all children with special educational needs should be identified and assessed as early as possible and as quickly as is consistent with thoroughness.
- *Individual education plan* (*IEP*). All SEN pupils are entitled to an IEP that outlines the strategies adopted for their educational support and development.
- *Pupil referral unit* (*PRU*). LEAs provide education for children of compulsory school age who have been excluded from school, or who may not otherwise receive suitable education, by operating PRUs.
- *Special educational needs co-ordinator* (*SENCO*). A teacher with the responsibility of co-ordinating a school's special education provision according to the Code of Practice.
- *Statement of Special Educational Needs*. Document drawn up by the LEA, following assessment, outlining a pupil's special needs and means of access to appropriate support.
- *Whole-school policy*. The SEN policy for a school as developed and adopted in consultation with all staff and governors. Since everyone is involved in the development and implementation of the policy all staff are aware of their responsibilities and duties.

are the issues of civil rights and equal opportunities. The debate about equalising access to education irrespective of gender, ethnicity or social class has increasingly been extended to those who might be disadvantaged by a disability. Thus special education has not only become a broader educational concept, it has also become part of a broader social and political debate.

(1992, p.13)

SEN is a blanket term that does not seek to indicate that a pupil is different from other pupils, only that they have needs that are. Between the 1944 Act and the Education Act 1981 came other Acts and reports that helped to change and formulate opinions and attitudes towards children who have special needs. The words 'child' and 'children' are used at this point because children from the age of 2 can be assessed for SEN purposes, and they have yet to become school pupils. The 1981 Act did away with the eleven categories of handicap and replaced them with a definition of special educational needs that is broad in meaning and does not seek to exclude via narrow definitions. The 1981 Act states that a child has special educational needs if he or she

> has a significantly greater difficulty in learning than the majority of children of his or her age . . . or has a disability which either prevents or hinders him or her from making use of educational facilities of a kind generally provided in schools, within the area of the local authority concerned, for children of his or her age or is under five and could fall into either of these categories if special provision were not made.
>
> (HMSO 1981)

The 1981 Education Act has had a far-reaching effect on children who have special educational needs and on the parents of SEN children. The Act imposed on parents the responsibility of ensuring that their children receive full-time education suited to their age, ability and aptitude and also to any special educational needs the child may have. The Act also provided for all children with special educational needs to be educated in ordinary schools, provided it is reasonably practical. That is, provided the child will receive the special educational provision that has been decided on, that the school's resources will be used efficiently and that it will be compatible with the efficient provision of education for other children. The Act also imposed on governors of ordinary schools the duty of providing appropriate support for SEN children – at least they have to aspire to do so.

PROCEDURES AND STRUCTURES

The statementing process

SEN pupils are those who cannot access part or all of the curriculum. There can be many reasons for a pupil's inability to do so. To ensure that a child is given access to all appropriate provision, and that resources are used fairly and efficiently, a *Statement of Special Educational Needs* will be made. This is a document prepared by the LEA when it has been decided that the child's needs cannot be met by the ordinary schools in the area. The legal structures and processes which lead up to the statement can be confusing to a newly qualified teacher. Although it may seem tedious, becoming familiar with the terminology can speed your ability to ask pertinent questions and find your way round some of the documents you will have to read. So far you will have read about the change in attitude to SEN pupils, and how some provision has changed to include pupils who would once have been regarded as ineducable. What is relevant to you now is to be able to recognise and interpret the language of special educational needs. Much of it has been created by legislation: the 1981 Education Act, the 1988 Education Reform Act and the 1993 Education Act. The 1993 Act requires the Secretary of State to provide LEAs, schools and some other agencies with practical guidance on their responsibilities to children with special educational needs and how those responsibilities are to be discharged. This is done through the Code of Practice which became effective in September 1994. It provides guidance on:

- the procedures to be followed once a pupil has been identified and assessed as having special educational needs;
- the planning, teaching and any other provisions needed to meet the special educational needs of the pupil;
- the responsibilities of all concerned agencies (LEAs, schools, the Health Service, Social Services Departments, etc.) to work in partnership with parents and each other to respond to children with special educational needs.

Stage 1

As a trainee teacher you may be asked to contribute to the procedures that help identify a pupil who has special educational needs. You may feel concerned about a pupil who is not meeting classroom expectations, and pass a memo to the SEN co-ordinator (SENCO) or the pupil's form tutor. This is the first identification of a learning difficulty, and as such will prompt assessment under Stage 1 of the Code of Practice. This means that information will be gathered to see whether the pupil is causing concern in any other areas. The information will be recorded and the child's special educational needs will be registered. This will include the teaching response and how it is planned. The Stage 1 process can be instigated by parent, teacher or another professional who has contact with the pupil. A Stage 1 pupil will have two reviews and the options that follow depend on the outcome of the reviews. If the pupil has made adequate progress two more reviews will take place. If progress has been maintained the pupil will be removed from the SEN register. However, if progress has not been satisfactory after the first two reviews, Stage 2 will be triggered.

Stage 2

Stage 2 will normally start after two terms of the pupil being on Stage 1. The SENCO will initiate the processes of Stage 2. More information will be sought about the pupil, further assessment will take place and advice sought. This will help to create the pupil's Individual Education Plan (IEP). The IEP should set out the nature of the child's learning difficulty, specific learning targets, the materials and resources to be used (and any special provision), staff involvement and how often support will be forthcoming, a time scale within which work is to be carried out, monitoring and assessment arrangements and a date for review. The review should take place within a term, and parents are to be invited. Consultation with parents must take place if the pupil is to be moved to Stage 3.

Stage 3

Stage 3 is more complicated, and it is the time when the school will ask for specialist help, normally from external agencies. The class teacher, the SENCO and outside support teachers – for example, educational psychologists (sometimes called ed psychs) – all share responsibility for pupils with SEN. Advice on teaching approaches, technology or classroom management and material, direct teaching and classroom support may be offered by external agencies. The SENCO has to organise a review within a term. The review will include and involve parents and if appropriate the pupil. The focus of the review will be on the progress made. It will include a report on how effective the IEP is and current information about progress made and any future planning. The IEP should have details about the following areas: strategies to be used and teaching targets, what assessment has been carried out, methods tried and the known outcomes, how experiences derived from Stage 2 have been built on for teaching arrangements and the arrangements for monitoring, reviewing and evaluation.

Stage 4

The head teacher, having consulted all the relevant people, may consider referring the pupil to the LEA for a statutory assessment if satisfactory progress has not been made. For a statutory assessment to take place documentation and evidence will be required to support the referral. It is at this point that the staging process ceases to be completely school-based; the LEA and the school share responsibility and have to co-operate with each other to ensure that the assessment and provision of education meet the pupil's needs. Stage 4 is the collection and collation of evidence, documentation and professional advice to determine whether the pupil's needs should be subject to the statutory procedures set up under the 1993 Education Act. This procedure does not automatically lead to a Statement of Special Educational Needs being issued. The LEA may decide to take advice from a range of professionals about the best way to meet the pupil's needs. Should the LEA decide that there is no foundation for requesting a statutory assessment, it must state its reasons. If the pupil's parents have requested the statutory assessment the LEA must respond within a given time.

Stage 5

The first four stages are an ongoing process and lead into each other should the pupil not make satisfactory progress. It does not mean that a pupil who is at Stage 1 will automatically be given a Statement of Special Education Needs. If a pupil is at Stage 4 it also does not follow that they will be 'statemented'. Stage 5 is reached when the LEA is satisfied that there is sufficient evidence to warrant a statutory assessment, and that advice has been collected from professionals, including teachers, doctors, social workers and educational psychologists. The two options that are available to the LEA are: (1) to decide that the pupil's needs can be met at school, as the resources are available, or (2) to issue a Statement of Special Educational Needs.

Whichever option is decided on, the aim will be to provide and meet, fully and appropriately, the pupil's needs as identified. The first option means that the pupil's needs and the provision for meeting them will be set out in a note, which is in place of the statement. It also means that the pupil's special educational needs have to be met from resources already available in the school.

The statement of Special Educational Needs

The Statement of Special Educational Needs constitutes a legal document and as such functions as a contract. The contract is between the LEA and the school on one side and the parents and the child with special educational needs on the other. The contents of the statement must be understood by all concerned and the relevant parties must ensure that its requirements are met. Following on from the statement are various procedures which are designed to ensure that the requirements are being met, and that they remain pertinent and relevant to the SEN pupil. The annual review is one such structure. This is a formal meeting in which statements are revised and updated, and at which progress is reported on.

Figure 7.2 The format of a Statement of Special Educational Needs

A Statement of Special Educational Needs constitutes a legal document, and is set out in six key sections, which focus on:

- biographical details;
- details of the special educational need, including the pupil's strengths and weaknesses, levels of functioning and a summary of their special requirements;
- an outline of the special educational provision to be made, including broad teaching objectives, the level of staffing support to be made available, and details of the monitoring and review arrangements;
- information concerning the school's responsibility in providing for the pupil's special educational needs;
- any relevant non-educational needs;
- any other provision that is required, e.g. speech therapy.

Integrated SEN education

Integrated SEN education has become more prevalent since the Education Acts of 1981 and 1988. Both Acts, in different ways, changed how SEN education is delivered in mainstream schools. A child who is statemented can receive full-time education in a mainstream school, provided the school is able to meet the pupil's special educational needs efficiently. Within a school the SEN pupil will find various procedures set up to deliver the education that the pupil will benefit from most. It often includes classroom support and/or withdrawal from some lessons. This is discussed more fully in the following paragraphs.

Special schools are discussed briefly above, and their importance for some pupils should not be ignored. However, the type of special school, its location and the number of pupils it has are dependent on many factors. The main factor is financial. Classes in a special school will be small, sometimes no more than twelve pupils, sometimes even fewer; class size is sometimes determined by the pupil make-up. Children who have Emotional and Behavioural Difficulties (EBD) are sometimes put in very small classes of four or five. Pupils who have MLD may be in classes of twelve or slightly fewer. Each class will need a class teacher who may teach the pupils English, Maths, Geography, History. The school may also have specialists for Technology, Art, Science and PE. The school will be organised in exactly the same way as a mainstream school – that is, it will have a head teacher, teachers with responsibility points, a school secretary, a premises manager, dinner staff, cleaners, governors and classroom assistants. The school could have, depending on the type of pupil, as few as eighty pupils. Since some Education Authorities pay teachers more for working in a special school, the cost of educating a pupil is considerably more than in a mainstream school. The 1988 Education Act introduced Local Management of Schools (LMS), which took money away from LEAs and made it difficult to finance some special schools adequately. The number and range of special schools vary from LEA to LEA. Some may have schools that have been purpose-built for children with physical disabilities, some may have schools that specialise in teaching children who are hearing or sight-impaired.

THE SEN DEPARTMENT

Policy and structure

The SEN policy of a school is an important document. The Department for Education's Circular 6/94, *The Organisation of Special Education Provision*, gives advice and guidance on schools' SEN policies, support services and how SEN provision should be co-ordinated (DFE 1994b). There are three parts to the circular: Part 1 is concerned with the annual report to parents and the issues to be considered when drawing up the report; Part 2 deals with provision and financial matters; Part 3 is concerned with the co-ordination of special education provision.

The structure of any SEN department is frequently determined by the number of SEN pupils and the types of SEN provision they need. The physical layout may also be determined by the number of SEN pupils and how frequently they are withdrawn from lessons. To take two extreme examples may be the best way of demonstrating this.

CASE STUDY 1

Low-level SEN provision

Imagine a mainstream secondary school with approximately 800 pupils. About twenty have been Stage 1, and are on the school's SEN register. Some have reached Stage 2 or 3, but not many. The SENCO will have to maintain the register and carry out the other responsibilities that go with the post. The SENCO may also go into classes and give pupils support in areas that have been agreed on. Some pupils may be withdrawn from specific lessons to receive extra help on a one-to-one basis, or to work in small groups. Other members of the teaching staff may assist with classroom support within their own specialism. That is, a science teacher with one or two lessons over the non-contact time allowance may be asked to support a pupil with SEN in science lessons. In a school with few SEN pupils the head teacher or a deputy head may be the SENCO.

CASE STUDY 2

High-level SEN provision

At the other end of the spectrum imagine a mainstream secondary school of 800 pupils with 200 on its SEN register. Twenty of the pupils are statemented, and another twenty or so are at Stage 4. The SEN department becomes a focal point in the education of 25 per cent of the pupils. The SENCO will have an enormous administration job just in keeping the SEN register up to date and co-ordinating case conferences. The withdrawal, in terms of class support and the classroom assistants' timetables, has to be worked out and co-ordinated with any teachers who have to add SEN support lessons to their timetable. The SENCO will need to have a number of specialist SEN teachers, who may be known as the SEN co-ordination team or the learning support team, within the department, and the administrative workload could well be shared between them. The SENCO with twenty pupils may have a small classroom area dedicated to special educational needs; the SENCO with 200 pupils may have a whole suite of rooms in which different groups of children who have been withdrawn from lessons receive the SEN provision set out in their statement or IEP.

Withdrawal and classroom support

In some cases it is appropriate for SEN pupils to be withdrawn from mainstream lessons to work individually or as members of a small group. In some schools RE is taught in one lesson a week. The SENCO should be aware of this and avoid withdrawing pupils from RE lessons. If it is not avoidable the head of department should supply the SENCO with some work for the pupil to do that is RE-based. It is important to know if a pupil is being withdrawn, as you have to keep your register up to date. Check with the SENCO and/or your head of department, not with the pupil, to find out if the pupil is being withdrawn. Pupils have been known to use withdrawal from some classes as a way to truant from others, or to avoid lessons in subjects they dislike. Even if pupils show you their timetable in a homework diary, check it out with a member of staff.

Classroom support, or in-class support, is another approach to helping SEN pupils. It is sometimes seen as being appropriate, as SEN pupils are educated with their peers. Pupils with special educational needs are sometimes allocated a support teacher or a classroom assistant. It is advisable to discuss their role before you teach the pupil. Some pupils will have an adult with them for specific lessons. If a support teacher or classroom assistant is to be present during the lesson, make sure you have discussed the lesson content with them. This makes it easier for them to assist the pupil and makes their assistance far more effective.

SENCO and specialist support staff

The SENCO has specific responsibilities under the Code of Practice. They are, as the title suggests, co-ordinating SEN provision within a school. They may do this with the help of a specialist team, or they may be able to fulfil their role in a couple of hours a week. It depends entirely on the number of SEN pupils in the school. Apart from maintaining the school's SEN register, the SENCO also has responsibility for:

- overseeing the daily operation of the school's SEN policy;
- organising the records on all pupils with special educational needs;
- co-ordinating provision for children with special educational needs;
- advising and liaison with colleagues;
- liaison with the parents, guardians or responsible adult of children with special educational needs;
- contributing to in-service training;
- liaison with external agencies.

The SENCO also has to gather information about pupils who have been staged, and co-ordinate SEN provision for the pupil. The SENCO has a major role to play in advising and consulting the head teacher, parents and outside agencies to ensure that SEN provision is appropriate and that all records are accurate and up to date.

Task 7.1 Auditing SEN provision: finding documents and identifying people

When you first arrive at your teaching practice school(s) it is easy to focus on what appear to be your most immediate concerns at the expense of preparing to deal with SEN provision in your teaching. In order to help you avoid this trap, this task provides a checklist of documents to collect and staff to identify during your first week in school.

Essential documents:

- school staff handbook;
- department/faculty handbook;
- school policy documents on special educational needs.

Essential staff:

- head of department/faculty;
- SENCO;
- SEN support staff;
- classroom assistants;
- other members of the department/faculty with responsibility for SEN provision.

YOUR ROLE AS AN RE TEACHER

Identifying SEN pupils

When starting your school experience you should be provided with specific documents: a school handbook, a departmental handbook and registers, which may also be called set or class lists. It is essential to know if you are teaching a pupil with special educational needs. To find out, ask the head of department or faculty whether there is a folder containing pupil IEPs that you can consult. You should check the lists you have been given and note if any of your pupils have special educational needs. In some schools pupil lists are marked with highlighters of different colours to indicate specific types of pupil, for example those who are known truants or pupils with special educational needs. Read through the IEPs for all the pupils you will be teaching. IEPs take many forms and can contain different information. What they will all have in common is that they will contain targets for the pupil to achieve. The targets can be wide-ranging – from a pupil having to increase his/her spelling ability by a specific number of words a week, improving concentration, staying on task, to being less confrontational or arriving for lesson on time. Each target will have a success criterion.

Teaching

Having identified SEN pupils on paper, you have to find a strategy for identifying them in the classroom. The SEN pupil is probably not the one swinging on the light fitting, or climbing up the window frames. Being familiar with the school policy on discipline will be an asset at this point! Once you have the class sitting and are able to register them, how will you know which is the SEN pupil if you have your head buried in the register? Introduce yourself to the class, smile at them and show you are friendly – but firm and not to be taken advantage of. Ask them to stand up when you call their name out, so that you can start to put faces to the list in your register.

The pupils you will need to notice – and try to remember – are those whose names are highlighted in the register. Try to note something about the pupil – unusual school bag, hair style or colour, where they are sitting – that will help you to remember them for the next lesson. After you have identified the SEN pupils try to go back and reread the IEP for them. Note in your register anything which you feel may jeopardise your handling of the pupil in class. Some pupils will have very low self-esteem, and very low expectations of how a teacher will respond to them. They may feel that all teachers they come into contact with will shout at them at some point because their work is badly presented, or their spelling is phonetical, or they simply cannot write about a subject but have presented you with a picture that shows they understood the topic you were teaching.

Language

Teaching RE to pupils who have special educational needs does present problems that are not faced by other subjects. The teacher of RE uses words like 'miracle', 'faith', 'worship' and 'God'. Many of the pupils you will teach will have little or no concept of the religious meaning of these words. Many pupils will have no concept of religion in that they come from backgrounds where they have been given no guidance and no intimation that religion can be part of everyday life. They will find the whole area hard to access because of the secular way in which they have been brought up. Some pupils may have had RE at primary or junior school stage, but they may not have thought deeply about it, for reasons that are about to become obvious. A class of Year 9 pupils read about the Immaculate Conception. They have heard the story before – possibly before they had sex education and found out how babies are conceived. At the end of the lesson two female pupils ask if they can talk to you. They tell you that they do not understand how Mary could have conceived if she was a virgin, because you cannot be a virgin and get pregnant. A virgin, they inform you, very seriously, is someone who has not had sex. How do you answer them? You can try to explain that the Immaculate Conception was a miracle and is a matter of faith – of being able to believe in something that does not normally happen. By comparison with some of the questions you can be asked this would be an easy one. How would you deal with 'My Mum says I'm Church of England – so why have I got to learn about Jesus Christ?'? It could be argued that as far as RE goes a proportion of pupils are unable to access the curriculum, and therefore have special educational needs. Almost everything you say is open to misinterpretation. Having spent a term teaching a Year 7 class the story of Genesis, a teacher asked the pupils to draw their favourite bit. They were to keep the subject of their drawing a secret, because the class would try to guess the bit of Genesis illustrated. Only one drawing defeated the class and the teacher. It was of a chauffeur-driven Rolls-Royce with two passengers. When the pupil was asked to explain which bit of Genesis the drawing represented he replied, 'It's God driving Adam and Eve out of the Garden of Eden'!

Planning

The RE department should supply you with schemes of work and lesson plans. These should fit in with the curriculum and the Agreed Syllabus for RE used by all schools within the LEA. You may also be given copies of worksheets to be used in class, sample pages from the textbooks you will be using and other relevant material. Using the information you have about any SEN pupils, you will have to ensure that the material is appropriate. This needs to be planned well in advance, as do strategies for using different types of worksheet for different pupils. School and departmental policy on this also matters, as you need to fit in with and work around existing school practice. The earlier you prepare for your lessons the more chance you have of planning successfully. If you have any worries or doubts about the topics and level of work you are expected to deliver you will need to discuss them with the head of department. Time is therefore an element that also needs to be considered, as you may need to negotiate how best to deliver specific areas of knowledge to pupils with special educational needs.

Should you find yourself in the situation of being able to plan your own lesson structures around the topics the department head has told you will be studied, you need to think through many things. You may have to put your lesson plan down on a form that prescribes specific areas that you have to consider. The areas could include: a time plan of the lesson, introduction, the main aim of the lesson ('by the end of the lesson you will/be able to/know about/understand/evaluate'), the learning resources you will need (artefacts, textbooks, worksheets, overhead projector, video, pencils, rubbers, rulers, stencils, posters, postcards). There may be an area on the lesson planning form that asks the teacher if the lesson was a success or a failure, and you may also be expected to evaluate your lesson. Planning is an integral and inescapable area of teaching. It vitally effects your performance, confidence and professionalism. It also reminds you how the class performed in previous lessons. You will also find out what they respond to best, the type of teaching method and learning resources they find interesting and that engage their attention. It can be, and frequently is, an exciting and invigorating experience. And in the middle of all of this you are aware that you have a pupil, or pupils, whose special educational needs have to be addressed in the lesson. You may have to write a report about the pupil, and you cannot do it if you have not included the special educational needs of the pupil, or pupils, in your scheme of things.

Planning a lesson seems, sometimes, to be very easy. All the information you need is at hand, and you have the expert knowledge to back up the written lesson plan. The area that may cause you problems, and create difficulties, is the time plan. Dividing a lesson of an hour up seems to be an easy thing to do: five minutes for registration, five to recap the last lesson, five to introduce the topic of the lesson, ten to read through information sheets, and so on. It always looks good on paper, but the reality can be very different. It can take ten minutes to register a class, and it can also take fifteen to recap the last lesson, especially if some pupils were absent. Lesson plans need to be flexible and should reflect your knowledge of the class you will be teaching. Always have some extension work at hand for the pupil who does all the set work when there are still twenty minutes to the end of the lesson. The work should be related to the main topic, and extend the pupils' knowledge and understanding. SEN does not define a gifted or more able pupil. Some schools may Stage 1 a more able pupil, as it is one method of monitoring how the pupil progresses. It is as well to be aware that, even if the school you are in uses streaming, you may find that some pupils will far outstrip others in the same set in their capacity for work. You will need to plan for them as well.

Recording

As mentioned earlier, as a student teacher you may be asked to comment on a pupil you have been teaching. You may be sent a form to fill in, asking you to write down your observations about the pupil under specific headings. These may be concerned with motivation, attitude to work, homework response, behaviour, interaction with staff and pupils, the pupil's strengths and weaknesses, positive features and attendance. The form may also ask what, if any, strategies you have used to help the pupil access the curriculum. The form may be the result of a colleague sending a memo that starts a Stage 1 procedure, or it could be the SENCO having to prepare material for a statutory assessment. Whatever the reason, you will not be able to fill it in accurately if you have not kept your records up to date. As a student teacher it may be that you only taught the pupil once or twice, for a fifty-minute lesson. Even so, you should know whether homework was handed in and from that have gained an insight into the level of understanding shown by the pupil, the standard of presentation of the work and have some idea of the pupil's interaction with yourself. It could be significant if the pupil has not interacted, and so worth recording. All the procedures concerned with SEN pupils rely on teachers having evidence to support the fact that a pupil has special educational needs. It is not enough to say that a pupil is not progressing or learning. How and why they are not learning or progressing needs to be demonstrated. As a student teacher you may feel you have not developed the expertise and confidence to make such judgements accurately and fairly. If so, ask the head of department or head of faculty for advice if you are unsure about any of the comments you are asked to make. It may also be of use to speak to the pupil's regular teacher and find out if they have any comments they would like to put down. As many of the forms concerning special educational needs are crucial to a pupil's future, and the procedures to be followed are so complex, it is essential that the information on any form is accurate and up to date.

Task 7.2 Keeping SEN records

In your school you will be expected to keep full records of pupil attendance, behaviour and academic achievement. Clearly you will need to achieve a balance in such recording between being too brief and too detailed in your notes. It is important to prepare yourself for this by exploring different methods of recording pupils' progress. It is vital for such records to recognise and comment on the specific issues surrounding SEN pupils. In developing a method of collecting relevant SEN data it may be helpful to follow the following steps:

1 Audit the methods of recording adopted by your mentor(s) and other experienced teachers.
2 Decide on a method and trial it during your first school placement.
3 After the placement make a list of the strengths and weaknesses of your approach.
4 On your second placement trial a refined version of your method of recording, adapted from the original in the light of your critical review of previous experience.

Your own personal recording procedures should include, as a minimum, the following information:

● whether a pupil is present or absent;
● if a pupil is late for class;
● submission of assignments;
● marks for classwork and homework;
● any rewards, merits or commendations;
● any detentions, punishments or sanctions;
● any SEN pupils and their particular needs;
● the strategies adopted to support the SEN pupils;
● the progress of SEN pupils measured against their specific needs;
● the effectiveness of these strategies.

Assessment

As a student teacher you will have to work within a whole-school policy when dealing with certain aspects of school life. As a student teacher of RE you have to meet the demands of the faculty or departmental handbook, and of a marking policy. It will be worth your while to find out if you have to mark pupil's work only on their understanding of the RE topic you have taught them, or whether you also have to take into account their spelling, punctuation and grammar. The distinction is this: if you only have to assess the pupils on their religious knowledge, understanding and grasp of the topic you have been teaching, you may find that you can give them a better mark than if you have to take account of spelling, punctuation and grammar. The National Curriculum requires teachers to assess pupils' work as a whole, not on a collection of achievements. This can present problems for any teacher who is trying to help pupils with special educational needs create a positive image of themselves. Some SEN pupils will have undergone many tests and assessments to ensure that the SEN provision they receive is pertinent to their needs. Being continually under the spotlight can have a negative effect on a pupil.

Task 7.3 Pupil assessment and special educational needs

Find out the type of testing your school uses to assess pupils: age equivalent, norm-referenced tests, curriculum-based assessment, criterion referenced tests, etc.

Find out any special arrangements staff use to test SEN pupils. Do these arrangements replace standard procedures or supplement them?

Ensure that you are aware of the range of practical procedures the school adopts for assessing SEN pupils.

Remember your responsibility for developing a critical awareness of these various testing methods and procedures.

Reporting

Building up a pupil's self-esteem and trust in you as a teacher is very hard – destroying either can be very easy. How you approach pupils can be a vital ingredient in classroom dynamics. Handing books back in class creates specific problems that you must be able to deal with. Pupils compare their work and will exchange information about the marks they have been given. However, if you have followed the school or department marking policy, you should not find yourself in the situation of pupils saying that the marking is unfair, and asking you to justify the marks you have given. There are strategies for dealing with this. You could say that you will not discuss one pupil's work with another, or that you mark each pupil as an individual and do not compare their work. You could also avoid the situation by writing a comment about their work, saying why you have given them the mark. For instance, a pupil who has special educational needs and has very bad handwriting has completed the work you set, and has most of it correct. You award a mark that reflects the pupil's effort in completing the work, and for correct content. You write this down next to the mark. You have another pupil whose work is very badly presented. You have looked through their exercise book and have noted that previous work was well presented, neat and accurate. The content of the work is acceptable. When you give the pupil a mark you make it quite clear that you feel the work does not reflect their ability, and that they have lowered their standard. Ensure the pupil knows you have looked at their previous work. Telling a pupil that their work is bad because of the presentation can be negative, but not when you have an example of good presentation in the pupil's book. Look for the positive aspects of their work, their understanding or insight into the topic you are covering. All pupils' work has a positive side to it. Sometimes it can be very difficult to find, but it is vital to look. How you handle a pupil whose work does not seem to have any positive features is very difficult, especially if the pupil has put time and effort into the work. Praising a pupil for time and effort is positive, but that can leave the pupil expecting praise for the work itself. Handling pupils' delicate self-esteem is a very sensitive area and there are many factors that have to be taken into account. These areas are sometimes covered by the IEP; if they are not, you need to seek advice. You may be asked to complete a set of assessment records or reports. Some schools use a computer system of reports. You will be handed a pile of cards and comments to select from to complete the assessment/report. It is possible that not all of them will say what you feel ought to be said, and in that case you will need to seek advice. Hand-written assessments/reports also need to be thought out.

Task 7.4 Writing SEN reports

Think about the assessments/reports you received when you were at school. Write down the first comments you can remember from the reports. Are they negative, positive or destructive? What do they say about the teacher who wrote them?

Writing reports often says as much about the teacher as it purports to say about the pupil. The following comments have all been used on SEN assessments/reports. What do they say about the teachers who wrote them? How effective are they as summative comments, enabling the pupils to understand their actual level of achievement? How effective are they as formative comments, motivating and guiding the pupils to allow them to make progress in the future?

- Her main ambition seems to be to do as little as possible. So far she has achieved this with singular success.
- Could do better.
- Shows an in-depth knowledge of the main subject area studied this term.
- Spelling and presentation appalling.
- Has made enormous progress, well done.
- Despite difficulties she has made a real effort to improve her knowledge and understanding of the subject. I am very pleased at the overall improvement in the presentation of her work.
- I have never seen this pupil.

Confidentiality

Confidentiality is an area that has to be taken seriously. To some pupils, and their families, having special educational needs still carries a stigma of shame. Some special educational needs pupils refuse to have any classroom support because of the possibility of peer group mockery and the shame they feel at being different. All the information you gain about the pupils you teach is privileged information. You are told of a pupil's situation because you need to know, and because you will be in a better position to make the pupil's education more effective. How and where you discuss specific cases and problems is not always up to you. You may find yourself discussing a problem with a senior colleague whilst walking down a busy school corridor rather than in the security of their office. As a student teacher you will not always be able to predetermine when and where sensitive material can be discussed. However, you can take care that none of the sensitive material that is written finds its way into pupil territory. Work out a system for yourself about how and where you will keep sensitive papers. Do not think that anything you take into a classroom will be sacrosanct – pupils can be very curious and may see no harm in having a rummage through your case or school bag. They will probably have no dishonest intention, just curiosity about the new teacher in their life. If you are asked to fill in a form, and you need to refer to a pupil's work, ensure that you do not leave the form in the pupil's book. It sounds unlikely, but it has happened and causes enormous problems when a pupil sees a frank and honest appraisal of their personality and ability.

Figure 7.3 The National Association for Special Educational Needs

The National Association for Special Educational Needs (NASEN) publishes handbooks to help with practical classroom situations. Called *Spotlight on SEN*, they cover particular areas of difficulty such as EBD, hearing impairment and learning difficulties. NASEN will also supply a detailed reading list. The National Association for Special Educational Needs can be contacted at NASEN House, 4–5 Amber Business Village, Amington, Tamworth, Staffordshire, B77 4RP. Telephone: 01827 311500, fax 01827 313005, e-mail nasen @bbcnc.org.uk.

SUMMARY AND KEY POINTS

Teaching is a very rewarding profession that brings laughter and sometimes tears. This is especially so for the teacher of pupils with special educational needs. At the heart of this chapter has been the idea that as an RE teacher you are also an SEN teacher. You cannot afford to shrug off your responsibilities and pass them over to the specialist SEN teacher.

This chapter has identified and unpacked the key issues and language surrounding SEN teaching. It has outlined the history of SEN provision and current policy and procedures. Finally it has focused on your role as an RE teacher, outlining a range of responsibilities and strategies and making suggestions for implementation in the school and classroom.

FURTHER READING

Farrell, M. (1998) *The Special Educational Needs Handbook*, London: David Fulton. An extremely useful compendium, containing an A–Z of terminology, an outline of legislation, many useful addresses and an excellent bibliography.

Gains, C. (1996) *The Special Educational Needs Co-ordinator*, Stafford: National Association for SEN. This outlines the different aspects of the SENCO, details various methods of liaison with external agencies and provides an insight into the role.

Jones, N. and Docking, J. (1992) *Special Educational Needs and the Education Reform Act*, Stoke on Trent: Trentham Books. Solid, clear and highly recommended.

Ramjhum, A. F. (1995) *Implementing the Code of Practice for Children with Special Educational Needs*, London: David Fulton. A good practical guide.

8 Learning to Teach Religious Education at Key Stage 4

Angela Wright and Taira Mohammed

The essential questions which we must always ask of religion in our schools are these. Is it behaving in a way which is truly educational? Is it tending towards balance and broadness? Is it enhancing the moral and mental development of pupils and of society? Is it deepening the human qualities of children and young people by encouraging an independent quest for truth and, at the same time, transmitting a broadly based and balanced understanding of the religious traditions of humanity?

(Hull 1989, p. 4)

The lowest standards occur where RE is taught within Personal and Social Education. There is evidence that this practice is declining, but it still exists in nearly half of schools, particularly in Key Stage 4. The highest standards in RE lessons are found among pupils preparing for public examinations

(OFSTED 1998, p. 159)

Teaching RE at Key Stage 4 has often been described as a 'graveyard' experience! The OFSTED report cited above confirms that there are problems for the subject at this phase and yet the potential for exciting teaching and learning is great. The questions raised by John Hull need to be thought through carefully in relation to Key Stage 4 RE and our practice needs to be moulded in relation to the answers we give. It is hoped that this chapter will offer something of a vision of just how innovative and challenging RE at Key Stage 4 can be. It charts recent developments in RE at Key Stage 4 and introduces the various options available, both examination and non-examination. In particular, it compares and contrasts the GCSE Religious Studies and GCSE (short course) Religious Education syllabuses. The process of planning and managing a Key Stage 4 curriculum is investigated, starting with how to choose an appropriate syllabus, and moving on to consider how to translate it into effective practice. The question of appropriate pedagogy is explored in relation to the questions of relevance, motivation and academic rigour.

OBJECTIVES

By the end of this chapter you should:

- have some knowledge of recent developments in RE at Key Stage 4;
- be aware of the various options for RE available at Key Stage 4;
- have considered how to translate syllabus content into effective and challenging practice.

RECENT DEVELOPMENTS IN RE AT KEY STAGE 4

The recognition of under-provision

The 1988 Education Reform Act heralded immense changes with the introduction of the National Curriculum. RE was to be part of the Basic Curriculum, continuing to use locally Agreed Syllabuses. Sir Ron Dearing led the first review of the National Curriculum and looked also at how RE was faring. It became clear that there were problems regarding the quality of teaching and the lack of provision in many schools, in terms of staffing, time and resources. The prescriptions of the National Curriculum were not applicable to RE. The subject did not use the same terminology, the same assessment methods or the same organisational structures. All these factors increased the sense of difference between RE and 'proper' subjects. The phase that was highlighted for the most obvious deficiencies was Key Stage 4. Many schools had no provision at all, whilst only a minority of schools offered RE as an option and often the take-up was small. However, church and many independent schools frequently entered the whole Key Stage 4 cohort for GCSE Religious Studies, and in county schools where RE was encouraged and supported there were some shining examples of good practice. Yet the most familiar occurrence was to see the RE provision being shared in a carousel arrangement with subjects such as personal and social education, careers and sex education.

In response to such underprovision Dearing made recommendations on adequate time for RE within the curriculum. Hours for each of the Key Stages were specified: thirty-six hours per year at Key Stage 1, forty-five hours at Key Stage 2 and Key Stage 3 and 5 per cent of available curriculum time at Key Stage 4. If schools were to take the timing issue seriously it would have a knock-on effect in terms of staffing needs and the allocation of resources. Such improvements take time and OFSTED's *Review of Inspection Findings 1993/94* still reported that

Figure 8.1 The status of RE (Reproduced with permission from Blaylock, L. and Johnson, C. (eds) (1997) *A Teacher's Handbook of Religious Education*, Derby: CEM, p. 5)

> The low priority given to religious education in recent years means that resources for teaching . . . inservice provision, and accommodation in some secondary schools is often unsatisfactory . . . There is not enough curriculum time for basic religious education lessons in many primary schools and in secondary schools especially at Key Stage 4 and Post-16 . . . A third of schools fail to provide specific religious education at KS4.
>
> (OFSTED 1995b, p. 4)

Responses to underprovision

Improvements to provision throughout the various phases became a key focus. The Model Syllabuses were published to guide the work of Agreed Syllabus Conferences, and Agreed Syllabuses themselves were required to be rewritten and regularly reviewed. The new focus on school inspections, and the inclusion of the Dearing recommendation of 5 per cent curriculum time at Key Stage 4 into many new Agreed Syllabuses, making it obligatory, put pressure on schools to ensure that their RE provision was appropriate.

With all these initiatives, many in the RE world were optimistic about the future of the subject. However, the lack of motivation towards RE from many Key Stage 4 pupils still presented itself as a very real problem for many RE teachers. It is possible to distinguish between extrinsic and intrinsic factors contributing to the problem. In relation to the extrinsic factors of time, resources and staffing, some progress was being made. The intrinsic factors were concerned with ensuring that the curriculum itself is appropriate, 'encouraging an independent quest for truth and, at the same

time, transmitting a broadly based and balanced understanding of the religious traditions of humanity' (Hull 1989, p. 4). This was the most important thing which
needed to be 'got right'. RE needed to be asking the right questions of the pupils,
engaging them with the fundamental questions of life, and ensuring that any such
enquiry was relevant and challenging.

Research done by PCfRE in 1995 showed that teachers were largely in agreement
that such fundamental questions and religious responses to ethical and social issues
were the most appropriate focus for the curriculum at Key Stage 4 (Blaylock and
Mayled-Porter 1996, p. 2). However, the problem of intrinsic motivation was not
helped by the lack of extrinsic motivation in the form of public examination accreditation, given the relatively few pupils opting for full GCSE RE courses.

There were examples of attempts to combat this problem through locally accredited schemes, such as the DARE project (Dorset Achievement in RE), developed
along these lines which were very successful. However, it was the development of
criteria for a new GCSE (short course) in RE and the new syllabuses which followed
that were to be a significant attempt to respond positively to the perceived needs at
Key Stage 4, addressing in their aims and content these intrinsic issues. It was now
possible, senior management willing, to offer all pupils an appropriate and challenging examined course, which uses the common currency of the GCSE.

CURRENT OPTIONS AT KEY STAGE 4

As we have seen, the opportunities in this phase have increased. In your school you
are likely to be offered one of the following options:

- a 'compulsory' GCSE for all pupils, following either the full or the short
  course;
- an optional GCSE full course, together with 'compulsory' non-examination
  provision for non-opting pupils (either as a discrete subject with 5 per cent
  of time or as part of a carousel system, which may be discrete or may be
  integrated with PSE);
- an optional GCSE full course (5 per cent), alongside a 'compulsory' GCSE
  short course for non-opting pupils (5 per cent);
- a GCSE full course option and no other provision;
- non-examination provision for all, either as a discrete subject with 5 per
  cent of time or as part of a carousel system, which may be discrete or may
  be integrated with PSE.

GCSE Religious Studies or Religious Education?

What is the difference between Religious Studies and Religious Education? The distinction is an important one, though in many schools little attention is actually paid
to it. Figure 8.2 draws on a comparison between the two drawn up by Lat Blaylock,
CEM Professional Development Officer. In 1995 CEM ran a major conference of

Figure 8.2 The distinction between 'Religious Studies' and 'Religious Education'

Religious Education	Religious Studies
• starts with the student	• starts with the religions
• emphasises learning from religion	• emphasises learning about religion
• has a curricular agenda set by life	• has a curricular agenda set by religions
• emphasises the processes of learning	• emphasises the content of learning
• challenges pupils on the basis of their encounter with world religions	• avoids the personal, challenging students to academic excellence
• succeeds when education leads to spiritual development	• succeeds when knowledge and understanding of religions are developed
• concerned with world views and their development	• concerned with one or two world religions

RE teachers which considered options at Key Stage 4. The group discussions which took place considered a number of propositions. One of these was 'Religious Studies only indirectly addresses the student's own experience. New accreditation should centre on the personal search for meaning which is at the heart of good RE'. Of the teachers present 42 per cent strongly agreed, 34 per cent agreed, 10 per cent didn't know, 10 per cent disagreed and 4 per cent strongly disagreed (Blaylock 1995).

However, despite the perceived differences between Religious Education and Religious Studies at Key Stage 4, these are not always reflected in the syllabuses of the examination boards. Consider the following selection of aims and assessment criteria, drawn from a range of boards :

Aims

GCSE (short course) Religious Education:

- Acquire and develop knowledge and understanding of the beliefs, values and traditions of one or more religions.
- Consider the influence of the beliefs, values and traditions associated with one or more religions.
- Consider religious and other responses to moral issues.
- Identify, investigate and respond to fundamental questions of life raised by religions and human experience.

GCSE Religious Studies:

- Stimulate interest in and enthusiasm for a study of religion.
- Develop knowledge and understanding of at least one living religion.
- Identify and promote exploration of, and reflection upon, questions about the meaning and purpose of life.

- Consider religious and, where appropriate, other responses to moral issues.
- Develop skills relevant to the study of religions.

Assessment criteria

GCSE (short course) Religious Education:

- Recall, select, organise and deploy knowledge of the syllabus content.
- Describe, analyse and explain the relevance and application of a religion or religions.
- Evaluate different responses to religious and moral issues.

GCSE Religious Studies:

- Demonstrate knowledge and understanding of the key elements of religion(s) studied, including beliefs, practices, sources of authority and organisation.
- Demonstrate knowledge and understanding of the effect of religion(s) on individual or corporate moral behaviour, attitudes, social practices and lifestyles.
- Produce evidence and arguments to support and evaluate points of view.

Task 8.1 Exploring the distinction between 'Religious Education' and 'Religious Studies'

Compare the perceived differences between 'Religious Education' and 'Religious Studies' as outlined in Figure 8.2.

Now get hold of an RE examination syllabus and an RS examination syllabus from the same examination board (see Appendix B).

List any differences you can see between them.

In what ways do the differences between the syllabuses correspond to those highlighted in the table?

Having looked at examples of the different syllabuses, work out your own response to the following proposition:

- GCSE RS only indirectly addresses the student's own experience, while GCSE RE centres on the personal search for meaning that is at the heart of all good education

---

Selecting a syllabus

In selecting a syllabus it is vital to have all the key information readily available. In order to aid this process Appendix A includes a list of the addresses and contact numbers of the examination boards, and Appendix B outlines the content of all available GCSE Religious Education and Religious Studies syllabuses. Even as a newly qualified teacher you may well find yourself involved in making important decisions about programmes of study and examination syllabuses at Key Stage 4. Obviously examination boards change syllabuses in response to uptake by schools, and you will need to ensure that you constantly keep yourself updated regarding developments. Appendix B offers an overview of the syllabuses available for examination in summer 2000.

The number of religions to be studied?

The syllabuses allow candidates to study no more than one (GCSE Religious Studies) or two (GCSE Religious Education) religions in addition to Christianity and also allow Christianity or one other principal religion to be studied alone. (This enables maintained schools, church schools and independent schools to adopt a syllabus which meets their needs and meets legal requirements.) If a particular denomination is to be studied, it must be placed in the context of the broader religious tradition to which it belongs.

The GCSE Religious Studies full course

The full course GCSE syllabuses offer systematic coverage of individual faiths with the option of some textual papers and some papers covering Christian responses to ethical issues. There has been some criticism of the syllabuses being quite dense in content, and therefore creating pressure in terms of effective delivery in the time available. As has been intimated, some teachers see the full course as offering limited opportunities for personal reflection, the 'learning from' element of RE. The full course benefits from sharing the same status as all other GCSEs. The EDEXCEL full course now integrates the systematic coverage of a religion with the RE focus on ultimate questions and ethics.

The GCSE Religious Education short course

The short course syllabuses are of two different types. The first type is essentially half a full course in the nature of the content. The idea is that it should be possible to run a full course as an option and a short course for all concurrently. The second type, the new breed of RE syllabus, introduces pupils to questions relating to philosophy of religion and ethical issues, from the point of view of one, two or three religions, depending on which syllabus you choose. The benefits of the short course specifically relate to the subject matter being seen as of more interest and relevance to all pupils. There remain issues regarding the status of short courses. This is particularly true for schools in which no other short courses are being run. The 0.5 nature of the course means it cannot appear in the exam league tables unless it can be joined with another short course to appear as a whole GCSE! However, early evidence indicates that the short courses have already been adopted by many schools. Some schools, which are still working with inadequate time at Key Stage 4, have chosen to begin teaching the short course in Year 9. A number of interesting textbooks and teacher resource books have been written to support both teaching and learning.

The Welsh certificate in Religious Education

It is worth noting here that there is also the certificate in RE offered by the WJEC which targets the less able pupil who is unlikely to achieve a GCSE. This can be taught in conjunction with their GCSE syllabus.

Non-examination RE

The non-examination route is one which whilst being problematic for many has been developed in innovative ways in some schools. Indeed, it was local developments in this area which proved to be the forerunners and to some extent models for the short course syllabuses. Many of these are still in operation and are very successful, in particular the DARE project (Dorset Achievement in RE). One head of department commented that the real hallmark of innovative and effective RE is successful non-examination RE, benefiting from being free of restraints. This freedom is particularly related to methods of assessment. For some pupils examination and coursework can be challenging. The DARE project builds in opportunities for pupils to produce work for assessment in a whole variety of ways, including the use of ICT, drama and art. Pupils are not only able to show their knowledge and understanding of topics covered but are also able to use imaginative ways explicitly to explore the 'learning from' aspect of RE.

Figure 8.3 Case study: non-examination RE at Key Stage 4

Cath Brooke is an RE teacher in a school in south London. She works in a well resourced department and in a school where RE is valued. She has been teaching a non-examination course for all pupils alongside a GCSE option group for several years. The course is successful and the girls really enjoy it. She puts much of the success of the course down to careful planning and resourcing. The modules of work are chosen because they are considered to be particularly relevant and interesting to the pupils. Examples of modules include one which explores the role of women in religion, and one which explores the way religion is portrayed in the media. The problem of lack of motivation is not encountered with many pupils. Cath has her own thoughts on why this should be.

'I think much of the positive pupil response is due to the fact that the pupils do actually enjoy the lessons. I acknowledge that the course is not an examined course as such (though work is still marked thoroughly but in a different way). Let me explain. The pupils have journals rather than books. Much of the work is discussion-based, but every lesson I give them an opportunity to make a written response to a Key Issue or question that we've been exploring. This response is often personal, very much focusing on the 'learning from' elements of RE. In effect, I ask permission to share their work. I respond not with grades but with thoughts and ideas. I always try to be as positive as I can. It's ironic that this kind of writing often reveals clearly how well they have understood the topic we have been covering, without requiring them to write reams of notes. On my part the monitoring and

Figure 8.3 Continued

> marking are quite demanding. It is vital that they have responses from me.
> I also get them to do regular self-assessment activities, and also assessment
> of the lessons too. Their feedback is very useful in helping me to evaluate
> the various units of work and to make changes as I go along. The planning
> and resourcing of lessons also need to be spot-on. Imaginative and exciting
> activities, using artefacts, visits and visitors, conferences, videos, are all really
> important and it's also important to give pupils the opportunity to be cre-
> ative themselves. Personally, these lessons are some of my most enjoyable
> teaching experiences. We have flexibility. We avoid the pressures of exam
> work. I think the pupils really enjoy the "space" these lessons offer.'

Task 8.2 Assessing options at Key Stage 4

Consider the range of options available in Years 10 and 11: full course
GCSE, short course GCSE, non-examination RE and various combina-
tions of the three.

Using the checklist of questions set out in Figure 8.4, make a list of
the strengths and weaknesses of the various options. You may wish to
categorise your lists in two columns headed 'For the teacher' and 'For
the pupil'. Which option would you ideally like to adopt and why?

TOWARDS EFFECTIVE PRACTICE AT KEY STAGE 4

Evaluating current provision

How then do you go about developing the provision of RE at Key Stage 4? At this
stage in your career you are unlikely to have much direct control over this beyond
your own personal teaching. However, once you gain a first teaching post you should
expect to be consulted on the nature of provision, and once you achieve the status
of subject co-ordinator or head of department you will find yourself having to make
some vital decisions. Consequently it is important to develop a critical awareness of
the quality of the Key Stage 4 provision you encounter during your initial training.

Remember before you start that you need to consider carefully what your
school's philosophy of RE teaching is. What does the RE department want to
achieve through its teaching at Key Stage 4? Is it examination results? Is it to create interesting and challenging learning experiences for the pupils? Both can be
achieved if syllabuses are delivered with high-quality teaching, providing stimulating learning opportunities for the pupils. Figure 8.4 offers a checklist to guide your
thinking as you begin the process of reflection on the quality of RE provision you
encounter.

Figure 8.4 Selecting options at Key Stage 4

The questions below offer some criteria to guide you in your choice:

- What does your Agreed Syllabus require you to do?
- Does the nature of your school require you to follow a specific curriculum, i.e. is your school denominational or of a particular foundation?
- Are there particular expectations from the school, SMT or governors to be taken into consideration?
- What has been covered in Key Stage 3 and how can you ensure progression and continuity?
- What curriculum time is available?
- What resources do you have available already?
- What resources are available to support the syllabus in question – particularly in relation to a core textbook if you wish to work with one?
- What capitation will be available?
- What are the staffing implications for introducing a particular syllabus?
- What are the strengths of the RE staff?
- Are there significant characteristics/interests of your Key Stage 4 cohort which need to be taken into account?
- Do you want a syllabus that relates to one, two or three religions?
- What is the most appropriate form of assessment for your cohort? Do you want 100 per cent examination or do you want to include coursework – if so what is the balance between them?
- What types of opportunities are there which follow GCSE RE/RS? How do you ensure progression from one to the other?

Task 8.3 guides you through a diagnostic evaluation of the Key Stage 4 provision in your school. In completing this task you will not only have focused your enquiry as to what the most appropriate syllabus for the school is, but you will also have begun the process of creating an action plan specific to the department in question. Such action plans are an important part of the work of a department. Although they are normally the responsibility of the head of department, it is important from the start to have an insight into and be prepared to make informed contributions to such forward planning. At the heart of such planning and decision making is a shared vision of the most appropriate nature and aims for Key Stage 4 RE. It will be this vision which informs your choices and it is well worth articulating the vision formally as a 'mission statement' for the department. Such a vision needs to be realistic yet bold. It needs to be clearly argued and backed up by evidence from a careful process of evaluation and review. A five-year action plan needs to be broken down into yearly development plans that are used to implement changes. Be aware that GCSE courses and options cannot be introduced overnight. It takes planning and careful thought as well as the support of as many of those involved as possible, from pupils and parents to the senior management team.

Task 8.3 Diagnostic evaluation of current Key Stage 4 provision

This task is best carried out in each of your teaching practice placement schools three to four weeks after you first arrived, once you have had the opportunity to settle in. Its aim is to help you move beyond mere awareness of the nature and extent of Key Stage 4 provision towards a critical evaluation of that provision. You should attempt to complete the following diagnostic table clearly, honestly and reflectively.

Diagnostic chart: analysing Key Stage 4 RE provision	
Positive factors	*Negative factors which I can change*
	Negative factors which I cannot change
Recommendations for future development	

Focusing your options

It may well be that from the process above you have identified the particular type of examination course you believe to be the most appropriate for your department to adopt, i.e. a full course, a Religious Studies–style short course or a Religious Education-style short course. You should also have narrowed down the choice of papers by identifying which religions you are going to focus on and how many, and the nature of assessment too. Having done that, you are likely still to be faced with a choice of syllabuses from various boards. Which to choose? There are no clear-cut criteria here. You should, however, consider such issues as:

- How user-friendly is the syllabus?
- Is it specific in communicating what it is demanding?
- Does it offer specific content to be covered, including references to textual material where appropriate?
- Is it too prescriptive for you?

- Does it offer a good balance between learning about and learning from religion?
- Is it easy to see how you would divide it up to teach it?
- Is there support available from the examining board?
- Are there good resources that have been written with the syllabus in mind?

Planning your programmes of study

This relates to being able to transfer your vision of what RE at Key Stage 4 should be into practice. You have now identified the syllabus you feel is most appropriate to your situation, and the choice has been informed by your vision. The next step in the process is curriculum planning. This means effectively translating the syllabus into carefully planned schemes of work which in turn can be translated into lesson plans. This planning stage is essential and the programmes of study, schemes of work and lesson plans are an essential prerequisite of running a successful course. The process will allow you to grapple with your concerns, identify your priorities, consider appropriate activities in relation to content and allow you to introduce key skills and to develop them effectively throughout the course. The process of lesson planning and preparation has already been dealt with in Chapter 3. Here we will focus on issues particularly relevant to GCSE teaching preparation.

At the heart of the planning process stands your ability to work with your syllabus to ensure that you are taking account of the:

- most effective use of timing;
- best ways of carving up the syllabus into various bite-size units;
- nature of the content and how best to decide when to teach what, i.e. is there a natural progression from one subject to another? Is any of the content and its related concepts more difficult than others?
- identification of aims and learning objectives which are specific to each particular unit of work, and yet clearly linked with the overall aims of the syllabus;
- nature of the teaching and learning opportunities to be used;
- opportunities for assessment, both summative and formative, unit by unit;
- experience of practising examination questions regularly.

At this planning stage it is also important to get hold of examiners' reports for your particular syllabus from previous years to ensure you have a clear idea of what it is the examiners are looking for. They also offer an insight from across the country as to which issues and concepts pupils found most difficult and those which were answered most appropriately. This may affect your choice as to how much time to spend on any particular issue. Another important source to inform your planning is past exam papers, useful for ensuring your planning is accurate and allowing you to build in appropriate examination practice throughout the course.

Task 8.4 Developing a curriculum map for GCSE RE/RS programmes of study

Select a GCSE examination syllabus and from it produce a curriculum map, based on the following pro-forma, identifying:

- what is to be taught – programme content;
- when it is to be taught – programme timetable;
- why it is to be taught – programme aims and learning outcomes.

GCSE RE curriculum map: Year 10					
Autumn term		Spring term		Summer term	
Module 1	Module 2	Module 3	Module 4	Module 5	Module 6
Title: Aims: Content:	Title: Aims: Content:	Title: Aims: Content:	Title: Aims: Content:	Title: Aims: Content:	Title: Aims: Content:

GCSE RE curriculum map: Year 11					
Autumn term		Spring term		Summer term	
Module 7	Module 8	Module 9	Module 10	Revision	Examination
Title: Aims: Content:	Title: Aims: Content:	Title: Aims: Content:	Title: Aims: Content:		

Effective teaching and learning at Key Stage 4

Motivating pupils is a primary task for teachers of RE at Key Stage 4. Given that you have chosen a syllabus, researched issues around it, divided the syllabus into manageable units to coincide with half-term blocks, and built in sufficient revision time at the end of the course, you now have the task of considering pedagogical issues. What are the most appropriate teaching and learning opportunities, having identified specific content and working with the specific assessment objectives? Again we return to your understanding of the aims and nature of RE. It is important to ensure that your teaching tackles the underlying suspicion in relation to RE that often lingers in the minds of pupils, other staff and parents. Your teaching of RE needs to take seriously the pupils, their opinions, ideas and convictions, the context and content of RE and the educational task of RE.

Taking the pupils seriously

You need to ensure that you are honest about the ambiguity of religion. Pupils understand that all that is religious is not necessarily 'good'. Religion may be a potent force in the world and is open to misinterpretation and misuse. In the name of 'religion' atrocities have occurred. Teaching needs to deal honestly with these issues. Pupils need to have opportunities to articulate their own world views, offering a broader context and grounding for their 'opinions'. This will almost certainly mean that opportunities need to be built into your teaching for the exploration of non-religious interpretations. These need to be presented as an intellectually valid and acceptable option. All these points bring us to the realisation that it is vital to begin with the pupils, to find out what they know already, to give them opportunities to articulate their own insights.

Taking the context and content of RE seriously

At Key Stage 4 it is important to ensure that the religions being studied are taught with integrity. Such an approach will need not merely to take into consideration description of ritual and practice but to consider the nature of the truth claims on which the faith is built and which inform and motivate the actions of believers. The teaching approach needs to tackle these issues, facing up to the ambiguities and controversy which will inevitably be raised as pupils grapple with the possibility of truth and engage meaningfully with the issues.

Taking the educational task of RE seriously

With a commitment to taking both the pupils and the religions being studied seriously, you will find yourself engaging with your educational task with purpose and clarity. Your RE teaching will be challenging and will help pupils develop their knowledge and understanding of religions and the implications of faith for believers and for non-believers. As pupils engage with these issues and are given opportunities to articulate and respond to issues, you will be helping them towards becoming religiously literate. This will involve skill development as they learn to express ideas and views in a balanced and considered manner.

Figure 8.5 The pedagogical process at Key Stage 4

It is possible to take the GCSE syllabus content and ensure that it is being taught with the principles discussed being taken into account. The process highlighted below offers one model that can be used to direct your planning and teaching of content at Key Stage 4.

1   Engage with the issue or theme in question, seeking to introduce it in innovative and interesting ways without offering any specific interpretation at this stage.
2   Allow pupils to articulate their personal, and often provisional, responses to the topic.
3   Look at how a range of religions and non-religious systems respond to the topic, selecting them in light of your syllabus and the interests and backgrounds of your pupils.
4   Explore why the range of religious and non-religious systems respond in that way, thereby introducing pupils to different world views, and different understandings of truth, authority and beliefs about God, humanity and the world.
5   Grapple with the implications of these answers, facing up to ambiguity and controversy.
6   Give the pupils an opportunity to revisit their initial reaction to the issue and to reconsider it in the light of the insights they have gained from other world views.

Task 8.5 Applying the Key Stage 4 learning process model

In pairs or small groups select a typical GCSE topic to work with. Ideally it will be one which both/all of you are due to teach during a school placement. Review the Key Stage 4 learning model set out in Figure 8.5.

Now sketch out a series of six teaching/learning blocks, one for each of the stages of the model, identifying appropriate activities for each part of the process.

Reflect critically on the learning package that you have drawn up. What are its strengths and weaknesses? What went well during your planning? What problems did you have to overcome? To what extent did the model help or hinder the process of developing a programme of study?

Assessment

Effective assessment happens when, having in your mind *assessment criteria*, you plan interesting *activities* which will engage the pupils and which relate specifically to learning clearly stated learning objectives. You will need to give them clear opportunities to show their knowledge, understanding and ability to evaluate. The assessment process needs to be carefully thought out and continuous and progressive in nature. Let's use the GCSE (short course) Religious Education assessment criteria as an example and apply them to a specific unit of work: 'Euthanasia in Relation to Christianity'. The three assessment criteria are:

1   Recall, select, organise and deploy knowledge of the syllabus content (RE 1).
2   Describe, analyse and explain the relevance and application of a religion or religions (RE 2).
3   Evaluate different responses to religious and moral issues (RE 3).

The example in Figure 8.6 is based on a unit of work in *Religion in Focus: Christianity in Today's World* (Clinton *et al.* 1998a). It was developed using the process identified in Figure 8.5.

Figure 8.6 Assessment criteria at GCSE: case study, 'Euthanasia'

Learning Objectives	Pupil activity	Assessment criteria
To understand what euthanasia is	Identifing, exploring and recording definitions of euthanasia	RE 1
To consider different legal responses to euthanasia in various countries	Exploring and recording details of the status of euthanasia in Britain and Holland	RE 1
To identify key questions which euthanasia raises for Christians	Brainstorm and initial discussion of key questions, e.g.: Does free-will give someone the 'right to die'? What is the most compassionate response to someone who wants to die? How can Christians best care for the suffering and the terminally ill? How can you judge someone's quality of life?	RE 1–2
To respond personally to a particular case study of someone whose life was ended by euthanasia	Individual reflection, followed by group discussion: Do you find the death morally acceptable? Do others in the class hold different opinions? Pairwork: explain your position to someone who opposes it	RE 1 and 3

Figure 8.6 Continued

To investigate a number of sources which give different perspectives on euthanasia	Evaluation of examples given from different perspectives within Christianity, e.g.: Quaker, Salvation Army, Catholic teaching and a personal response of one individual Christian. Pupils to record whether stories are examples of relative or absolute morality	RE 1, 2 and 3
To weigh up these various responses in the light of Christian principles	Evaluation of Christian principles which can be given for and against euthanasia Pupils are to consider the 'weight' of the different arguments and in doing so to show, in their opinion, how the scales balance. Class debate: 'Should voluntary euthanasia be allowed in Britain?' Essay: 'People have the right to end their own life when they wish.' Discuss	RE 1, 2 and 3
To explore alternatives to euthanasia, through a case study of a hospice, and to consider what is quality of life	Exploration of sources of doctors, patients and families who have benefited from the hospice movement. Pupils to role-play a conversation between someone pro-euthanasia and someone pro-hospice care. Creation of a poster which explores the question 'What is quality of life?'	RE 1, 2–3

Coursework

> The purpose of coursework is to provide an opportunity for candidates to show what they can do when they are not limited by the time constraints of a written examination and are dependent on recall.
>
> (NEAB, 1997, p. 1)

Coursework needs to be planned carefully if you are going to ensure that the candidates have the best opportunity to show what they can do. You need to ensure that it is an integral part of your course, not something tacked on the end. Ensure that pupils have opportunities for planning, investigating and drafting. Follow carefully the guidance given by the exam boards. Be clear about your role as teacher. This is identified in the NEAB guidance as fourfold: to enable, to empower, to supervise and to authenticate (NEAB 1997, p. 4). Give pupils deadlines for different stages of writing. Be consistent and fair by keeping to them. If you are unsure of any issues regarding teaching and assessing a GCSE course, do not hesitate to contact the exam board for assistance.

Figure 8.7 Teaching at GCSE: some concluding practical tips

- Avoid too much note taking.
- Make sure pupils use appropriate quotations.
- Avoid superficiality and teaching so much to the exam that you concentrate on process rather than content.
- Use visitors: it's not easy for pupils to empathise, so give them the opportunity to hear it from the 'horse's mouth'.
- Use artefacts.
- Encourage pupils to ask questions.
- Make sure you are secure enough in your subject knowledge to answer them.
- Build in the regular use of exam questions under exam conditions for each unit of work.
- Make the best use of homework, particularly for work to be assessed, consolidating discussion work and other class activities.
- Encourage pupils to use role-play and speech bubbles in ensuring that they have understood the relevance and application of religion to people's lives.
- Pupils often seem to struggle to understand the difference religious beliefs can make, so this will need to be directly tested.
- Ensure you provide good summary points at the end of units: 'If you forget everything else, remember . . .';
- Build in revision and study skills as you go along.

SUMMARY AND KEY POINTS

This chapter has surveyed recent developments in RE provision at Key Stage 4. It has investigated responses to underprovision, paying special attention to the GCSE short courses. The range of options available to you as a teacher in selecting and developing your RE curriculum has been teased out. In the second half of the chapter we concentrated on methods of establishing and enhancing effective classroom practice. There is, of course, no substitute for classroom experience as you seek to develop your professional skills in this area. Its importance should not be overlooked, since the overall quality of RE provision in a school is often clearly reflected in the status of the subject at Key Stage 4.

FURTHER READING

There are no books written specifically on teaching RE at Key Stage 4. There are, however, a number of new textbooks, some of which are accompanied by useful teacher resource books. The list below identifies some examples.

The *Religion in Focus* series reflects much of the thinking presented in this chapter: it covers all the GCSE short course syllabuses available, is based on the pedagogical process identified in this chapter and is full of practical suggestions for classroom activities; The Teacher's Resource Book has many photocopiable worksheets to accompany and consolidate classroom discussion and there are also examination practice questions on each of the topics covered and model answers. The publication of a volume on Islam and Judaism was imminent at the time of writing.

Alongside these textbooks it is also worth investigating some of the best of the locally accredited courses. Be aware too that your pupils may access the GCSE revision guides and also the subject support offered by the BBC.

Clinton, C., Lynch, S., Orchard, J., Weston, D. and Wright, A. (1998a) *Religion in Focus: Christianity in Today's World*, London: John Murray.

Clinton, C., Lynch, S., Orchard, J., Weston, D. and Wright, A. (1998b) *Religion in Focus: Christianity Today's World. Teacher's Resource Book*, London: John Murray.

Clinton, C., Lynch, S., Orchard, J., Weston, D. and Wright, A. (1999a) *Religion in Focus: Islam in Today's World. Teacher's Resource Book*, London: John Murray.

Clinton, C., Lynch, S., Orchard, J., Weston, D. and Wright, A. (1999b) *Religion in Focus: Islam in Today's World. Teacher's Resource Book*, London: John Murray.

Harrison, M. and Kippax, S. (1996) *Thinking about God*, London: Collins.

Lovelace, A. and White, J. (1996) *Beliefs, Values and Traditions*, London: Heinemann.

Mayled, J. (1977) *People and their Gods*, London: Nelson.

Watton, V. (1996) *Religion and Life*, London: Hodder & Stoughton.

Williams, B. (1997) *One World, Many Issues*, London: Stanley Thornes.

9 Establishing and Enriching Religious Education at 16-plus

Vanessa Ogden

> Making social cohesion a prominent goal of education also has a powerful
> rationale in economic terms. There has been a growing acceptance by
> economists of the centrality of human and social capital in economic
> success . . . law, contract and economic rationality provide a necessary but
> insufficient basis for the stability and prosperity of post-industrial societies;
> these must be leavened with reciprocity, moral obligation, duty towards
> community and trust. It is this 'social capital' which has a large and
> measurable economic value. A nation's well-being, as well as its ability to
> compete, is conditioned by a single pervasive cultural characteristic – the
> level of social capital inherent in the society.
>
> (Kennedy 1997, pp. 5 f.)

Kennedy's compelling vision of an inclusive system of further education which contributes to the social capital, as well as to the economic capital, of a learning society
fit for the twenty first century has to be one of the most powerful arguments for the
importance of Post-16 RE in sixth forms, sixth-form colleges and colleges of further
education (FE). If it is the ultimate goal of our society, in planning its future, to build
a prosperous, creative, critically self-aware and cohesive civilisation, then RE's contribution to enhanced and enlightened working practices and an enriched social and
community life is fundamental.

The skills of recognising and interpreting ambiguity, diversity, subjectivity and
hidden meaning which arrive with the transition from adolescence to adulthood
may never, if left to chance, reach maturation (Hyde 1990, p. 52; Grimmitt 1987,
p. 59). RE at post-16 deals directly with the development of what Vygotsky
terms the higher-order semiotic skills, enabling pupils to transcend objective for-
mal-operational thinking and empowering them as independent learners to
unravel the intricate interwoven strands of public and working life (Wertsch
1985, p. 15).

To create and establish a post-16 RE course which answers these demands, and which is vibrant, rigorous, enriching and exciting, is a challenging and rewarding experience. It will test your mettle as a subject specialist, a manager and a classroom teacher, but the personal and professional gains will be extensive, and your invested time and energy should prove to be very worthwhile. This chapter seeks to support your work. It provides information to facilitate planning, suggestions for teaching and learning strategies and practical examples.

OBJECTIVES

By the time you have completed this chapter, you should:

- have a solid grasp of the field of post-16 education and be able to anticipate its potential changes to your advantage in planning;
- be able to argue convincingly for the importance of RE in post-16 education;
- be able to plan several types of post-16 RE courses and be aware of their limitations;
- be able to teach a vibrant, challenging, exciting and diverse RE programme at post-16 level.

RE IN THE CONTEXT OF POST-COMPULSORY EDUCATION

This section provides information about the field of post-16 education and RE's position within it. It will help you to understand the legal and statutory requirements governing pupils' post-16 entitlement to RE and it will set out some of the developments of the new framework which will influence its provision. This information should help you to plan the development of your post-16 courses, as well as providing you with some arguments to use in support of your bid to establish RE provision at your school or college.

The legal and statutory requirements for RE at post-16

RE is a statutory requirement of the curriculum at post-16 for every pupil in grant-maintained, voluntary aided and maintained county/community schools and City Technology Colleges. Both the 1944 Education Act (HMSO 1944, Section 25(1)) and the 1988 Education Reform Act (HMSO 1988, Section 7) legislate for the inclusion of RE throughout the schooling of young people in England. Of the colleges, only sixth-form colleges are required by law to provide religious education under the regulations of the 1992 Education Act; tertiary colleges and other colleges of further education are exempt from offering a full entitlement.

In many schools and colleges across the country provision of the full complement of post-16 RE is chequered. The reasons are complex and derive principally from the historical development of RE as regards both its pedagogy and its status. Issues of funding, in what is clearly an under-resourced sector of the education system, also contribute to the poverty of provision of religious education at this level (SCAA 1996a; OFSTED 1996). However, a sea change in post-compulsory education is under way, the implications of which are exciting for the RE practitioner.

The new qualifications framework

In 1996 Sir Ron Dearing unveiled his proposals for a new framework of qualifications at post-16 in a document entitled *Review of Qualifications 16–19* (Dearing 1996). Although not radical, it suggested a measured change leading to the rationalisation of qualifications under one overarching certificate, whilst retaining the three distinct pathways of achievement that already existed: Advanced Level General Certificate of Education (A Level GCE), General National Vocational Qualification (GNVQ) and National Vocational Qualification (NVQ). These three routes are termed by Dearing 'subject-based education', 'applied education' and 'vocational education' respectively. In addition, the review directly referred to the need for a spiritual and moral dimension to post-16 education (Dearing 1996, pp. 125 f.). Consequently the awarding bodies of all post-16 qualifications have been required to make the spiritual and moral dimensions of learning implicit in their syllabuses or specifications.

The three pathways towards qualification at post-16, which together with Key Skills and the National Record of Achievement make up a student's entitlement to education at this level, are delineated here, along with the opportunities for accreditation which they provide for RE. (See Figure 9.1.) It should be noted that there is no opportunity for a discrete, i.e. separate and specific, qualification in RE within the applied education and vocational education pathways. The accreditation of discrete RE is confined to the A Level and A/S Level pathway, which excludes a very large number of the young people now engaging in post-16 education. For those embarked on the applied and vocational tracks RE must be taught within broader programmes of study. This is a fundamental problem and it requires all the creative resources of RE practitioners to find ways of offering post-16 pupils a full, accredited entitlement.

However, there are indications that it is planned to develop the framework to incorporate all qualifications from 14 to 19 within one system. Also, the suggestion by Dearing that students should in future be able to mix and match their qualifications from among the three pathways appears to be gaining ground and A Levels are becoming modular to facilitate this (Dearing 1996, p. 17). This model has the power to completely refresh and enrich the provision of RE at post-16: it creates a wealth of opportunities to offer relevant and vibrant RE which, in a modular format, can be tailored to the diverse needs of all pupils at this level. For the moment, though, whilst it is useful to be aware of this potential development, RE practitioners have to work with the means of accreditation available to them as outlined above.

Figure 9.1 RE within Dearing's proposed post-16 framework

Route one: subject-based education
A Level and A/S Level
in two or more of the following subject areas:

● the sciences, technology, engineering, mathematics;
● the arts and humanities (including English and Welsh);*
● modern languages (including Welsh if not the first language);
● the way the community works.*

NCVQ Units to Level 3
in key skills such as:

● communication, application of numbers, information technology.*

An asterisk (*) denotes where RE may be studied.

Route two: applied education
General National Vocational Qualification (GNVQ)

(a)   in a broad vocational area such as:
    ● business;
    ● health and social care;
    ● art and design;
(b)   in key skills such as:
    ● communication, application of number, information technology.

RE can be studied as integral to GNVQs or as discrete parts of key skills.

Route three: vocational training
National Vocational Qualification (NVQ)

(a)   in a specific vocational occupation such as:
    ● banking services;
    ● funeral services;
    ● animal care;
(b)   in key skills such as:
    ● communication, application of number, information technology.

RE can be studied as integral to NVQs or as discrete parts of key skills.

The National Record of Achievement in Education and Training Post-16
Institutions are expected to promote and contribute to the spiritual and moral development of their students in Dearing's proposals. Accredited RE courses run internally by schools/colleges could be certified for the National Record of Achievement.

The accreditation of post-16 RE

Accreditation is of fundamental importance to the success of your programme. Those studying at post-16 are unlikely to value learning which does not add to their chances of gaining employment or a university place. This is understandable; most are governed by the pressures of an increasingly competitive post-industrial and global job market. It is vital, therefore, to consider the public accreditation opportunities available to you at post-16. Though Dearing's proposals may open up some key opportunities, accreditation opportunities at present are more restricted. They currently exist within the following awards:

- *A Level* and *A/S Level* in Religious Studies; or General Studies;
- relevant units of *GNVQ*;
- the *Key Skills* qualification (particularly communication and inter-personal skills, working with others);
- *National Record of Achievement Certification*, which can be provided: (a) internally by the individual school or college; or (b) externally by awarding bodies such as ASDAN, Bristol, that run general programmes of study sometimes related to Key Skills; and (c) work which contributes to certificated recognition of spiritual and moral development opportunities.

Accreditation through GNVQ and Key Skills qualifications is the least explored opportunity in post-16 RE for those for whom A Level is inappropriate, or for those who have chosen not to sit for it, and so the next section devotes some space to a consideration of these as methods of public recognition for study undertaken as part of the general entitlement to RE.

THE GENERAL ENTITLEMENT TO POST-16 RE

This section is devoted to an examination of the options available to you regarding pedagogy, content and structure when planning a course designed to offer a general entitlement to RE at post-16. Although it begins with a discussion of the structural and planning issues concerned with establishing a general programme, these considerations should be included in your strategies for introducing inclusive public accreditation through GNVQ and Key Skills, since they will undoubtedly affect your success in such an initiative. Most of these ideas can be used with or without the accreditation option.

The general entitlement to post-16 RE and pedagogy

It is important to recognise that before offering any post-16 RE programme you must establish your pedagogy. You need to ensure that your course is founded upon educational aims that sustain the rigour and integrity of religious education, and that these are not compromised by the process of tailoring your course if you decide to accredit it.

To help you devise your aims you should refer to your local Agreed Syllabus and the SCAA publication *Religious Education 16–19* (1995b). Bear in mind that: (1) your aims need to be relevant to the whole-curriculum aims for post-16 education; and (2) that you are making a direct progression from your work with pupils at Key Stage 4. It is imperative that students should build on the conceptual understanding they have gained in previous Key Stages; they should also develop their use of the tools of interfaith dialogue in RE, theological and philosophical reflection, and religious language, thus aiming to further their religious literacy (Wright 1993, p. 79). Pedagogical approaches which further this aim encompass both systematic and thematic teaching in addition to an experiential element to learning, which involves faith communities themselves.

Content

The content of the programmes of study should reflect the aims of RE, rather than merely attempt to fit performance criteria and syllabus specifications of vocational qualifications. If you teach in a county maintained school or CTC, to an extent your choice of content is limited by the law. The 1988 Education Reform Act requires you to 'reflect the fact that the religious traditions of Great Britain are in the main Christian, whilst taking into account the teachings and practices of the other principal religions represented in the country' (Section 7). In addition you will need to teach in accordance with your local Agreed Syllabus. Under the 1992 regulations for sixth-form colleges, governing bodies may stipulate which syllabus shall be followed, regardless of area.

As with your aims, content should also build on progression in learning from Key Stage 1 to Key Stage 4, thus reflecting the complexity and diversity of RE appropriate to Key Stage 5. It should not be repetitious of elementary learning: it should be developmental, capitalising on the students' increasing awareness of social, employment and personal responsibility in a plural, diverse and often conflicting context. Students should learn:

- about the importance of religion in directing belief, action and behaviour;
- how to critically analyse information and articulate their own beliefs;
- about world religions in the context of faith communities;
- the significance of such religious commitment for all aspects of life in Britain, personally, socially, occupationally and globally.

Structure

The structure and style of your course will be determined by a number of practical management issues, and this will inevitably affect the kind of accreditation which you can offer too if you do decide to pursue that route. You may find that your course will have to be run through a programme of day conferences. This will have implications for grouping, staffing and budgeting. The following are the key issues that you need to consider.

Resourcing

Inevitably, you will have to operate on a tight budget, which limits the kinds of activities which you can do. Also, you will find that there are very few appropriate resources for RE at this level.

Timetabling

If the subject's allocation achieves the government recommended 5 per cent minimum of timetable time then you should expect a timetable allocation of one hour per week or six one-day conferences per year. This will give you scope for developing assignments which can be accredited through general studies, vocational education routes, Key Skills or the National Record of Achievement. If, however, your allocation is restricted to less than this, opportunities for accrediting RE will be more sporadic.

Staffing

There are strong arguments that only specialist staff should teach RE units, as with other subjects, particularly since many staff will have had no significant RE themselves on which to draw. The confidence of non-specialist staff may need to be boosted by INSET, since the quality of teaching will make or break a post-16 RE programme.

Size of groups

If you are working with a large sixth form you may find that you have large teaching groups, particularly if you are structuring a conference-based RE programme. You should carefully consider your teaching strategies and the kinds of activities which are manageable with the group size you have.

The ability of your pupils

You should also be aware of the ability level of your pupils; groups may well be of mixed ability. If you have prior knowledge of your pupils, use it to gauge the level of work. You will need to pitch your teaching accordingly and to differentiate just as you would do in other key stages.

Teaching and learning strategies in general post–16 RE programmes

Once you have formed the basic structure of your course and planned for accreditation if necessary, the final success of your programme in upholding the integrity, rigour and vibrancy of RE rests with the teaching practices employed in the classroom. This is the key to sustaining the motivation and interest of your pupils. The talents and tastes of a group are important; you should always consider them when

planning teaching and learning activities. You could consider the teaching and learning strategies set out in Figure 9.2.

When developing these strategies into learning activities for an RE programme,
you should take account of the maturity of post-16 pupils and their increasing
awareness of the complexities of adult public and private life. Tasks which are
matched to political or cultural issues and raise existential questions stimulate both
learning about and learning from religion. One developed example of such teaching
and learning activity is set out in Figure 9.3.

Figure 9.2 Teaching and learning strategies at post-16

- Make a video.
- Audio-visual resources.
- Plan and deliver collective worship.
- Business presentation for the National Record of Achievement.
- Courtroom drama.
- Debate.
- Visiting speaker.
- Plan and organise a charity event with informative publicity about the religious principles involved in caring for those in need.
- Display on a religious theme, e.g. the 'misinformation' about Islam in the media.
- Planning and running an awareness week, e.g. disability.
- Planning an ethical advertising campaign linked with local business.
- Producing a magazine on moral issues or local faith communities' news.
- Producing a photo-story.
- Pupils planning and organising their own conference.
- Carrying out a survey on religious belief in the school.
- Using puzzles and games.
- Pupils leading seminars for others.
- Reading and writing with textbooks.

Teaching and learning activities such as this can be easily related to assessment
tasks for a general post-16 RE programme. Although assessment tasks at post-16
should aim to provoke a more sophisticated response than at other Key Stages, nevertheless it is good practice to stimulate learning from religion in a variety of ways, so
it is useful to note that preferred methods of assessment in vocational education and
training mirror those which are already common practice in RE. Evidence in a
GNVQ portfolio might include outcomes from many of the teaching and learning
strategies suggested above: artwork, extended writing, surveys, interviews, video-
recorded role-play or drama, newspaper work, display, a fully documented record of
an event such as a disability awareness day, business presentations, and so on. Such
assessment tasks should be familiar to the RE specialist, who as a matter of course
has to find resourceful methods of eliciting evidence of pupils' understanding of spiritual and moral concepts and the development of 'dispositions'; portfolio tasks could

Figure 9.3 Model teaching and learning activity

Topic. Social exclusion
Text. Jesus at the home of Simon the Pharisee, Luke 7:36–50
Activity. Discussion or role-play
Hand out the roles to be played, written on card with a summary of the likely beliefs of the person you will be representing, in this case the sinful woman or prostitute, Simon the Pharisee, the respectable dinner party guests from the establishment, the disciples representing Jesus's view. (Care should be exercised about representing Jesus as himself, since some faith groups would regard that as blasphemous.) Using the cards, students must undertake to represent the views of the person they are playing in a discussion of the event. Then groups must make a formal presentation of those views and the outcome of a detailed consideration of Christian responsibility in the face of social exclusion.

Learning points

- Beliefs in Judaism about sin and social organisation.
- Jesus's view about how literally rules should be applied when people need love.
- The rise of conflict through belief.
- Depth of feeling in religious belief.
- Empathy, appreciation of difference and social exclusion.
- Christian responsibility.

---

be borrowed and adapted to the pedagogical aims of a general post-16 RE programme.

Options for the accreditation of RE through key skills and GNVQ qualifications

Vocational education has rarely been considered as a route to the accreditation of RE, if at all. Where links have been made, they have on the whole been restricted to health and care qualifications, but in fact there are a number of possibilities available for the accreditation of RE through GNVQ and Key Skills qualifications (see Figure 9.4) which are exciting. These possibilities have been created by casting a spiritual/moral perspective on working practices and asking, why are they necessary?

Writing assignments for GNVQ qualifications

If you choose to pursue this, it should be remembered that writing assignments for accreditation in GNVQ qualifications is technical. You should work closely with a staff team involved in teaching GNVQ before venturing to set your own. You must

Figure 9.4 Accreditation possibilities through Key Skills and GNVQ modules and units

Key Skills

● Communication	● Seminar and business presentation through RE, assessing use of image, communication of information and response to questions, etc.
● Information technology	● Preparing databases in RE, preparing documents for RE using desktop publishing, etc.; use of the internet for communication and information gathering
● Personal skills: working with others	● Exploring belief and practice and their effect upon life and work within a local faith community

GNVQ module: Advanced Health and Social Care

● Equal Opportunities and individuals' rights	● Religious attitudes and moral responsibility
● Interpersonal interaction	● Conflict and resolution in belief and care practice between practitioner and patient, e.g. participating in or advising on abortion, dealing with confidentiality, child abuse, etc.
● Psycho-social aspects of health and social well-being	● The effects of life in modern society upon the individual, her/his belief and practice, and interaction with health and social well-being
● Educating for health and social well-being	● Human responsibility and initiatives in health and social education, e.g. healing the sick, the hospice movement, dealing with controversy, etc.

GNVQ module: Advanced Business and Finance

● Business in the economy	● Faith community and its influence locally, nationally and globally, e.g. co-operatives, Traidcraft, langar, zakah, etc.
● Marketing	● Spiritual and moral issues in advertising and influencing customer choice; what makes for successful long-term marketing?
● Human resources	● See worked example in Table 9.3.
● Employment and production in the economy	● Religious attitudes to employment and the importance of work; prohibited work, service, the spiritual life, e.g. the 'Protestant work ethic', dealing with unemployment, etc.
● Business planning	● Ethical considerations

familiarise yourself with GNVQ teaching and learning styles, course specifications and assessment procedures. Records of continuous diagnostic feedback to pupils on their work need to be well documented. Pupils must be able to show written evidence of how they have planned their work, and how in their assignments they have covered the performance criteria and range of skills specified to attain each element of your unit. You can take an assessor training qualification which will help you to understand how pupils' evidence of work and your records of it should be presented in order to qualify for a GNVQ.

This mastered, the process of teaching and assessing a GNVQ becomes unproblematic for the RE specialist, although it must always be borne in mind that, to qualify, the appropriate demonstration of performance must be provided within the GNVQ subject area itself. For example, candidates will be expected to show practical knowledge of business practice in human resourcing, and not merely a philosophical understanding.

The model which is presented here (see Figure 9.5) shows how RE applies to vocational education and how it can be accredited through performance criteria in already existing qualifications. It does not claim that GNVQs in Business can be taught entirely through RE; it merely demonstrates the links that enlightened employers would deem appropriate in relation to their responsibility for the work force.

Figure 9.5 Suggested GNVQ accredited RE programme at post-16

Following GNVQ Business at Advanced Level, City and Guilds Specifications, 1996/7.

Mandatory Unit 4: Human Resources

Topics covered	Related areas of RE
• Rights and responsibilities of employers/employees	• Valuing the individual: what makes us human? Reverence for life: where does responsibility for others come from? What is the extent of our responsibility for others to help them fulfil their human potential?
• Legal and ethical constraints influencing the behaviour of public/private sector	• Valuing the community: the concept of service; stewardship; the needs of the community versus the individual; the common good; leadership and power
• Ways to uphold the rights of employees/employers including the role of trade unions and staff associations in negotiating conditions of service and resolving conflicts	• The relationship between belief and way of life
• The changing nature of roles and the challenges of introducing and implementing changes at work	• Conflict and resolution
• Interviewing and appraisal	• Inter-faith dialogue

regarded as a rigorous test of academic ability. As well as the capacity to write incisively, it examines how well a pupil can manipulate knowledge and understanding to support a well informed theological and philosophical exploration of specified areas of in-depth study. The assessment objectives include the notion that candidates should deal with critical scholarship, and demonstrate understanding of the reasons for diversity in the response, judgement and practice of both corporate and personal religious activity. The use of technical religious language in candidates' writing and extensive quotation is expected as a matter of course.

Choosing your syllabus and papers

Your selection of examining board and syllabus is important: your choice will influence the success of your candidates in the final examination. When choosing a syllabus you should think about content and the style of examination and how well these will suit your candidates. In the first instance, you will need to consider whether to enter your candidates for a modular or a linear syllabus. Modular courses have several advantages: candidates may be motivated by cumulative successes in modules; candidates may resit modules, if they wish, for a limited period of time; and candidates may gain partial accreditation, completing later within a limited time period. However, the modular course does require the candidates to be of A Level standard when they sit for a module, regardless of the stage they have reached in the course. This is a consideration which should not be underestimated; it is common for the Religious Studies A Level course to be a maturation process which culminates in a final test of the candidate's mettle. Many pupils may be disadvantaged in this respect by a modular course.

Once you have chosen your syllabus you should select your units of study carefully and base your choice on several criteria: candidates' prior knowledge of the topic, the number and quality of appropriate resources and textbooks available for study, and your own expertise. Examination papers can vary in layout and the kinds of questions which are set; they can be general or specific; it is wise to obtain a variety of samples and discuss them with post-16 pupils before making a selection. Some may have an optional coursework element which will help candidates who find a straight examination difficult. Reflect upon the assessment criteria for marking and how your candidates, given their abilities, will best address these in their responses to the style of question set. Some awarding bodies set more general criteria, intending to give candidates the freedom to argue creatively from a wide variety of angles, whereas others have a more specific technical agenda. The latter is often easier to work with if your pupils' strengths lie in literacy; more general criteria can lead a talented candidate to drift into irrelevance.

Exam boards also vary in the support which they offer to teachers who are entering candidates for examination with them. Some are very approachable and provide INSET support, supplementary notes, examiners' reports, resource lists, guidance on marking and a subject officer whom you can contact. You should be quite demanding of them, since they are paid by your school or college for each candidate you enter. Also, consult them about other schools in your area which teach the same syllabus and papers. Most schools welcome visits from other practising teachers who need advice and the chance to see the practical implementation of the syllabus.

Teaching and learning strategies at A level

There is sometimes an assumption that with A Level Religious Studies we leave behind any learning that does not centre on note-taking and textual reading. Whilst those teaching and learning strategies are fundamental to A Level, if they are used exclusively, study becomes monotonous and religions lose their richness and vibrancy.

Candidates do need to assimilate comprehensive factual information, and cultivate the art of fluent and refined critical writing. A pupil's staple diet of learning should include the following features: plenty of reading around the subject; independent research; systematic review and testing; committing to memory quotations and extracts from their own essays which focus on key themes; and, most important of all, constant essay practice. Issue pupils with bibliographies, addresses of libraries and Internet website addresses, to promote their autonomy in research and writing.

Pupils will require thorough coaching in essay technique. They need to feel confident that they can set out complex arguments in a structured and logical fashion under pressure, and one way to ensure this is to drill them to: (1) repeat quotations and extracts from their work on key themes; and (2) write timed essays to set structures. Those pupils whose talents lie in critical writing should be encouraged to embellish the set structures and provide commentary on extracts they have learned as they write; those pupils who find freedom in critical writing difficult will at least feel clear about what they should be writing in an exam. Whilst it does not certify good RE, well rehearsed essay technique under pressure will be the key to success in the final examination.

Use a model or writing frame for the structure of an essay that is appropriate to the experience and calibre of your pupils. For example, with a group whose literacy skills are less sophisticated you could use a 'hamburger model'. In this model the 'bun' relates to the introduction and conclusion, which are similar but not identical, and which when read together should form a summary and evaluation of the main arguments deployed in the essay. The layers of meat represent the main arguments, while the salad, cheese and onions represent the factual information and quotations used to support the arguments. Finally, pupils can be shown how to add the 'relish', in other words, you teach them how to polish their writing. This is a simple model for pupils who have never encountered academic writing before; there are others which you can construct to suit your own candidates.

Many pupils will not have written academic essays at this point and so they will find it very difficult to begin with. They will need tutorial guidance and support to help them begin to develop critical reflection on their own learning and writing, and to generate the skills of analytical enquiry which are fundamental to religious studies at A Level. Pupils will need to be able to challenge their own thought processes as well as the thinking of others, and you will need to provide them with the cognitive strategies to do so. This can be achieved in several ways, two of which are suggested below.

1   *A symposium.* Pupils are given a religious philosophical or theological question, for example 'Is God real or imagined?' Very much in the manner of Plato's *Symposium*, pupils are expected to take on a role each and give an exposition of the arguments of Feuerbach, Freud, Jung and others. Pupils should then, with your help, critically analyse the arguments together in discussion. Initially you may need to support them with resource material, although ultimately pupils should be encouraged to conduct their own research and symposia independently. If there are funds available, you could suggest that they take their symposia to the Internet and hold network discussions.

2   *A seminar.* Pupils are given a flexible learning package which invites them to prepare a seminar on a particular question, e.g. to critically discuss arguments against the existence of God from psychology. The question is broken down into three parts designed to enable pupils to show their depth of knowledge and understanding, critical judgement and aptitude for logical argument. A list of resources to consult should be included, together with a mark scheme showing how marks will be awarded, and you could incorporate an element of fieldwork among the faith communities. Pupils are expected to give their seminar using overhead projectors, slides and handouts, as well as submitting a written copy.

There are a variety of creative teaching and learning strategies that you can interweave with textual work and writing to stimulate motivation and inspire pupils' thinking. Although they are more practical they will not diminish the intellectual challenge, provided they are carefully thought through. They will improve motivation and they will give pupils models – visual images – on which to 'hang' much of their conceptual learning. Use audio-visual resources such as video and music; explore artefacts; engage visitors from the faith communities or organisations; arrange trips; invent games; organise quizzes and use prizes as an additional motivation; and use independent learning through research and fieldwork. Encourage pupils to attend conferences and to subscribe to magazines such as *Dialogue*, a philosophical journal for sixth-formers. The effective use of creative strategies will provoke the classroom interaction and debate necessary to help refine skills of logical argument, as well as making lessons lively. Combining this with continuous constructive feedback and positive reinforcement will enhance pupils' confidence, and consequently their performance in the final exam.

Candidates with special educational needs

It is likely that your pupils will be of mixed ability, although not to quite the same extent that you would expect to experience in teaching groups at Key Stage 4. However, the differences between candidates become polarised at A Level because of refinement of the criteria for achievement and the skills required for the attainment of each level. Be aware that you will still need to differentiate work; some of the language can be extremely difficult to comprehend for many pupils, particularly at first while they are making the transition between GCSE and A Level.

Try to think of ways in which this problem can be overcome: the use of glossary sheets and dictionaries; modelling concepts with drawings, charts or posters; simple learning and testing of words; peer tutoring. There are many more. For those who are of marked ability, you will need to ensure that they are continually challenged to extend their powers of written argument and analysis, and to apply their knowledge and understanding to support their evaluations.

Schemes of work and teaching materials

Planning an effective A Level course should involve you in writing a comprehensive scheme of work which takes account of timing and the spread of content. Once you have allocated time to each topic area, allowing space for teacher-led revision, you should think carefully about assessment tasks and how they relate to the assessment criteria of the syllabus and the content. Ensure that you plan tasks which effectively develop pupils' examination technique and all the skills which they will need to deploy. Include these in your scheme, together with your assessment criteria, and then plan teaching and learning activities to correspond with them. In this way, the

---

Task 9.2 Differentiation at A Level

Select three students from your A Level group who are representative of the top, middle and bottom bands of the ability range. Write a sketch of each pupil's strengths and weaknesses as learners in your subject area.

Carry out a baseline assessment test, at the beginning of your next unit, which examines their ability to write a critical, structured and incisive answer to an essay question.

On the basis of this test, identify methods of differentiating learning activities to improve their performance and write resources to address these, e.g.:

- how to structure an essay;
- how to learn quotations;
- how to learn set extracts;
- how to develop critical analysis;
- how to plan an essay.

Reassess your pupils' performance at the end of the unit. Establish how far your pupils' performance has improved and review the effectiveness of your strategies.

criteria for assessment will be made explicit to pupils throughout their course of study. Plan a revision course and, at the same time, create revision booklets, and specimen question-and-answer manuals which pupils can borrow.

Although as a general rule A Level teaching is perhaps more formal in style, nevertheless by virtue of the nature of Religious Studies as a subject area, your A Level course has the potential to be a vibrant, exciting and enriching experience for your pupils. The non-textual resources available to you within the faith communities, museums and art galleries are manifold, and they provide pupils with a real opportunity to engage directly with the subtleties and intricacies of belief in a diverse and conflicting society, and a role in bridge building and interfaith dialogue.

SUMMARY AND KEY POINTS

As a practitioner given the responsibility for establishing and enriching the provision of post-16 RE, it is your task to develop stimulating and relevant courses which are rigorous and which protect the integrity of the subject. Within this brief, there are exciting possibilities which have the potential to regenerate RE's contribution to post-16 education. Already, in Dearing's new framework, there exist opportunities to create new perspectives on the links between RE and the world of employment and public life.

RE at post-16, like many other subjects, has traditionally been offered at A Level and provided as a general entitlement in much the same style. As the new framework develops, a new vision of the future of post-16 education is emerging, characterised by fluidity, flexibility and diversity. The potential for more dynamic and more inclusive RE within such a framework is considerable and exciting. RE can offer diverse modules of a subject-based or vocational character, permitting students to study the subject in a variety of contexts at a number of levels according to individual needs and requirements.

Some modules could reflect traditional A Level content. Some could aim to develop critical thinking skills through philosophy or epistemology in relation to theistic and non-theistic belief. Others could concentrate on religious issues that affect the workplace or national and global public life, such as human resourcing or international team working. Others could explore the religious dimensions of community life and citizenship, and so on. This new perspective on post-16 RE reveals a wealth of learning opportunities which will enable it to fulfil its key role as a significant contributor to social and economic capital, and as an investment in the enrichment of individual, community, social and working life. RE post-16 is concerned with belief, and with the cultural, creative, transformative, critically reflective and cohesive dimensions of social well-being and work that enable civilisations to prosper. As practitioners, the responsibility to uphold this is ours.

FURTHER READING

Grimmitt, M. (1987) *Religious Education and Human Development*, Great Wakering, Essex: McCrimmon. This book examines the contribution of RE to human development and how learning in RE itself develops within the individual.

Hyde, K. (1990) *Religion in Childhood and Adolescence: a Comprehensive Review of Research*, Birmingham, Alabama: Religious Education Press. This text charts a history of theory on human psychological development and RE.

Kennedy, H. (1997) *Learning Works: Widening Participation in Further Education*, London: Further Education Funding Council. This document analyses the provision for general education at post–16 and makes recommendations to the government for improving the uptake, as well as arguing for the central role of further education in a learning society.

Ogden, V. (1997) *The Role of Religious Education at 16–19 in the Ascendancy of Work-related Learning and a New Framework for Post-compulsory Education*, Abingdon: Culham College Institute. This is a report prepared on behalf of the Sir Halley Stewart Trust into the nationwide provision of post-16 religious education, together with a critical analysis of the relevance and potential of RE as a general entitlement. The report discusses the aims of post-16 RE and its future character.

SCAA (1995b) *Religious Education 16–19*, London: Schools Curriculum and Assessment Authority. An influential discussion paper which makes suggestions for appropriate provision for RE at post-16. Copies may be obtained from the QCA.

Wright, A. (1993) *Religious Education in the Secondary School: Prospects for Religious Literacy*, London: David Fulton. This text gives an account of RE which forms a basis for the progression at post-16 towards the interfaith dialogue and theological/philosophical thinking outlined in this chapter.

10 Spirituality in the Classroom

Clive and Jane Erricker

This chapter aims to introduce you to the concept of spirituality as it is variously understood and currently debated in society and education. It will present the legal requirements for addressing children's and young people's spiritual development in state education and the requirements and guidelines produced in the Office for Standards in Education (OFSTED) and the documentation of the School Curriculum and Assessment Authority (SCAA), which has now become the Qualifications and Curriculum Authority (QCA). It will survey different understandings of the nature of spirituality and the relationship between spirituality and religious belief with reference to the development of spiritual education in state schooling. This will lead us to consider ways in which you may address spiritual development in practice within your school, the curriculum and RE.

OBJECTIVES

By the end of this chapter you should:

- be familiar with the legal requirements, directives and guidelines for the development of spirituality in education;
- be able to debate the value of different approaches to the nature of spirituality and its role in education;
- begin to identify ways in which spiritual education can be implemented in the curriculum.

SPIRITUALITY, EDUCATION AND THE REQUIREMENTS OF THE 1988 EDUCATION REFORM ACT

Circulars 3/89 and 1/94

The 1988 Education Reform Act identified spiritual development as one of the main aims of state schooling, which should underpin the curriculum. The national system of education was to be one that both

- Promotes the spiritual, moral, cultural, mental and physical development of pupils at the school and of the society, and
- Prepares such pupils for the opportunities, responsibilities and experiences of adult life.

(HMSO 1988, p. 1)

These aims were restated in the two official government circulars that followed the Act: Circular 3/89 and the subsequent Circular 1/94 (DES 1989, p. 4; DFE 1994a, p. 9). Together these documents (1) reinforced the concern of the 1988 Act to ensure that spiritual development reasserted its presence in education, and (2) confirmed 'the government's commitment to strengthening the position of Religious Education and collective worship in schools' (DES 1989, p. 4).

Circular 1/94 further stated that 'The Government is concerned that insufficient attention has been paid explicitly to the spiritual, moral and cultural aspects of pupil's development and would encourage schools to address how the curriculum and other activities might best contribute to this crucial dimension of education' (DFE 1994a, p. 9). This emphasis on the importance of addressing spirituality caused some concern in the teaching profession. In order to clarify some of the problems concerning the nature of the provision required, further directives and guidelines were produced by OFSTED and SCAA.

OFSTED guidance on inspection

In its *Framework for the Inspection of Schools* OFSTED provides the following definition of spiritual development:

> Spiritual development relates to that aspect of inner life through which pupils acquire insights into their personal existence which are of enduring worth. It is characterised by reflection, the attribution of meaning to experience, valuing a non-material dimension to life and intimations of enduring reality. 'Spiritual' is not synonymous with 'religious'; all areas of the curriculum may contribute to spiritual development.

(OFSTED 1994, p. 8)

You should recognise that it is the school's provision for spiritual development that is the subject of inspection rather than the pupil's spirituality. With this in mind the

Framework document identifies the contexts in which such development could occur:

- through the values and attitudes the school upholds and fosters;
- through the contribution made by the whole curriculum, RE, acts of collective worship and other assemblies;
- through extracurricular activity, together with the general ethos and climate of the school.

One of the obvious difficulties that this movement towards inspection created was that of identifying the criteria and context in which development could be assessed. Whilst the OFSTED framework amplifies previous guidance it has been criticised for not supplying any specific assessment criteria or identifying how spirituality should be addressed in particular curriculum contexts. It has also been attacked for stressing throughout the importance of the development of the individual and the uniqueness of what is meant by spirituality to each individual rather than relating spiritual development to community, religious belief or theological principles.

SCAA on spiritual and moral development

The School Curriculum and Assessment Authority was set up under the Conservative government in 1994. It took the place of the National Curriculum Council (NCC) and as one of its initiatives republished the NCC's *Spiritual and Moral Development: A Discussion Paper* (SCAA 1995a). This formed the basis of a major conference on 'Education for Adult Life: Spiritual and Moral Aspects of the Curriculum' which took place in London on 15 January 1996. Following this a National Values Forum (NVF) was established, which resulted in the publications *Education for Adult Life: The Spiritual and Moral Development of Young People* (SCAA 1996a) and *Findings of the Consultation on Values in Education and the Community* (SCAA 1996b).

The initiatives of SCAA have been important because they have raised the profile of spirituality, linked with morality and values, in education. The approach has been one of consensus, drawing together informed opinion across different areas of society: education, youth work, industry and employment, faith communities, parents and government. Its agenda, as outlined by SCAA's chief executive, Dr Nicholas Tate, at the London conference, is as follows:

> The issues we are here to discuss are not just ones for schools. Moral and spiritual education in schools is only possible if the society which maintains these schools is clear about its ends . . . As the statutory custodian of the school curriculum, the School Curriculum Assessment Authority is perhaps uniquely placed to initiate a national debate on these issues. But we hope to do more than just that. Our objective today is to come up with an agenda for action.
>
> (Tate 1996, pp.1 f.)

> **Task 10.1 SCAA and the debate on spiritual education in schools**
>
> The two SCAA documents referred to, *Spiritual and Moral Development* and *Education for Adult Life*, have set the context of debate on spiritual education in schools. Review each document and identify:
>
> - what changes you observe between the two documents;
> - whether the changes would be helpful to you as a teacher in implementing spiritual education alongside moral education;
> - what specific principles, in approaching spiritual and moral education in the classroom, you think you need to employ to conform to the SCAA model;
> - whether the SCAA approach is deficient in any respects, in relation to addressing children's spirituality or as guidance for classroom teaching.

Tate's concern is to stop what he identifies as the moral decline of modern British society, a decline he attributes in part to the spread of moral relativism and an 'anything goes' mentality. He weds moral values to the importance of religious faith.

THE NATURE OF SPIRITUALITY: SPIRITUALITY, RELIGIOUS BELIEF AND EDUCATION

This section considers the positions of six writers concerned to establish the approach that should be taken towards spiritual education: Jack Priestley, David Hay, Adrian Thatcher, Dennis Starkings, Clive Erricker and Andrew Wright.

Jack Priestley: spirituality as a dynamic process

Jack Priestley notes in his Hockerill Address of 1996 that the key moment in the use of 'spiritual' in modern education was its appearance in the 1944 Education Act, preceding 'moral, mental and physical' in the first sentence of the Act's preamble; he goes on to argue that it owes its presence to 'a simple piece of archiepiscopal jiggery-pokery' (Priestley 1996, p. 2; cf. HMSO 1944). Priestley explains this by relating how the author of that part of the preamble, Canon J. Hall, the Chief Officer of the National Society (NS), was chosen for the post by Archbishop William Temple to gain 'the confidence of local authorities, directors of education and the teachers in their organisations' in seeking a partnership between church and state schools (Priestley 1996, p. 8). When Hall was asked why he had used the word 'spiritual' rather than 'religious' he replied, 'Because it was much broader . . . If we had used the word religious they would all have started arguing about it' (p. 8).

Priestley also relates how the word was almost lost when in 1977 the DES published a list of key areas it believed to be fundamental to sound education (DES/HMI 1977a, b). One view offered in a supplement to *Curriculum 11–16* was that the word 'spiritual' 'is a meaningless adjective for the atheist and of dubious use to the agnostic' (Priestley 1996, p. 2). Priestley observes that such views often flew in the face of, or were simply ignorant of, relevant educational research. This, as we shall see, is not an uncommon phenomenon.

The most significant points to note about Priestley's observations are: (1) how the notions of spiritual and religious are overlapping but distinct; (2) how contentious the word spiritual is in modern society; and (3) how the notion of the spiritual has a particularly ambivalent place in relation to the curriculum. Priestley's own position focuses on the way we talk about education. Drawing on the philosophers Ludwig Wittgenstein and Alfred North Whitehead, he argues that the language we use to speak of education imprisons us in an impoverished conception of it. We have reduced education to a thing we call 'curriculum' rather than understanding it as a process which is creative and dynamic. It is for this reason that we have such trouble placing spirituality in education, since:

> to dwell on the spiritual is to emphasise the subjective, to dwell on the process of being and becoming. Discussion of the curriculum, however, centres around knowledge. Knowledge is seen as objective, something which exists outside of ourselves but which we can take in through learning and contain through memory. That is one of the key dangers of reducing education to curriculum and one of which we have suddenly become aware again. The documentation of the past decade has been depressing because of its limited vocabulary. It is dominated by notions of teaching and learning. There has been precious little attention paid to thinking, creating, imagining, becoming.
>
> (Priestley 1997, pp. 29 f.)

The emphasis in Priestley's understanding of the spiritual is not related to a particular faith stance or the distinction between the religious and non-religious. Priestley even refutes the need for definition in an attempt to open up our understanding of the possibilities of education once it is understood in its fullest (spiritual) sense of being a life-giving process.

David Hay: challenging the secular suspicion of spirituality

David Hay has been an important voice in addressing the spiritual in education prior to and since the 1988 Education Reform Act. You will encounter his most recent research into children's spirituality in the next section, but his concern with our suspicion of the spiritual in an age in which secularity dominates is a key theme in his earlier writing.

In 'Suspicion of the Spiritual: Teaching Religion in a World of Secular Experience' (1985) he argues that there is a detachment from the spiritual in the teaching of RE.

both society and state schooling lack commitment to Christian belief and an education grounded in Christian nurture. The fear of secularity and relativism, he argues, is unfounded. Relativism is not, *contra* Tate, to be equated with the idea that 'anything goes', but is a recognised philosophical standpoint that affirms divergence of view and on this basis calls for a consensus of values whilst accepting the distinctness of different epistemological and faith stances. This is not to be equated with the SCAA consensus, which ignores the divergence and thus is overtly concerned with morality rather than spirituality. Erricker's argument is that spiritual development is concerned with helping student's to reflect upon their own experiences and those of others in order to investigate the process of spiritual development itself. This position therefore opposes the idea of attempting to arrive at a shared definition or common theological basis upon which provision for spiritual development can proceed. Erricker reasons that to do the latter would result in precisely the opposite of what we are attempting to achieve educationally as well as bringing about the disaffection of students.

Andrew Wright: embodied spirituality

Wright situates himself between the positions of Thatcher and Erricker. In 'Embodied Spirituality: The Place of Culture and Tradition in Contemporary Educational Discourse on Spirituality' (1997a) he draws on Alasdair MacIntyre and Paul Ricouer in stating:

> The story of my life is always embedded in the story of those communities from which I derive my identity. I am born with a past; and to try to cut myself off from that past, in the individualistic mode, is to deform my present relationships. The possession of an historical identity and the possession of a social identity coincide.
>
> (MacIntyre 1985, p. 221, quoted in Wright 1997a, p. 16)

Wright goes on to point out that it is necessary to understand spirituality in terms of communal identity, which must begin with 'recognising and nurturing children into the specific spiritual tradition they bring with them to the classroom' (p. 16). In contrast he suggests that a 'spiritual education that seeks to dislocate itself from any specific tradition' will end up 'indoctrinating children into the spiritual tradition of romanticism' (p. 17), which he identifies with the teachings of Rousseau and those of progressive child-centred educators.

Task 10.2 Approaches to spiritual education

Consider all the approaches outlined in the main text and construct a classroom activity for each one that will convey the spirit of the approach in terms of its educational aims. Examine the results of this set of activities in the classroom.

> *Jack Priestley*. You might use a poem that would connect with the children's experience and imagination
> *David Hay*. You might introduce a contemplative or meditative activity
> *Adrian Thatcher*. You might identify how a parable can advance children's understanding of spiritual insight
> *Dennis Starkings*. You might identify how the performing arts and artistic expression might result in spiritual reflection
> *Clive Erricker*. You might interview children on the question of what really matters to them in their life
> *Andrew Wright*. You might wish to ask children to explain with which religious tradition they identify and how that contributes to their lifestyle or world view.

UNDERSTANDING CHILDREN'S SPIRITUALITY

This section presents different approaches to researching spirituality in children's development and therefore different approaches to its inclusion in the curriculum. It considers the work of Robert Coles, David Hay and Rebecca Nye and of the Children and Worldviews Project. All three approaches are empirically grounded in fieldwork that provides the basis of their understanding of children's spirituality. You should consider how their research can relate to your practice in the classroom as a teacher who is also engaged with discovering and reporting on the spirituality of your pupils.

Robert Coles

In Robert Coles's book *The Spiritual Life of Children* (1990) he explains how he began carrying out research into children's lives after witnessing the effect of race riots on children in New Orleans in 1960. At that point he turned from his training as a psychoanalyst to become a field worker, talking to children going about their everyday lives 'amid substantial social and emotional stress' (p. xi). His work specifically concerned with children's spirituality took the form of a research project begun in 1985 spanning the Americas, Europe, the Middle East and Africa, and covering conversations with children of various faith backgrounds and others belonging to no faith community. His approach was based on the view that the construction of religious ideas was a valuable aspect of people's identity and that children themselves already evidenced this original and creative activity rather than simply being the receptors of adult ideas. Coles was influenced by the writings of Dr Ana-Maria Rizzuto and her view that 'it is in the nature of human beings, from early childhood until the last breath, to sift and sort and to play, first with toys and games and teddy bears and animals, then with ideas and words and images and sounds and notions' (p. 6). He understood this activity as deriving from 'our predicament as human beings, young or old – and the way our minds deal with that predicament, from the earliest years to the final breath' (p. 7).

Coles's approach can be characterised by the three distinct features.

1   *Qualitative.* Conducted through semi-structured interviews with individuals and groups.
2   *Anti-reductionist.* Not imposing a pre-established theoretical framework on the interpretation of findings.
3   *Non-judgemental.* Not subjecting respondent's views to a rational or systematic scrutiny.

Coles reports his conversations with children in detail in his book. A brief example is given in Figure 10.1. He does not seek to place the children's comments and observations within any pre-determined theoretical framework, or to draw from them any general conclusions about the nature of children's spirituality.

Figure 10.1 An example of Coles's research into the spirituality of childhood

The following extract is from an interview Coles carried out with a Hopi Indian girl (1990, p. 25). The girl is reporting a conversation she has had with her teacher.

Child. The sky watches us and listens to us. It talks to us and listens to us. It talks to us and hopes we are ready to talk back. The sky is where the God of the Anglos [white Americans] live, a teacher told us. She asked where our God lives. I said, 'I don't know.' I was telling the truth! Our God is the sky, and lives wherever the sky is. Our God is the sun and the moon, too; and our God is our [the Hopi] people, if we remember to stay here [on the consecrated land]. This is where we're supposed to be, and if we leave, we lose God.

Coles asks if she explained this to the teacher.

Child. No.

Coles. Why?

Child. Because she thinks that God is a person. If I'd told her, she'd give us that smile.

Coles. What smile?

Child. The smile that says to us, 'You kids are cute, but you're dumb. You're different – and you're all wrong!'

I have no doubt that psychiatric interpretations of much that children say about religious and spiritual matters can, in a sensitive doctor's hands, be of great interest; and I have no doubt that a cognitively based analysis of the manner in which the moral and religious and spiritual thinking of children changes over time can also be of great interest. Do I risk pomposity when I describe this work as phenomenological and existential rather than geared towards psychopathology, or towards the abstractions that go with 'stage theory', with 'levels' of 'developement'?

(1990, pp. 39 f.)

David Hay and Rebecca Nye

Below is an extract from Hay and Nye's work, carried out at the University of Nottingham, illustrating its purpose and method:

> We have been working with children aged six and ten years in Nottingham and Birmingham and have had to consider how spirituality might be given expression at the fringes of its traditional vehicle in European culture, the language of Christian theology. . . Where the language and institutions of formal religion are absent or unconvincing for many people, we had to try to identify the areas of children's language and behaviour where the 'sparks of spirituality' may be found.
>
> For this purpose we needed to create a hypothetical map as a kind of template to guide our conversations with children. We examined the converging evidence of writers on spirituality and on child psychology, as well as our own experience of talking with children in the pilot stage of the project. As a result we proposed a set of three interrelated themes or categories of spiritual sensitivity which were basic enough to allow expression within or outside the familiar (usually religious) languages of spirituality. The intention is to make possible the identification of spirituality in a wider and more abstract context than has been achieved elsewhere. We will thus be able to move beyond an understanding of children's spirituality based on 'knowledge' towards a more general psychological domain of spirituality as a basic form of knowing, available to us all as part of our biological inheritance.
>
> (1996, pp. 9 f.)

Hay and Nye constructed a table of categories of spiritual sensitivity, referred to as 'a geography of the spirit', which is set out in Figure 10.2. Hay and Nye's approach can be characterised as follows:

- It seeks to uncover children's spirituality in a social context identified as secular.
- It affirms a belief in the innate spirituality of children.
- It seeks to relate children's spiritual experience to that traditionally expressed in religion.

The Children and Worldviews Project

This approach stems from the belief that the way in which children learn cannot be separated from who they are and the experiences that have shaped their identity. Children's experiences, and their interpretations of those experiences, form the vehicle by which all subsequent experiences (including formal learning experiences) are moulded and readjusted in order that the child can make sense of them. This selective patterning of experiences and reflections forms the child's world view, the

Figure 10.2 Hay and Nye's categories of spiritual sensitivity

- *Awareness sensing.* Being aware of oneself in the present moment. This can be understood in religious terms in the practice of meditation and contemplative prayer.
- *Mystery sensing.* Awareness of our experiences of realities that are in principle incomprehensible. They include experiences of fascination, awe and wonder.
- *Value sensing.* This concerns feelings of what really matters to us. Here strong feelings are a measure of matters of importance.
- *Relationship.* This refers to an awareness of our relationship with ourselves, with others and the world around us in a holistic sense.
- *Meaning.* This concerns questions of existential importance. Typically these may be 'Who am I?' 'where do I belong?' 'what is my purpose?'
  (Hay and Nye 1998, p. 57)

window through which he or she looks out on the world and which protects his or her sense of identity. This understanding of spiritual and moral development can be placed within a 'process approach' to education.

The personal construct theory of learning suggested by Kelly (1986) holds that an individual invariably approaches any situation in life with a personal theory of explanation. If these ideas, either explicitly taught or implicitly assimilated by the child, are ones which deal with existential issues, then we may be said to be considering children's spirituality. After looking at the information provided by conversations with children the project developed the idea that the way to access children's understanding is to look at the metaphors that they use when talking about important issues. Affirming Cooper's suggestion that 'Metaphor's essential role is a cognitive one, sustained by our need to explain and understand through comparison' (1986, p.18), the project sought to engage with matters of importance to children and facilitate their accounts and explanations of their experiences. From these they identified children's use of metaphor as the key to unpacking their spiritual understanding.

The Children and Worldviews Project's approach can be characterised by the following features:

- It adopts an open-ended and process approach to enquiry into the development of children's spirituality.
- It identifies metaphorical language as a key to the expression of children's spirituality.
- It does not equate spirituality with overtly religious concepts and thinking.

These three approaches each have distinctive perspectives but also provide overlapping concerns and methods. They make it clear that spiritual education has to be pursued in a way that is often very different from the usual delivery of a curriculum subject, and offer models on which classroom practice can be based.

> **Task 10.3 Teaching spirituality: principles to employ in the classroom**
>
> Using this chapter as an initial guide and means of orientation, consult:
>
> - Robert Coles's *The Spiritual Life of Children*;
> - David Hay's and Rebecca Nye's *The Spirit of the Child*;
> - The Children and Worldviews Project's *The Education of the Whole Child*.
>
> Discuss and write down what you think are the essential principles to employ in the classroom on the basis of these three approaches. Now construct a classroom activity that reflects one of the approaches in practice and report your findings.

APPROACHES TO SPIRITUAL EDUCATION IN RE

This section and the one that follows are essentially practical in nature. The issue being addressed is how we can translate the approaches and theoretical stances presented above into the classroom context.

Broadly speaking, commentators divide into those who believe that spiritual education must be addressed by first giving pupils a religious framework within which to investigate spirituality and those who believe that spirituality is present in the experiences and reflections of children as a matter of course, or even innate.

The SCAA Model Syllabuses for RE proceed according to the first perspective by constructing two attainment targets: learning about and learning from religion (SCAA 1994a, b). Within this model 'learning about religion' (the understanding of accurate information concerning religious teachings and practice), should proceed to 'learning from religion' (reflection on the spiritual, or faith awareness). The following classroom suggestion, based on this religion-centred model, uses an example drawn from the Buddhist tradition.

The Buddhist journey and children's journeys

The theme of journeys is often used in religious education. In the Buddhist tradition and in the Buddha's teachings it acts as a metaphor for life. We journey in Samsara (our worldly existence) as we pass from one life to the next. The Buddha's teaching is presented as the Noble Eightfold Path, which provides direction and leads us out of Samsara towards Nirvana (Enlightenment). This is illustrated in the 'wheel of becoming' (Figure 10.3), which depicts Buddhist teachings in a visual way.

In the picture the wheel is divided by six spokes which connect to its hub. Around the circumference of the wheel is its rim. Within this structure the Buddhist world

Figure 10.3 The wheel of becoming (© Dharmachari Āloka – Friends of the Western Buddhist Order)

view is illustrated. The hub shows three animals clinging on to one another: a pig, a cockerel and a snake. They represent the three forces that create our worldly existence: ignorance, desire or greed and aversion or hatred. They are the basis of Dukkha, unsatisfactoriness or dis-ease, which the Buddha called the first noble truth. These give rise to the six realms of existence that are depicted between the spokes of the wheel. At the top is the realm of the gods, which is a place of pleasure and happiness but prone to the influence of pride and delusion, which are the forces that produce its nemesis. Below and to its right is the realm of the asuras, or jealous gods. They are afflicted with envy, which produces enmity and conflict characteristic of their world. Working clockwise, the next realm is that of animals, ruled by ignorance and instinctive desire. At the bottom is the realm of hell, full of pain and fear. Moving upwards, we reach the realm of the hungry ghosts who are ruled by unquenchable desire. They can never be satisfied. This is illustrated by their huge stomachs and thin throats. They can never eat or drink enough to end their craving. The last realm is that of human beings. Here we find scenes of birth, work, enjoyment, conflict and death, as well as figures in meditation, reflecting on these experiences. The scenes relate to the four sights Siddhartha experienced when he travelled beyond the palace walls before seeking the end of suffering, which can also be found in the pictures on the rim of the wheel. This is the realm in which the possibility of enlightenment presents itself. It is why a human birth is so precious. We travel through these realms in our different rebirths according to the law of karma.

We can also understand this whole picture psychologically. During our lives we experience these different states of mind, associated with the different realms, and by identifying them we can deal with them appropriately, rather than becoming caught up in the emotions they invoke. In this way we learn how to make the best use of our lives and progress toward enlightenment. Pleasure, anger and jealousy, instinctive desires, fear and pain, craving, all these no longer control us. We recognise them for what they are: passing states. We do not cling to them or reject them. In this way we practise 'letting go', the basic Buddhist attitude.

Task 10.4 suggests an activity through which you can experiment with enabling children to bring their own experiences, imagination, thoughts and feelings to the picture.

Task 10.4 The wheel of becoming: classroom activity

Get your pupils to think of the wheel as a big picture story, like a cartoon. The idea is to enter the picture imaginatively themselves. Talk through what is happening in the different realms and what it would be like to be there.

- How would you feel?
- What would you like to be doing there?
- Where would you most like to be?
- Where would you least like to be?
- Who would be there with you?
- What would you want to happen?
- What would you not want to happen?
- What would you be thinking and doing?

If your pupils are confident enough you can introduce the connections between passing from one realm to another, i.e. moving from one state of mind to another. Sometimes we feel happy and sometimes sad. Why does this happen? Sometimes we feel safe and sometimes scared. Why does this happen? According to what the pupils say, you can ask them to think about that, how they deal with it, and the results can be shared in the class or a group. If they get this far they will offer many suggestions which you can use to introduce further activities. You now have an opportunity to explain further the Buddhist ideas in the picture, to which they can respond.

You may use the activity given or a different stimulus. Report back an evaluation of your session(s): it is important to bear in mind that you are reporting on the value of what you did for the development of your pupils' spirituality. You will need to consider how you were able to assess this. Pay particular attention to what you think worked and what you could have done more effectively.

SPIRITUAL EDUCATION ACROSS THE CURRICULUM: STORY AND SPIRITUALITY

Working with children's experience or innate spirituality can be undertaken by assuming their capacity to implicitly relate to spiritual ideas, rationally, emotionally and imaginatively. The approach outlined here accords with this understanding. Story is used as the vehicle to address spirituality and adopts the procedure of telling a story which is passed on to the pupils as potential storytellers in their own right. What is important is not their literal understanding or factual recall of the story but their capacity to pass it on as a matter of importance to the community of listeners. The story of the temple bells, as set out in Figure 10.4, has an implicit relationship with religion, but that need not be the case with other stories that could be chosen. When telling the story in the classroom you can introduce moments at which everyone stops and listens and sees images in the story with closed eyes – in other words, use the story as a form of meditation. The purpose of the ritual and sharing, at the end, is to transfer the story to the listeners and encourage them to link it with their own experiences and reflections. This can lead into further expressive and creative activities.

At the end of the story and the activity that follows it you may wish to distribute a shell to each of the listeners and say that they can now tell the story to someone else by using the shell. Thus the story can start from the object that has become a

Figure 10.4 The story of the temple bells (Reproduced with amendment from *The Song of the Bird* by Anthony de Mello. © 1982 by Anthony de Mello, S.J. Used by permission of Doubleday, a division of Random House, Inc.)

When he was young a boy used to have a story read to him in bed about a temple and, because it was his favourite story, his parents read it to him again and again. The story told of a temple in a far-off land that had a thousand bells. When the bells rang they made the most beautiful sound in the whole world, and people came from all over the world to hear them. As the boy grew older the story stayed with him. But in the story there was a moment when the temple was destroyed by a huge wave and the ruins were carried to the bottom of the sea. Yet, so it was said, it was still possible to hear the bells if you sat on the shore and listened patiently and silently enough. When he grew up the boy set out to go and hear the bells. He travelled a long distance to the island, where he sat quietly on the beach to hear this most beautiful of sounds. For a whole year he sat there every day, but all he heard was the sound of the gulls in the air, the wind in the trees and the waves on the shore. After a year he decided to go home, disappointed. But before he did he went to the beach to sit for one last time and listen to the sounds which had become so familiar and which he had come to love: the gulls, the wind and the waves. As he did so, sitting silently and still, he heard, at first, one faint bell, then another, and another, until he could hear the sound of the whole thousand bells. It was the most beautiful sound he had ever heard.

symbol or image by virtue of embodying a story. One variation is not to tell the ending but to ask the listeners to imagine their own ending. Did the boy hear the bells? In time and with many tellings the story has come to incorporate embellishments – for example, a cafe/inn where the boy stayed when he first arrived on the island, people in the cafe whom the boy asked about the bells, etc. This involves listeners in the role of playing these people. Responses then become incorporated in the next telling of the story, and so on.

Task 10.5 Story and spirituality in the curriculum

After telling the story of the temple bells in Figure 10.4 you might ask your pupils to do the following:

● Close their eyes and go back through the story in their minds.
● Choose their favourite moment.
● Put their hands out with their palms up next to one another.
● Transfer their favourite moment from your mind into their hands and close them together.
● Turn to the person next to them and tell them what they have in their hands and why.
● Discuss their conversations with the whole class.

Carry out the above activity or adapt the process to a different story and report back to your fellow students on how it worked in the classroom and what you think was achieved.

   The important thing is, of course, not the particular story nor the specific activities but the process employed, especially adapting the content and the process to the age of the group and the curriculum. It is important to be aware how the process depends on the involvement of the listeners.

SUMMARY AND KEY POINTS

Understanding the place of spiritual education in the classroom depends on your recognition of the approaches that are available, the processes of application that you can employ, the aims you wish to pursue beyond subject knowledge and the relationship you have with your pupils. Most important, you must identify spiritual development not as something that arises from curriculum knowledge, but as something you facilitate on the basis of specific aims, objectives and strategies you employ directed toward that end and consonant with both pupils' development and subject understanding.

FURTHER READING

Best, R. (ed.) (1996) *Education, Spirituality and the Whole Child*, London: Cassell. Contains a range of articles devoted to different approaches and strategies that can be employed in addressing spiritual education and its associated areas of values and moral education. It is a stimulus to furthering development in social, moral, spiritual and cultural education.

Coles, R. (1990) *The Spiritual Life of Children*, Glasgow: Harper Collins. Coles's work consists of interviews with a wide range of children from different countries and faith communities. He reports on his findings and the way he went about speaking to them. It is valuable not just for its content but as a model of conversation with children on spiritual matters.

The International Journal of Children's Spirituality, Abingdon: Carfax. Edited by Clive and Jane Erricker, this is the only journal devoted to spirituality in education. It contains a range of contributions across its issues from writers and practitioners in the UK and beyond who have addressed the debate on spirituality during the 1990s.

Erricker, C., Erricker, J., Ota, C., Sullivan, D., and Fletcher, M. (1997) *The Education of the Whole Child*, London: Cassell. A report on research interviewing children in England on what mattered to them and the significant experiences in their lives. It addresses policy, theory and practice in relation to spiritual and moral education.

Francis, L. and Thatcher, A. (eds) (1990) *Christian Perspectives for Education*, Leominster: Gracewing. A collection of essays focusing on approaches to the curriculum, religious education, morals and spirituality in education from Christian perspectives. There is a specific section on spirituality in the curriculum, comprising three chapters, but the whole book gives a good grounding for understanding the idea of Christian studies and theological approaches to education.

Hay, D., with Nye, R. (1998) *The Spirit of the Child*, London: Fount. An account of research into children's spirituality and its connections with religious understandings and practice. It argues for the innate spirituality of children and offers a model for facilitating it.

Starkings, D. (ed.) (1993) *Religion and the Arts in Education: Dimensions of Spirituality*, Sevenoaks: Hodder & Stoughton. A collection of papers organised in four sections: 'Introducing the spiritual', 'Personal and cultural dimensions', 'Religions, the arts and the spiritual' and 'Religious education and the pursuit of meaning'. It offers important insights, perspectives and approaches to spirituality in education.

Wright, A. (1998) *Spiritual Pedagogy*, Abingdon: Culham College Institute. This book defends an 'orthodox' Christian understanding of objective spirituality against Romantic and post-modern subjectivist interpretations. It also provides a useful and comprehensive survey of the current debate from the author's own critical stance.

11 Collective Worship

Derek Webster

> School worship stretches pupils, asks them to look beyond themselves and hear what may interrogate. If human society resembles a circle of people on a floating island, all looking inwards, then school worship is an opportunity to turn around and face an unknown, illimitable and mysterious ocean. Obviously worship is demanding of head and heart. It is like reading the *Phaedo* for Plato asks his readers to ponder an argument and respond to the sweep of a vision
>
> (Webster, 1991, p. 251)

School worship has been a feature of school life in Great Britain for centuries. Yet it was not until the 1944 Education Act that it became a legal requirement. This requirement was reaffirmed and modified in the 1988 Education Reform Act and the 1993 Education Act. It offers teachers an opportunity to raise important questions of meaning and value for their pupils. These questions arise from teachers' specialist subject areas, e.g. Science, Geography, Information Technology, as well as their own experiences. Such questions are significant for pupils in secondary schools because they offer a means of thinking about themselves, of forming their values, developing their attitudes and coming to terms with their own feelings. Indeed, at its best collective worship contributes to the understanding of how to live in the global society of the new millennium. Seen in this light, it is an asset available to all teachers. Instead of being a tiresome daily ritual, an irritant to the senior management team or the RE department, it can be an exciting instrument to be used by schools as they work to achieve their educational ends.

should be taken to have its natural and ordinary meaning. That is, it must in some sense reflect something special or separate from ordinary school activities and should be concerned with reverence or veneration paid to a divine being or power.

(DFE 1994a, p. 21)

This view, which does not have the force of law, is a disputed interpretation. Some see behind it the influence of 'right-wing' Christians in politics and education determined to impose a particular understanding of worship on the nation's schools. Others feel that it offers schools an opportunity to deliver what their young people have a right to receive. This definition could be called a strong one. It has historical roots but is felt by many schools, particularly those with no denominational allegiance or affiliation, to be inflexible. It assumes the existence of a supernatural being and suggests that the appropriate response to such a being is one of adoration. A more accommodating view is suggested by Brian Gates in his 1989 Hockerill Lecture, *The National Curriculum and Values in Education*. He sees worship as 'a generic activity of ascribing worth and value, identifying targets and ideals from and for life and work' (Gates 1989, p.13).

This fits well with the further view of worship in *The Shorter Oxford English Dictionary* as: 'to regard with extreme respect or devotion . . . to honour, to salute'. This definition of worship may be called a weak one. Yet it expresses a view which is common in the guidance given to their schools by Local Education Authorities.

A middle way is difficult to find and probably unnecessary, for informed opinion is coming round to the view that the legislation permits worship according to each definition. The second weak one is certainly the one that has the widest support among teachers and governors in non-denominational schools faced with organising worship. It enables them to frame aims for collective worship that take into account, in a very precise way, the social composition of their schools, the ethnic origins of their young people and the gifts and abilities of individual pupils. These aims give them the opportunity to deploy staff in ways that recognise their strengths and interests. Finally they permit schools to acknowledge the community and environment in which they are set. It is immediately obvious from this that the justification of worship in schools and the criteria of its success are educational. In the more usual corporate worship of Sikhs and Hindus, Christians or Jews within their own communities, the justification and criteria are, of course, theological. The weak definition, then, seems to give schools aims for collective worship which have the greatest flexibility.

COLLECTIVE WORSHIP IN STATE AND FAITH COMMUNITY SCHOOLS

State schools

A single and clear definition of worship with which everyone agrees does not, then, exist. Given that it is a contestable concept with deep historical roots, seen by some

as a socially or culturally conditioned idea at whose centre is an unverifiable experience, perhaps that is inevitable. Yet while there are those who regard it as wholly
reducible and explicable in behavioural terms, there are others who understand it as
the response of love to a Divine Person. Between these two ends of the spectrum
almost every position imaginable can be found. The problem this gives state schools
is easily put though difficult to solve. How can teachers, most of whom are non-
believing, devise models of worship which allow them to retain their own integrity
and which also suit the needs of largely agnostic pupils from a mainly non-religious
background? The model which emerges from a majority of secondary schools, seriously attempting to keep within the law and to use worship as an educational instrument, is one which takes as its starting point something akin to the weak definition
of worship.

It is a model deriving from a very loose positivist theoretical foundation. It places
greater emphasis on the human than on the divine and is sympathetic to those
approaches to worship which focus on the richness of human possibility. It sees society and the physical world in terms of what they are themselves rather than in terms
of a theologically based grand design. So nature is not an epiphany of God but an
instrument which, through technology, can be bent to serve human purposes. Society is not a divinely sanctioned structure of preordained groups but is pluriform,
owing to the effects of immigration, urbanisation and class differentiation. The model
takes religions not as an overarching frame of reference but as one thread among others set equally within human affairs. So religions have no authority outside their own
sphere and may not judge what lies beyond them. Finally the model sets reason, seen
at its best in scientific thinking, as sovereign in understanding society.

Despite many local variations, this model provides a common content for most
state schools. It covers three areas: socio-political matters of contemporary significance; personal and moral themes relevant to young people; and school and local
community issues. The first of these typically includes gender stereotyping, racial
prejudice, homelessness, unemployment, pollution and refugees. The second usually
covers rules of family and community living, responsibility in relationships, friends
and enemies, duties to others in society, especially those in the Third World, charitable giving and issues of public concern such as HIV/AIDS. The final one deals with
the local environment, including that of the school, personal achievements, the value
of people, disabled men and women, strangers in the community and service to
others.

This, then, is a model which looks for what redeems others from misery and injustice; it celebrates human victories over suffering and hardship. It enables many agnostic
teachers to share in collective worship without compromising their personal honesty.
However, there are those who criticise the model, pointing out that its emphasis on
human matters diminishes the Divine Being, its concern with social and political matters encourages controversy, and its simplistic presentation of complex issues can
amount to indoctrination. They fear that its elevation of reason is at the expense of the
affective and unconscious in human affairs; that in allowing religion to be a private matter it betrays the spiritual basis of the human person. Those who defend the model reply
that worship which arises out of human living is bound to witness to the concerns of
that living; that these issues, because they are important, will have a political dimension;

that reason is a safeguard against indoctrination and sloppy emotional thinking. They assert, finally, that the concept of worship is so broad that it can accommodate a model with a human emphasis as well as one which takes a divine perspective.

Faith community schools

The model of worship which emerges from the practice of faith community schools, the greatest number of which are Anglican and Roman Catholic, is a more theologically based one. The nature of these schools and the historic context of their religious foundation mean that generally they will see it as their role to nurture pupils into a particular faith. Sometimes, although not necessarily, this can also mean the assertion of traditional personal, social and political values. Schools of a faith community often have a philosophy which takes a hierarchical view of the structure of reality and presents spiritual values as paramount. It sees the world as a theatre for the activity of God and an expression of his creative power. Human beings are made in God's image and their society is an instrument of His will. These ideas do not go unchallenged, for some believers feel that there is an otherworldliness about this philosophy which fails to acknowledge the pluriform nature of society and is meaningless to pupils. They think that it imposes on young people controversial beliefs, and fosters an obsolete world view without intellectual credibility. However, the more traditional believers reply that their metaphysical stance is a witness to the eternal truths which stand above the fashions and contemporary fads of teenagers.

The content of acts of worship can be very traditional in a small minority of denominational schools. They may be led only by a senior member of staff or an authorised member of the religious community to which the school is attached. They can include the lections for the week, set prayers for the season and hymns which mark the religious pattern of the year. Worship in this mode can quickly subordinate educational common sense to theological rigorism. Less traditional worship employs a more modern idiom. Its prayer is informal, its Scripture is updated, its music has the rhythms and beats of the pop scene, and it uses material which moves easily from drama, film and mime to dance, drawing and poetry.

There are, however, some schools which eschew both these emphases, the traditional and the modern, in the Christian model. They look for a more exploratory approach to worship that affirms the place of questioning and seeking, investigating and challenging in religions. Taking seriously the view that all dogmas are only partial and all doctrines provisional, they prize the quest for truth and the energetic intellectual effort that goes with it. They are hospitable to new insights, acknowledge the ambiguities and sharpness of existence and know that the language of faith is only proximate and corrigible. This emphasis in the denominational model of collective worship is positive about the dialogue of the great religions of the world with one another. It allows that religions do not have all the answers and invites pupils to begin a quest. It is, however, an emphasis or a model which has drawn criticism upon itself. It appears to some to have a theological base which is too fluid; it can appear ambivalent in its witness to a particular faith, even partial; it may be suitable only to older, brighter pupils; and it tends to subordinate theology to education. Those who defend it stress its value in taking pupils to the point where they ponder mystery and build bridges between faiths.

For a very few schools such bridges would include the possibility of interfaith worship. The essential feature of the interfaith model of worship is a pattern of ideas which help world faiths to meet each other with sympathy so that a genuine attempt can be made to understand their different thinking and practice. In such a meeting they reflect on what they share, on the ideas they have in common and on the values which unite them. It is, however, a model viewed with deep suspicion, even hostility, and remains controversial. Believers in a faith worship in the context of a faith, not of no faith. So some would argue that there cannot be worship unless it is set in the context of a particular religion. To mix the faiths is to deny the distinctiveness of each and to concoct a syncretistic mishmash of ideas confusing to pupils. Those wishing to experiment with the interfaith model ask each of the religious traditions how far they can walk with other traditions, share the richness of their teaching with them and listen to them.

Task 11.3 Assessing collective worship

Attend acts of collective worship over a few days and write down the extent to which they are shared by:

- several members of staff or visitors;
- pupils of varying ages;

and the extent to which they:

- have an imaginative content;
- use a variety of media.

Note down your overall impression of their:

- strengths;
- weaknesses.

What would you change if you were the member of staff responsible for collective worship? Why?

EDUCATION, WORSHIP AND RE

Worship has a close relationship with other areas of the curriculum. It ponders the universe, wondering with the sciences how things come to be and what their purposes are. Probing the mysteries of time and place, it looks in awe at the ever-changing patterns of human history and geography and seeks their meaning. It stands in astonishment at human achievement in the arts: at poetry, whose words capture essences; at drama, which is revelatory of the human spirit; at music, which carries men and women to the threshold of mystery; at art, which becomes a theophany. Worship reflects on the values embedded in human ideals and aspirations as they occur in literature and philosophy. It sees what is noble and worthy as well as what is hideous and evil in the thinking and action of men and women. Of course, it sees with a particular slant and in a certain context. Worship is akin to wearing dark glasses which exclude some items in order to see other items better. So it looks for what integrates and is holistic, for what draws things together. It also sees with a prophetic eye and raises difficult value questions. Those who support it most ardently say that worship seeks the truth: those who deny its place in schools say it is a lie that distorts understanding.

RE in the secondary school curriculum aims to help pupils understand religions and offers a context in which they can reflect on their own beliefs and values. Worship echoes this and is supportive of it. Both RE and the act of worship at their best raise questions whose answers are never finally given. What is my origin and end? What is my duty to my neighbour? How may people find justice? What are truth, freedom and beauty? Can my guilt be cleansed? Both engage in a style of thinking which is compassionate, responsible and thankful, which sifts evidence and which does not claim to know all the answers. Both press to the limit and seek the boundaries of knowledge. Both have practical consequences in the lives of pupils. For they affect the attitudes they develop, their understanding of people and the responsibility they feel they have to themselves and others. Religious education and worship can differ sharply in content, in perspective, in the level of empathetic response they demand and in the instruments by which they are assessed. But what draws them most closely together is the foundation on which each stands, the warrant of the place each has in schools, for these are wholly educational.

The act of collective worship and RE share with the rest of the school curriculum the tasks of helping pupils to enlarge their horizons. They work towards that end by affirming the questioning and exploratory nature of the educational venture. They prize a quest for truth which stresses vigorous intellectual effort and honest reporting, for integrity does not take short cuts or trade in deceit. They acknowledge the uncertainties, the ambiguities and pain of existence, looking directly at human evil which many would prefer to veil. They testify to the paradoxes and illogicalities which hold sway among human beings, knowing that every system is imperfect and each life is unfinished. They espouse that critical openness which protests at victimisation, exclusion and destruction among human beings. And finally they refuse to regard as absolute the thinking of the past or overestimate that of the present in challenging current moral reflection.

Task 11.4 Organising collective worship

What issue do you feel passionately about or what interest totally absorbs you? Organise an act of collective worship for an age group of your choice about it, taking as your theme 'It really matters to me that . . .'

SUMMARY AND KEY POINTS

Fundamentally, when all the myths are shredded and all the slogans emptied, it is the only role of the school curriculum to enable young people to become human. Of course, in the sense that they belong to the species Homo Sapiens they are already human, but in another sense, through education, they may become more truly human. This is vital, for it is very easy to become less than human. As the legislation sees it, collective worship is a key element in helping pupils to achieve this deeper realisation of their own gifts and responsibilities. It allows the depths within young people to resonate with what they take to be ultimate in their world; it correlates symbols and images with a mystery that seems to inhabit every human being; it speaks of the freedom in involvement and the fulfilment in self-emptying. Although the legislation is imperfect and its aims are inadequately worked out, it steers in broadly the right direction. The practical problems it poses for schools can be worked through, given good will and a clearer understanding of the educational justification and developmental possibilities of worship.

Collective worship is, then, a treasure house and a superb opportunity for teachers of all subject areas. It is at its best when many and diverse enthusiasms are brought to it. It interrogates values and ideals, encourages creative growth and human achievement, recognises the principles beneath human actions and transmits new knowledge. Seen properly, it stands at the centre of the educational venture. It does not indoctrinate; rather the reverse, it challenges the prevailing secular humanism found in state schools and calls for consideration of competing world views. In doing so it deepens the humanity of pupils.

FURTHER READING

Brown, A. (1996) *Between a Rock and a Hard Place*, London: National Society. A thoughtful little booklet which is useful to those looking at the emerging issues relating to collective worship in schools. Although written from an Anglican point of view it ranges very widely and offers food for thought especially to those looking to the future with an eye to changing the legislation.

Copley, T. (1989) *Worship, Worries and Winners: Worship in School after the 1988 Act*, London: National Society/Church House Publishing. A constructive examination of secondary school worship which is helpful to teachers, parents and governors. Lively, accessible and humorous, it looks at both principles and practice and is useful to those faced with organising collective worship for the first time. It shows that it can be a positive experience for all involved.

Department for Education (1994a) *Religious Education and Collective Worship*, Circular 1/94, London: DFE. This is essential reading for those who need to be aware of the exact legal situation regarding collective worship. It is an interpretation from the DFE of the implications of the legislation of 1989 and 1993 for schools. Effectively it represents the intentions of the government of the time. It does not, however, have the force of law until it is tested in the courts.

Webster, D. (1995) *Collective Worship in Schools: Contemporary Approaches*, Cleethorpes: Kenelm

Press. This book is one of the few in this area to take seriously the possibility of interfaith collective worship. It also emphasises the educational nature of collective worship in schools as opposed to the theological nature of corporate worship in faith communities. Relating worship to the spiritual dimension of education, it offers an educational justification of collective worship.

Wright, C. (1995) *Delivering Collective Worship*, Bury St Edmunds: Courseware Publications. Chris Wright shows how to develop a policy for collective worship and then implement it in an energetic way. He discusses good practice and with excellent examples shows what is possible with pupils. A book to help the confused sort out their ideas and then work in a creative way. Theory and practice are well brought together.

12 Religious Education and Moral Education

Andy Angel

Any preoccupation with ideas of what is right and wrong in conduct shows an arrested intellectual development.

(Oscar Wilde 1983, p. 1205)

You can't prevent the heathen being converted if they want to be . . . this is an age of toleration.

(Saki (Munro 1976, p. 633))

What Wilde and Saki have to say is instructive to all Religious Educators, and their comments deserve to be pondered awhile. They represent the two poles of the fraught relationship between RE and moral education (ME). In between these two poles lies a minefield ready to explode underneath the unsuspecting. This ground is not simply hallowed but has been fought over for quite some time. Many would like to own it and to exclude others from it. As a new RE teacher, whether entering the field with fresh idealistic optimism or with world-weary cynicism, you are likely to find the task of picking your way through the field of ME a challenging one. The aim of this chapter is to provide you with a rough guide to the subject.

The area is not simple terrain to map out. There are many different things going on, and, to understand it, you need to have a good idea of what they are. Many factors influence the relationship of RE and ME. Trends in educational thinking strongly affect both RE and ME. The philosophy of education has largely determined the nature of ME, while RE theorists have often shaped RE. Of particular importance in educational thinking has been the desire to define and avoid indoctrination. These trends in educational thinking are themselves often influenced by developments in academic thinking, especially in the fields of ethics and philosophy of religion. However, neither RE nor ME takes place in a social or political vacuum. A knowledge of the social and political background to developments in RE and ME helps us to understand them. And finally, going from the sublime to the practical, the delivery of ME in RE requires the teacher to think through how ethical issues are taught and what tasks are to be set. And, of course, there are the pupils who, in their own inimitable way, normally manage to change the nature of any lesson one may wish to teach at some stage between the planning and the delivery.

OBJECTIVES

By the end of this chapter you should:

- understand the political and social contexts of moral education in RE;
- be able to pick your way through the basic ideas of the RE/moral education debate;
- understand the alleged dangers of indoctrination;
- be aware of practical issues concerning moral education within RE teaching.

THE POLITICAL AND SOCIAL CONTEXTS

There have been three basic models of the relationship between RE and ME. All three envisage RE as meeting a moral need in society. The first of these models, the *confessional* model, understands part of the role of RE to be the moral rejuvenation of the nation. The second, the *multifaith* model, sees RE as a vehicle through which the anti-racist cause may be furthered. The third, the *spirituality model*, sees RE as a much-needed counterbalance to the all-pervading materialism of modern Britain. Each of these models evolved out of its social and political context and the responses of those involved in RE to that social and political context.

Confessionalism

In the period 1934–39 RE was given fresh impetus. Until that time, it had been very much the Cinderella subject in schools. In 1934 a new journal, *Religion in Education*, was launched. The hope of many of the early contributors was that they could use RE as a vehicle for the moral rejuvenation of British society.

Figures like M.V.C. Jeffreys, M.L. Jacks and B. Yeaxlee perceived a decline in moral standards and a growing spiritual vacuum in society. They believed that this vacuum was being filled with materialistic philosophies and that the new nationalistic ideologies were becoming increasingly attractive to the common person. If this moral vacuum were not filled, and its attendant decline in moral standards not stemmed, the country could well be gripped by an undemocratic nationalism which would rob people of their freedom and dignity.

These thinkers were clearly worried at the rise of nationalistic philosophies and political parties across Europe. They saw the scientism and positivism of their contemporaries as harmful to spiritual and moral development, as pupils refused to believe in something that they could not prove, especially when proof was so forthcoming in other areas of the curriculum. Furthermore, they saw this as a problem not simply in schools but in society at large.

Such thinkers believed that the only sufficient answer was to breathe new life into what they saw as a tired old form of RE. As it stood, the subject tended to comprise the history and geography of first-century Palestine and a measure of rationalist ethics. This, they believed, had to be replaced. Rationalist ethics was cold and bloodless, and the history and geography of first-century Palestine were irrelevant to the mind of most pupils.

The suggested replacement was the well known confessional model of RE. In collective worship, pupils would find the Christian God, and in the classroom they would see that the Christian faith not only made sense but also made more sense than any other philosophy on offer. In large part, confessionalism was forged to meet the perceived social and cultural needs of the day. RE is to be a vehicle for stemming the moral decline of the people. And so ME as an integrated aspect of confessional RE was to nurture pupils into Christian attitudes and ways of behaving.

Modelling multifaith

The next model of the relationship between RE and ME, the multifaith model, was forged in response to tension within an increasingly multicultural society. This tension was reflected in the 1968 Birmingham speech of Enoch Powell, MP, in which he warned of impending 'rivers of blood' on the streets of Britain as a result of racial strife, and the Notting Hill riots. Racial tension had come to a head and had exploded. In the world of RE there had been calls for multifaith teaching since the mid–1930s but there had never been concerted support for it. In the late 1960s support for multifaith RE was beginning to gather momentum. In January 1969 it got just the opening it needed. Alice Bacon, Minister of State for Education and Science, wrote in her foreword to a special race relations issue of *Learning for Living*:

> But when the movement is of large numbers of immigrants, it brings not only opportunities for widening our experience of other races, but also problems of integration. We who are involved in education are well placed to contribute to the solution of this very difficult and delicate problem. The teachers in particular have a unique opportunity for implanting greater understanding in the minds of the young and for influencing opinions and attitudes. If advantage is not taken of the fact of the complete absence of racial prejudice in the very young, by nurturing and strengthening it, so that it is carried forward into young adulthood and beyond, the opportunity and the harmony may be lost.
>
> (Bacon 1969, p. 4)

The momentum towards multifaith RE galvanised. One way to contribute to mutual tolerance, understanding and acceptance between different ethnic communities was to try to promote mutual tolerance, understanding and acceptance between different faith communities. This could be partially achieved by teaching pupils about various faiths in a tolerant spirit and encouraging them to carry that tolerant spirit over into their everyday lives. Throughout the 1970s, with strong support from CEM, multifaith RE became the dominant form of RE in British schools.

Such RE teaches the moral lesson that tolerance, understanding and acceptance of minority ethnic/faith communities is of paramount importance in today's religiously and ethnically plural world. There has been limited questioning of whether it is right or fair to use RE as a tool for furthering the cause of 'positive discrimination', but in the main that multifaith RE ought to exist for this purpose has not been questioned by the majority of RE practitioners. ME in this kind of RE consisted of nurturing pupils' attitudes, in order that they might be able to combat racism.

New Age in a new world

The last model of the relationship between RE and ME is, for want of a better description, the anti-capitalist spirituality model. The background to this model was the rise of popular capitalism under the influence of Margaret Thatcher in the 1980s. The combination of individualism, materialism and capitalism created a social atmosphere of ruthless competition between people. Money seemed to become the benchmark of social status, and the love of it the root of all human activity. The opportunity for individuals to make something of their lives financially seems to have been the cornerstone of this culture. It also seems to have been the cause of its popular appeal. However, it found little support in the world of education, which strongly resisted it for as long as was legally possible.

In the wake of the 1988 Education Reform Act, RE reacted strongly against the idea that it might exist to teach pupils the Protestant work ethic. Indeed, it pitted itself directly against such a position. In a world which was dominated by Mammon, RE should lead people (via a multifaith path) to the living God. The role of RE in the individualistic, materialistic and capitalist modern world was to bring pupils face to face with the world of the spirit. Ironically, the modern world was seen to be spiritually poor, as it was lost in the worship of money. Pupils needed to learn that being human entailed more than having money. To be fully human required one to have found oneself. Finding oneself entailed the realisation that one can be fully human only in community, and this realisation, in turn, entailed a commitment to building up loving relations with one's neighbours, whoever they might be and of whatever colour and creed they might be (Hull 1995, pp. 130–2, 1996, pp. 66–8).

RE should help pupils to realise that a money spirituality (formerly known as avarice) was losing one's life to the pursuit of a false god and sowing seeds of destruction of social relations. Positively, it should show children that there was an alternative to this kind of materialism which could be found in the writings and practice of the world's major religious traditions. ME in this context is to try to persuade pupils not to adopt the materialism of the prevailing culture.

Task 12.1 Auditing Moral Education during your school placement

Write a profile of ME in the RE department where you are working, looking at:

- the departmental policy on ME (if any);
- the views of the members of the department;
- lessons, to see what comes across to and is learned by the pupils.

THE ROLE OF . . . EDUCATION WITHIN . . . EDUCATION

There are, then, three basic models for the relationship between RE and ME. They all perceive different problems in society, they all have different solutions to the problems they perceive and they entail quite different programmes for the classroom. The obvious question, therefore, is which one of these models is to be preferred? I wish to leave the question open here. To answer it is too difficult in such a short space. Instead, I wish to show how certain presuppositions will lead to one conclusion and certain other presuppositions will lead to other conclusions. Then you may decide for yourself where you stand in this debate and, maybe, work your way forward from there. The title of the section is deliberately open. Which way round should it read? 'The role of moral education within Religious Education' or 'The role of Religious Education within moral education'? This little conundrum encapsulates the main issue of the debate. In answering it, you will find that much will depend on your world view and on how religion, philosophy and education fit into that world view.

The 'Christian' thing to do

Let us imagine that God does exist and that He has revealed Himself fully in Jesus of Nazareth, who was also the Messiah. Ultimate truth is to be found only in Christianity. True spirituality is found only in being a Christian, and true morality is properly known and understood only by the church. Reason helps the human mind to find answers to the questions it constantly asks, but only when it is subservient to its elder sister, revelation.

What is the place of education in such a world? Education is the process of seeking truth and seeking to disseminate knowledge of it. Therefore, in this world, education has the role of nurturing pupils into the Christian faith. It helps them struggle through their questions in order that they can see for themselves that the doctrines of the faith are true. It enables them to see the rightness of Christian morality and so nurtures them as people that they are enabled to live by it. Philosophy, especially in the areas of ethics, epistemology and metaphysics, will be of incidental value to those students who have a bent for this kind of thinking. It might conceivably appear in lessons on Christian faith and doctrine as either a friend or a foe of the faith.

ME in this scheme of things is relatively easy. Christian morality is taught and discussed in the classroom. Secular morality may be brought in by way of contrast but the focus of the lesson is clear: to help the pupils see the sense that Christian morality makes. This programme is backed up by the school's requirement that all pupils act in a Christian manner and the practice of the school in disciplining pupils in a Christian manner. Explicitly and implicitly, ME is about nurture into the Christian faith.

Ethics in 'enlightened' times

Now let us change the picture a little. God may well exist but we are not sure about it and we do not wish to base our lives on what may turn out to be a false assumption. Religion is no longer central to our picture of the world. We remain questioning beings and so Reason takes the place that revelation has recently vacated, thus becoming the sole criterion of truth.

Education remains the pursuit of truth (or perhaps mere knowledge if our faith in truth is greatly weakened) and the passing on of our knowledge of it. Therefore schooling at a practical level is the passing on of knowledge. Knowledge is publicly agreed to exist in the academic disciplines and so, in schools, some watered down form of the traditional academic disciplines is served up to pupils.

In subjects like Geography and History this is a relatively easy task. In RE it is much more difficult. That is because the relevant academic disciplines (theology, philosophy and religious studies) are at war with each other. It only becomes more complicated when the social sciences (psychology, sociology and anthropology) join in the fray. Turning this into a school subject is a very hard task, and that is one of the reasons why RE has changed its identity (and name) so many times since 1944. One solution to the problem has been to relativise religious claims to truth by putting them on the map of the history of ideas and leaving them there.

RE, then, tends to become an attempt at a value-free evaluation of religion, the assumption being that something like this is more or less possible. Various religious traditions are explored and an attempt is made to show how religions are supposed to fulfil the spiritual or aesthetic dimension of humankind's nature. This study of religion is complemented by a perusal of various important ethical issues of the day, e.g. abortion, euthanasia, the North/South divide and issues of environmental concern.

The ME aspect of RE is contained within the study of topical issues. Pupils approach them from a 'rational' viewpoint. By that is meant a viewpoint that starts from a rationalist or non-religious base as opposed to a viewpoint which, while defended by reasoned arguments, may well start from religious premises. The ethical issues are defined and then the best possible solutions to the problems are (allegedly) discovered by means of putting forward and rebutting (normally utilitarian) arguments.

Letting the liberal agenda go

Let us change the picture once again. Imagine that non-religious ethicists cannot agree among themselves how one goes about distinguishing right from wrong. Imagine further that some philosophers believe this to be an impossible task or, even, that 'right' and 'wrong' are meaningless words. There would be no criteria by which good and evil could be discovered.

Of course, such a scenario is more than familiar in the world of twentieth-century ethics. It has given rise to another way out of the problem of creating a school subject out of all the academic disciplines that feed into RE. It has relativised all claims to truth: religious, philosophical and scientific. In this postmodern environment we have lost our faith in Reason, as we cannot work her out. She may have all the answers but she has not shown them to us, and all the people who claim she has disagree with each other. In such a scenario, who takes centre stage? The answer, more often than not, is the pupil as a reasoning human being.

So the nature of ME within RE changes again. When focusing on moral problems, more often than not the pupils are required to approach them from a number of different angles, both religious and secular. Pupils will learn about what Christians, Muslims, Jews, Hindus and humanists (read utilitarians) think about a particular moral issue. Then they will be asked to say what they think about a moral issue. Provided they give reasons for their answers, they are deemed to be on the right track. Then they move on to the next issue.

The key to the relationship of RE and ME concerns your understanding of truth. If Christianity is true, then ME is about nurturing into Christian morality. If Reason is the sole criterion of truth, then ethics must be discovered through the exercise of reason. If Reason (should it exist) be impenetrable to us, then pupils ought to be allowed to express their own view, provided they do so 'intelligently', because they are, after all, at school.

Task 12.2 The context of Moral Education: teacher and school

Write the following two summaries on one side of A4 each:

- a summary of your own ethical position;
- a summary of what you think it is legitimate for you to teach pupils, in terms of ME, in a: (a) non-faith school, (b) Christian school, (c) Jewish school, (d) Islamic school.
- Attempt to justify your point of view throughout the exercise.

THE SPECTRE OF INDOCTRINATION

There are some who may object to the idea that pupils are encouraged to justify their opinions, regardless of what they might be. What if they are racist? What if they are sexist? Is the teacher required to commend a pupil for being an intelligent racist or chauvinist? The natural reaction of many teachers to these questions is to determine to weed all antisocial attitudes out of pupils. Teachers ought, at least to some extent, to be teaching pupils what values they are to hold (whether by religious nurture or by rational argument). However, at the point of making this decision the teacher has entered the minefield of indoctrination and/or conditioning. Do we require pupils to say 'headperson' and 'chalkboard' and to use the female pronoun in their essays on morality? Or are these indications that the 'loony left' has infiltrated the classroom? Where exactly does neutrality lie?

One answer to this problem has been to claim that neutrality lies in weeding out all the value-laden material from education. Pupils are to meet only with uncorrupted, neutral evidence and they are to use pure logic in the making of their ethical decisions. Should a teacher try to do anything else in the classroom, she is indoctrinating. The name of the game, therefore, is how to spot indoctrination. Task 12.3 invites you to undertake an initial review of the nature and extent of indoctrination in schools. Everybody knows that it is bad but what exactly is it?

Task 12.3 Auditing the nature and extent of indoctrination in schools

Take out the lesson plans and/or schemes of work you have prepared for your teaching practice. Look at them with an eye to spotting any activity or assumption behind an activity that might be indoctrinatory. Try to rewrite that part of the lesson plan and/or scheme of work.

The method criterion

At this point in the search for indoctrination, consensus breaks down. Some hold that indoctrination is a special type of teaching which takes freedom away from pupils, a sort of pseudo-educational brainwashing. Consider the following scenario. In a chalk-and-talk lesson on social and marital problems in her course on 'Religion and Human Relationships', Ms Ann Spencer manages every year to persuade her Year 10 girls that men are abusive to women. Following this talk with video documentaries on wife battery and the failure of absentee fathers to support their children only serves to further drill in her view that men are evil and women are loving. The pupils are then required to write an essay on the breakdown of relationships on the basis of this material. The essays are bound to reflect and reinforce Ms Spencer's own view. If the criterion of indoctrination is that of teaching method, then the *way* Ms Spencer teaches clearly indoctrinates pupils.

On the other hand, this account of indoctrination may not work in all cases. Should Ms Spencer show videos of young mothers neglecting or abusing their children and introduce pupils to examples of good fathering before the essay is set, we would hardly accuse her of indoctrinating. The above methods, in themselves, do not constitute indoctrination. Moreover, drilling ideas into pupils is regularly used as a method for teaching such things as times tables and verb conjugations. Nobody calls that indoctrination.

The content criterion

Some others would have it that indoctrination is teaching pupils something that is not true, i.e. indoctrination has to do with the *content* of the teaching–learning process. Therefore, should Father John Bird teach that Christ was a revolutionary leader who overthrew the Romans and set an example for all his followers as a political revolutionary, excising neatly any Gospel evidence to the contrary from his lessons, he would be indoctrinating. It seems terribly clear-cut.

But perhaps it is not. When Father Bird retires an ex-pupil of his, Father Andrew Smith, comes to replace him. He teaches the same thing, but only because his education moulded him into thinking it. Is he indoctrinating? Many think not, because he is not responsible for his ignorance, Father Bird is. There is culpability only where the agent knows what she is doing.

The aim criterion

Therefore, others have claimed that indoctrination is better defined by the *aim* of the would-be indoctrinator. Ms Eleanor Powell is teaching Economics at a well known public school. Personally she accepts Marxist economic theory and is politically committed to bringing about a communist state in Britain. In order to practise her political beliefs, she enculturates her pupils into purely Marxist economics. She is obviously indoctrinating, as she fully intends her pupils to hold Marxist beliefs unshakably. Here indoctrination is to do with aim.

But is it really so? Her partner, Mr Frank Whistler, tries to foster spiritual feelings, and their concomitant anti-capitalist values, in pupils through his RE teaching. However, the pupils are very adept at debate, come from wealthy families and, perhaps on account of their backgrounds, disagree with him, out-arguing him at every point. Despite his aims he fails entirely to convert even one to his point of view. Can he really be charged with indoctrination, or is he, rather, an amiable fool?

The consequence criterion

Perhaps, then, indoctrination takes place only when the pupils are actually indoctrinated: indoctrination is defined by the consequences of the teaching programme. Imagine that Ms Sue Payne tries to convince her pupils that it is good to tolerate people of other faiths and not to try to proselytise them. Through her sympathetic approach to all faiths, her promotion of universalism through the syllabus content and teaching method, and her strong rebuttal of any fundamentalist viewpoint in the press, her school and her class, she wins her pupils over. She has indoctrinated them into that view. But, regardless of whether she has indoctrinated or not, consequence is not the only criterion of indoctrination here, as she has indoctrinated them *into a view*: content plays a part too.

The use of foregone conclusions

Another view is that indoctrination involves use of *foregone conclusions*. Mrs Leah Howson teaches her pupils that all religions describe the spiritual realm at the start of their secondary RE course. All her teaching leads from this basic premise. Her teaching programme thus involves two foregone conclusions: that there is a spiritual realm; and that all religions describe it. Pupils must accept these (hotly debated) 'truths' in order to engage in study. The fact that the two points are not publicly accepted truths but are presented as such makes them foregone conclusions. As Mrs Howson is not giving pupils a chance to question them, she is indoctrinating.

These, then, are the various definitions of indoctrination and the replies that have been made to them. You need to work out for yourself which definition makes most sense, and then you need to avoid doing that in the classroom, because everybody knows that indoctrination is bad. Or is it? The view that indoctrination is always bad is not universally accepted and the term has not always carried pejorative overtones. It used only to mean teaching pupils true doctrine, and surely there is nothing wrong with teaching the truth, especially when it may otherwise be inaccessible to people?

Indeed, the pejorative use of the term 'indoctrination' presupposes that there is a truth that all may discover through the use of reason and by looking at the evidence. It presupposes that there is a neutral way of looking at things. It assumes that indoctrination is the process by which someone is introduced to a subject from a particular perspective. Education, on the other hand, involves only the neutral assessment of evidence by way of reasoned argument.

Figure 12.1 Five criteria of indoctrination

Five basic criteria through which educators claim to identify indoctrination are as follows.

- *Method*. Indoctrination is the result of imposing ideas on pupils through inappropriate 'closed' teaching methods.
- *Content*. Indoctrination can be recognised when the knowledge and ideas passed on to pupils are untrue.
- *Aim*. Indoctrination occurs when a teacher deliberately sets out to impose a particular point of view on pupils.
- *Consequence*. Indoctrination takes place only when pupils are actually indoctrinated.
- *Foregone conclusions*. Indoctrination is the result of a learning process that proceeds forward to an inevitable conclusion.

There is a major problem with this whole approach to the subject of indoctrination. All study involves coming at fresh evidence with a preconceived idea of what we may find. Even where we allow the new evidence to reshape our old idea, we have slotted it into the basic picture of our subject, which we had beforehand. All teaching involves building up a picture in the pupils' minds into which we can slot evidence and theory in a meaningful way. Indeed, knowing how to plan your teaching so that the pupils are able to see how the concepts, facts and theories of a subject all slot together into the larger paradigms is an important part of good teaching. No teacher would expect the average pupil to be challenging intelligently the larger paradigms of any subject, at least until they embark on their first research degree. Be that as it may, there are some practical issues to do with RE and ME which now demand our attention.

PRACTICALITIES

Imagine that you have overcome the theoretical problems of ME within the context of RE and that you are ready to start the job. How do you do the job in practice? Let us visit an imaginary classroom where Ms Laura McLaughlin helps her pupils find their way in the difficult world of modern adolescence. She informs them of the unpleasant consequences that drugs and unsafe sex may entail. She even tells them of her own awful experiences and how she genuinely regrets them. She does not tell them that she still has not quite kicked the habits, despite being convinced that they are bad. One night, she is seen by the lower sixth purchasing drugs at a rave. The only moral lesson a child learns from such a situation is never to take that hypocrite seriously again. Harsh it may seem but real it is. To teach ME successfully, you need to embody what you are trying to put across. You need to be a role model.

Indeed, you cannot help but be a role model. If pupils respect you, they are very likely to take who you are seriously and they will follow your example to some extent. However, who you are and what you say may well be two very different things. Teach pupils to be loving by using sarcasm and 'attitude' and you will find your pupils become sarcastic 'with attitude'.

But don't forget that you are not the only role model a pupil has at school. The pupil probably likes, respects and imitates other teachers. Unless you are at a school with a very strong and clear ethos, and with the wherewithal to attract exactly the kind of staff that will embody that ethos, you are likely to find that what you are modelling to the pupil is quite different from what other members of staff are modelling to the pupil. Let us enter another imaginary school. Amelia Jonson epitomises middle-class Christian values and her pupils can see it. Dr Bernie Apps, the Biology teacher, is an out-and-out evolutionist and allows his biology to dictate terms to his philosophy and ethics. Any monkeying around in his classes and you soon learn what is meant by 'the survival of the fittest'. The French teacher (joint honours graduate with philosophy), Mr Angus Martin, could not be more postmodern, unauthoritarian and free in his approach to education. The pupils are given conflicting moral examples in every different classroom.

And don't be fooled into thinking that it is just other departments you need to worry about. Imagine an RE department with one theology graduate, someone who did their theology whilst training for the Christian ministry, one World Religions graduate, one atheist, one humanist and a Buddhist – all passionately committed to their own approach to the study and practice of religion. It is, of course, very large for an RE department, but it demonstrates the point. There are likely to be conflicting agendas within RE departments on how and why ME should take place within RE.

And the problems do not finish there. There is always the Personal and Social Education PSE programme, provided your school has one up and running. This will have a rationale/philosophy which may complement or oppose what the RE department is trying to do (assuming it knows what it is doing with ME). However, practice is such that PSE is likely to be handled differently by different members of staff. This will contribute to the plethora of moral examples and moral exhortations with which the pupils have to grapple (assuming that they do not give up and ignore them).

Added to these difficulties is the remarkable capacity pupils share with other human beings to talk one moral language but act according to another. In fact you are likely to find that, taking into account the enormous moral input to pupils in school (not to mention out of it), pupils are learning to behave in various ways in different situations and that they are capable of talking a number of different moral languages which may or may not correspond to their moral behaviour.

But this is all getting rather academic. We have forgotten the pastoral care system that most schools have. The way we treat pupils, the way we discipline them, will teach them yet more moral lessons. Again, are those lessons being reinforced in the classroom, through PSE, in academic subjects, or is it just another thread in the complex and confused web of ME in school? And, of course, pupils are children with minds of their own. Pupils will learn moral lessons only when they chew them over for themselves and decide that such-and-such a thing really is right and that they really ought to do it.

Thankfully, the RE department is not primarily responsible for monitoring ME throughout the school, but it is inevitably affected by it, as it is by the values of the local and national culture. It may be a depressing exercise but it is well worth attempting to understand the moral climate of your school, in all its contradictions, as that will help you to understand the moral understanding the pupils bring with them into your classroom.

So, now that you know what you want to say, and you understand the mind set of your hearers a little better, how are you going to say it?

Sense and sensitivity

Well, unless you are ideologically opposed to this, you ought to be sensitive. The need for sensitivity in teaching should be well understood. Pupils are human and thus frail in all sorts of ways. Blast them and they shatter. Nurture them and they grow. I believe the point is widely accepted by RE teachers looking at moral issues. If Father McDermott launches into a tirade on the evils of wealth and the stoking of the fires of hell he may upset his students, who like shopping and do not care much about social reform. They will not listen, and those living in poverty will be none the better off for his tirades. ME will not take place in his RE lessons on account of the fundamental lack of communication.

On the other hand, if Ms Sarah Jones addresses the issue of the North/South divide but cursorily before launching into '*Looking Good–Feeling Great*', a scheme of work on the importance of self-esteem, her pupils are unlikely to address an important moral issue seriously. They are more likely to become primarily concerned with the nurturing of their adolescent egos and the ordering of their private and social lives to that end, rather than becoming in any way politically aware and active. Failing to address an issue because it is unpalatable and addressing only the ones which will make your lessons popular with the pupils is not being sensitive but depriving pupils of their education.

Moral problems are difficult to address and addressing them hurts, that is why they are called problems. However, avoiding grappling with difficult subjects in the name of sensitivity is neither moral nor educative. There is a balance to strike between helping the child see the scale of the issues and giving the child no more than he or she can bear. It is hard but necessary if ME is to be real. Nurture children and they grow. Fail to prune them and they grow wild.

Evaluation

All good teaching, we are told, involves evaluation and feedback. Where does that fit into ME? How do we evaluate the ME component of our RE teaching? The most obvious and easy answer is to state current practice, that we give pieces of work on moral issues a mark, perhaps a percentage, perhaps a grade. And we give better marks to pupils who know the relevant facts and put the better arguments. And so we encourage pupils to believe that it is good to argue effectively and bad to argue ineffectively and that we need not worry about intentions and attitudes. It is more than a touch ironic that a schooling system founded ultimately on the philosophy of Plato should have reduced its ME to sophistry. Is finding the best argument all there is to ME? Or, putting it another way, do we want our school leavers to enter the adult world believing that they deserve to be successful if they can argue their way out of anything?

Perhaps there is more to ME than the ability to argue. Miss Linda Bell gets B+ for her essay arguing the case for and against retaining the Ten Commandments in modern society. She has learned (or, more likely, recapped) some ancient history. She has learned how to analyse a topic and argue a case. She has expressed an opinion. But has she learned anything moral (as opposed to learning about moral ideas)? Is she entering into moral debate or standing on the sideline? Or is she merely an observer? What are we asking her to do? What is our aim? If it has to do with ME, rather than ancient history or debating skills, then surely Miss Bell ought to be required to assess her own moral standing within the exercise. Perhaps the title should require her to go on from arguing the case for and against retaining various commandments to review her own behaviour in the light of her ideas. ME, if it has anything to do with life, involves looking at one's own behaviour and attitudes.

And exactly how are we feeding back? What does B+ for your views on retaining the Ten Commandments mean? Can a child be 79 per cent moral in his views on abortion at the end of the Year Ten examination? Grades and numbers are fairly meaningless indicators of moral learning. Perhaps it would be wiser to adopt some kind of verbal feedback, which describes the moral position children present in their work. Should we do so, we are faced with the difficulties of scale. How do we describe the moral positions of our pupils? And how does a pupil interpret our description of his or her moral position? If we are working within a faith, or a philosophical school, the faith or philosophy may provide us with a scale. Within Christianity, 'a loving way of approaching the problem' is obviously at one end of the scale while 'this reads as if you were possessed' is clearly at the other. And the work load implicit in this approach to evaluating is enormous, not just in marking work but also in standardising across the department.

Another issue follows from it. A pupil may well come to certain conclusions on various moral matters (whether by nurture into a perspective or by 'free thought'). Now the pupil has a position, can he stick to it? And if he, as so many of us do, finds that his moral performance does not match his moral ideas, how do we help the child to address this issue? And if we do not address this issue, is there any value in going further? If we lead a child across a field and into a ditch out of which it cannot clamber alone, surely we need to help it out before we can proceed. Likewise, if we wish our pupils to learn anything moral in RE, we need to help them to cross the rough terrain of moral difficulties. It may not always be possible but we need to recognise that when it does not happen the pupils are no longer learning moral lessons – they are detached from the subject matter. And it is at this point that we realise that we seem to be asking pupils to develop some sort of spirituality.

Indeed, the more we look into the practicalities of ME, whether we like it or not, the more it looks as if some form of confessionalism is not simply in order but inevitable.

Task 12.4 Developing a scheme of work for Moral Education in RE

Select a programme of study you are following for teaching practice and write a lesson plan covering one stage of the programme which deliberately sets out to relate the programme topic to moral issues. Try to set tasks and create teaching blocks which morally educate the pupil, rather than simply educating the pupil about morality.

SUMMARY AND KEY POINTS

In the garden of ideas the plots allotted to education are best likened to conservation areas where all things grow wild, competing against each other for space, and all in the cause of freeing Nature to be truly herself. If the interested person takes a look at how ME is faring in the RE bed, he will see that there are three variations on the RE/ME hybrid. They are Christian moral nurture, teaching pupils to be anti-racist and teaching pupils to look into the spiritual instead of basing their lives on money.

Some interested persons are keen to see the area dug over and re-landscaped. They have questioned the role of RE in ME but it seems inevitable that RE will at least contribute to ME (whether one likes it or not), as so much religion is ethics. It is difficult to determine what the place of ME should be in RE because the basic premises of different world views lead to very different conclusions on the matter. Nevertheless, it is fundamental to a liberal education that no ideology may demand that its premises should be held by anything other than rational conviction. Therefore the various models of the relationship between RE and ME outlined above remain educationally viable because, as yet, there is no consensus on which of the major (or minor) world views constitutes absolute truth. Until there is consensus, and all are convinced by good reason that this world view represents absolute truth, a liberal education system must inevitably allow education into different world views, provided that a rational defence is made of any world view into which pupils are to be educated. What is important for RE teachers is to recognise they have the right and the duty within this system to teach with integrity.

RE teachers, whilst holding a mandate to teach with integrity, ought to be aware of the dangers of indoctrination and so of what indoctrination is. Indoctrination is variously defined by criteria of content, method, aim and consequence. A more recent definition suggests that indoctrination is defined by the assumption of foregone conclusions in what is taught.

With knowledge of the way in which ME takes place in RE, and understanding of what it ought to be, and an understanding of the type of teaching to avoid, an RE teacher only needs practical skills to become a fully fledged moral educator through RE. Such skills involve understanding the way ME works in the school as a whole, the ability to be sensitive, a clear idea of how to set tasks which will actually contribute to moral development and a knowledge of how to evaluate them meaningfully.

This is all easily written down on paper, but it is a very tall order in practice. The RE classroom is no Eden. So perhaps it would be appropriate to end on a biblical note: 'Train a child in the way he should go: and when he is old he will not depart from it' (Proverbs 22:6). 'Come unto me, all ye that labour and are heavy laden, and I will give you rest' (Matthew 11:28). 'Let the reader understand' (Mark 13:14).

FURTHER READING

Hirst, P. (1974) *Knowledge and The Curriculum*, London: Routledge. A collection of essays which outline the educational philosophy underpinning the kind of RE developed in the early 1970s and still prevalent in many schools. Essays three, four, six, nine, eleven and twelve are of particular interest for those seeking to understand the logic behind multifaith RE.

Hull, J.M. (1998) *Utopian Whispers*, Derby: CEM. John Hull has been a leading figure in advocating the importance of the moral dimension of RE teaching, especially in terms of nurturing tolerance in a plural society, in his opposition to 'religionism' and in his critique of the spirituality of a materialist 'money culture'. This collection is a challenging and illuminating summary of the work of one of the most influential religious educators in recent years.

Scruton, R. (1985) *Education and Indoctrination*, London: ERC. A lively and thought-provoking booklet. It offers a new and useful definition of indoctrination, aimed at curbing the dangerous excesses of anti-racist and anti-sexist educational programmes and putting in their place courses which further the pursuit of truth.

Snook, I.A. (1972) *Concepts of Indoctrination: Philosophical Essays*, London: Routledge. A comprehensive collection of essays concerning the nature of indoctrination from the debates of the 1960s and 1970s. The conclusions drawn within them continue to define the term. Of interest to those who wish to understand in greater detail the way in which the various uses of the term have developed.

Snook, I.A. (1972) *Indoctrination and Education*, London: Routledge. An easy way into the indoctrination debate as it affects modern schooling in Britain. Of interest to those who wish to get a broad overview of the indoctrination debate in minimal time.

Thiessen, E.J. (1993) *Teaching for Commitment: Liberal Education, Indoctrination and Christian Nurture*, Leominster: Gracewing. An elegant defence of Christian confessional religious education against the charge of indoctrination, challenging many hard-held liberal assumptions.

Part V

Supporting professional development

13 Resources for Religious Education

Joanne Reed

This chapter examines the types of resources that are available in RE which you will need to familiarise yourself with. It gives advice on how to use those resources, how to look after them and what to avoid. By no means is it a definitive list – my experience teaches that classroom resources present themselves in the most surprising ways – but the main areas of books, videos, worksheets and artefacts are covered. Acquiring resources is often one area most likely to instil immediate panic in any teacher. Cost, availability and time are usually in short supply and the stress of preparation for a new term can be immense. Be advised that whilst variety is the spice of life, and varied resources should certainly enhance any learning experience, in the first instance you will be able to get by with relatively little. Building a good collection of resources takes time. Don't be too hard on yourself, give yourself that time and be organised.

OBJECTIVES

By the end of this chapter you should:

- understand the ways in which resources can be used to differentiate and enrich the learning experience;
- know how to acquire resources, both by making and purchasing;
- have a sound knowledge of the wide variety of resources that are available.

PLANNING FOR THE FIRST TIME

I once heard a colleague comment that the best resource teachers have is themselves. Your knowledge, your experience of life, your ability to be enthusiastic about any, if not all, subjects on the RE syllabus – these are the attributes that will get you through the lessons when more concrete resources are simply not available. Sometimes the resources are there but it's Period Six on a Friday afternoon and you know there's no way that your disaffected bottom set Year 11 class will use a worksheet except as basketball practice or for making paper aeroplanes. In such circumstances you instinctively turn towards yourself, to initiate class discussion, to talk about the subject or to ask them the right questions. And, in the right circumstances, it can work beautifully. Many teachers will report that some of their best lessons were on the hoof, relying on little more than a wing and a prayer.

However, such behaviour shouldn't really be considered an ideal substitute for planning, which necessarily involves taking stock of what resources are available. All too often they amount to precious little. Walking into a department that has sixty copies of a book outlining the life of Corrie Ten Boom and a video cassette of Zeffirelli's *Jesus of Nazareth* is every newly qualified teacher's (NQT's) nightmare. Worse still if the head of department has no ambition to improve the situation. Of course, there may not be a head of department. You may have already had the misfortune to discover that such departments do exist. At this point recognise that it's all down to you. Kiss goodbye to your social life and blow the dust off your PC. If you don't own a computer use the school's, and if you're not computer-literate then be friendly to the person in charge of information technology (IT). You will almost certainly need their co-operation at some point. If there is no computer available anywhere (unlikely and unfortunate) and no money to purchase textbooks I think I'd resign, unless I had already been briefed about the situation before accepting the position. In which case I'd make an appointment to get my head examined.

PRODUCING AND USING WORKSHEETS

Once you've worked out the scheme of work for the next few weeks and you've sussed out what exists in the department you can start to plan your lessons and worksheets. If you have decent textbooks (more on that later) you may find they contain useful tasks for pupils to do. However, if the tasks are of the 'see what you can find out about the life of a Jewish rabbi' variety and there is no information whatsoever in the book to enable the pupils to complete the task, then think again. Producing a worksheet with good customised questions or tasks for the type of pupils you're charged with teaching is your mission and it can be a highly productive and satisfying experience. You will need to do some homework, though, on what will be appropriate, particularly if you have pupils with special educational needs (SEN). Do find the time to talk to an SEN or classroom assistant and find out what the pupils can cope with. It may be that they are still learning to read and write. In such a case, a task which requires them to copy out a sentence (or five) and fill in the missing word chosen from a selection in a box may be the most suitable.

Teaching a mixed-ability class does not mean you have to produce three different worksheets for each level of ability. You can develop differentiated tasks on the same sheet. If the first task is kept simple you may find the more able pupils completing it before the less able have even written the title. However, that is not necessarily wrong. You simply ensure that the following tasks are pitched at a level that will develop the pupils' knowledge and understanding.

You can also differentiate by outcome. RE is a subject that lends itself to this in a way that few other subjects can. If you ask a pupil to describe how she would respond to being let down, or what is her perception of God or heaven, you encourage both creativity and opinion to develop. 'How do you think the leper felt once he had been healed?' or 'How do you think a Muslim child feels during Ramadan?' are questions that should elicit a response from every pupil. Allowing pupils to develop their imagination is a vital part of the religious education process. By provoking them to consider situations that they might not ordinarily experience, or indeed have difficulty in dealing with, you are providing them with the opportunity to think carefully about the impact that religion can have upon the choices that people make daily.

If you do have the time to produce varied worksheets for a mixed-ability class do ensure that you are sensitive to the feelings of the less able (or even the more able) when handing out the work. This is probably an occasion when you personally give worksheets to pupils, rather than allowing or asking a pupil to do so. Some pupils will pick up very quickly on the stigma of having to do easier work because they are deemed incapable of doing the same work as their peers. To be called 'boffin' or 'swot' can, of course, be just as distressing for the very able.

Try to avoid producing a worksheet comprising only text, or at least vary the look by putting boxes around the question or using subtitles in bold. If you can find a suitable illustration to break up the text, paste it in. If there's nothing suitable, have a go at drawing your own, or ask someone. Art teachers are good people to know. A simple cartoon or picture will make a difference to the way the worksheet is received. Pupils are often put off even attempting to start work if all they see is words. Try to make the worksheet look attractive but be wary of using a typeface that is too 'fancy'. Stick to something simple like Times New Roman.

Task 13.1 Analysing and evaluating worksheets

Acquire a selection of worksheets from your department, preferably from across Key Stages 3–5. With each worksheet consider and discuss the following points:

- Is the text easy to read?
- Are there any questions or tasks for pupils to do?
- Is the layout of the sheet interesting? Are there any graphics or illustrations to stimulate interest?
- How long do you think it would take to work through the entire sheet? Consider the differing ability of pupils when discussing this.
- How could the sheet be improved?
- What state are the worksheets in? Look for signs of wear and tear.

Most departments will already possess worksheets of some description. They are a useful aid to employ in RE but they vary widely in their standard. In theory, they should not be used too often. In practice, how often they are used depends on a range of other factors: the type of school and range of pupil ability, existing resources, the number of lessons per week for each class and the teacher's preferred style of teaching. It is clear, though, that an established pattern of handing out worksheets every lesson for pupils to complete generates a predictability factor to RE which could have a demotivating effect upon pupils.

Conversely, however, a folder full of worksheets containing all the necessary information and tasks required to complete a course, say at Key Stage 4, has the advantage of security for both teacher and pupils. If everything that needs to be learnt can be located in one place, then problems that arise because of absences are minimised. Very few textbooks meet all syllabus requirements, in terms of providing either relevant information or suitable tasks. More often than not, a teacher will use several books as preparation for lesson planning at GCSE level, whether it be the short course or full course.

I strongly advise that worksheets are placed in an A4 clear plastic wallet before handing them out to the pupils. This ensures that the life span of your worksheet extends beyond a thirty-minute lesson. Pupils receive something which looks good, they are less inclined to screw the paper up or graffiti it, and you should be able to use the worksheet time and time again, subject to the behaviour of the more psychotic element you may have the pleasure of educating. Admittedly, such wallets are not cheap, but when the alternative may well be constant reprinting or photocopying of existing worksheets, which in itself may become expensive, consider it as an investment. It also preserves your sanity; collecting back in thirty pieces of paper that are torn, crumpled and inkstained will do nothing for your general well-being.

If you plan to deliver a scheme of work using worksheets as a foundation for each or many of the lessons – one would hope with additional activity-based sessions built in – consider carefully purchasing a cardboard or ring-binder folder for each person in the class. Assuming there is cupboard or shelf space somewhere in your classroom, you then have the advantage that the work is easily accessible for pupils to pick up as they come in. Alternatively, you may prefer to place them on the desk before pupils enter the room. You need to be extremely organised to ensure there is time to do this, but especially if there is no break in between lessons. However, pupils from the preceding class can be persuaded to help, and the effect of having work already on the desk with instructions either written on the board or uttered verbally as pupils walk in should be significant. Pupils get the message that they are expected to work; they are given less opportunity to mess around, and the result should be that more learning takes place.

As you begin to build up your own stock of self-generated worksheets you will find that the use of a word-processor will become indispensable. It may seem an obvious thing to say, but a worksheet stored in electronic form can easily be adapted and revised, to meet changing circumstances or in response to its previous use in the classroom. Hand-written worksheets are really not acceptable, and are banned in many schools. Typed worksheets are, inevitably, 'one-off' affairs that do not allow for continuity and development in your teaching.

Figure 13.1 The question of copyright

> In producing worksheets, using the photocopier, and recording and playing back videos, it is absolutely vital to be aware of, and stay within the bounds of, copyright law. Clear guidance is readily available from your college and your schools, and should be displayed prominently next to the photocopier.

VIDEOS AND AUDIO-VISUAL RESOURCES

Videos in RE are an excellent resource for giving information, generating ideas and helping pupils understand more fully. A well made programme or film can convey a spiritual concept with more depth and far greater ease than a textbook. A few words of caution, though. Always watch the programme *before* the pupils. This may sound obvious but there may be nudity or swearing, even in a documentary, that simply would not be appropriate at Key Stage 3. You really don't want to find yourself racing for the pause or stop button mid-lesson, and then apologising to parents after little Johnny has gone home and relayed the afternoon's events to his family.

Furthermore, some pupils will find it difficult to concentrate for longer than twenty minutes at a time. If a video is longer than that, do plan a break in the proceedings every so often, either to question their perceptions or to follow through a particular line of thought that may have been raised. Using this technique sustains their interest and ensures that they engage with the video. Alternatively you can give out questions for the pupils to make notes on as they watch, and then stop after ten minutes or so to check that everyone is concentrating and to reinforce lesson content. Pupils should be encouraged to take notes at as early a stage as possible, preferably in Year 7. A video exercise can be a good place to start. Do make sure you know where television equipment needs to be returned to, and how it works, before the lesson begins.

It is important to make the link at some point in the lesson between the content of the video and RE. There is something wrong if pupils are unable to discern the educational value of a programme or film, even if they enjoyed watching it. If a pupil asks, 'What's this got to do with RE?' then, assuming the question is a genuine one and not a time-delaying tactic, take the time to explain. Pupils should be expected to develop a sound understanding of religious concepts. Unless such expectations are made clear from the start there is a high chance that they will leave the classroom entertained but not necessarily enlightened. As professionals we need to be able to gauge with some degree of certainty what progress has been made by the end of the lesson. If pupils are no further forward as regards their knowledge and understanding then we should be able to evaluate what went wrong or consider other ways of delivery and forms of lesson structure.

Videos can be accessed from a range of sources. They can be commercially purchased, hired from High Street shops and specialist suppliers, taped from television transmissions, loaned and/or hired from RE specialist suppliers and RE resource centres, and can even be home-made by your pupils. Your local or regional resource centre should be able to provide you with details of commercially produced videos intended specifically for the RE classroom. When taping or showing a video it is important to follow the advice on copyright in Figure 13.1.

TEXTBOOKS

Textbooks can and should be an excellent resource but quite often they do not provide everything that you want them to do. A textbook may lack vital content or be written in an inappropriately simplistic fashion. It may be too wordy in its look and lack any interesting graphic presentation. If you're trying to follow a locally Agreed Syllabus which specifies that you must cover Ramadan, and the seemingly perfect book you'd considered purchasing fails to mention this Muslim time of submission, what do you do? Well, if you've got any money at all – and presumably there's some if you're even thinking of buying textbooks – how about investing in a range of books on the same subject? Don't restrict yourself to the notion of one textbook per pupil. Granted, there's a lot to be said for giving a pupil a book to read and use, and in this age of increasing technology many pupils, sadly, use books less and less. One book is almost certainly better than no books at all.

There is a different model of learning, however, which forces pupils to engage with the text by ensuring that they have to develop their research skills. If you give a pupil one book you automatically limit the level of answer you can reasonably expect them to produce. If you give a pupil several books, though, you can encourage and expect them to read around the subject in rather more depth.

This system can be organised in a number of ways but one which I have seen work especially well made use of fifteen to twenty different books on one subject, say Islam or Judaism. In this particular department a total of 120 books (roughly) were purchased. The books were then divided into six boxes, one box for each table or group of about five or six pupils. Thus each group used about fifteen to twenty books to research from. Those that were very wordy in content and more suitable for A Level or GCSE students were few in number. Maybe one or two such books were found in each box. The books which were more accessible for the Key Stage using them were, logically, greater in number. Each group comprised pupils of mixed ability and the pupils were encouraged to share information between themselves. The tasks set were quite adventurous for the Key Stage but questions and guidelines were provided for each element. Consequently, although pupils may have been expected to research and write about the Holocaust, they were provided with easily manageable short tasks. For example, what was it that Jewish people had to wear on their arm? Where did the trains take them?

It will take a while to set up a system like this – quite possibly a number of years – and it is not the cheapest system. One also has to invest a fair amount of time in finding a range of books to cater for all abilities in the Key Stage as well as structuring quite carefully the sort of tasks to be set. The storage of such resources can be a problem also. However, in terms of learning and developing Key Skills it is an ideal practice which should yield many benefits. Also, in the long run you will spend less money and time on photocopying.

There are a number of excellent books designed for use at Key Stage 4, particularly for those following a GCSE short course syllabus. This is explored more fully in Chapter 8. There has been criticism that no one book presents the complete syllabus in sufficient depth or that certain main faith traditions are lacking adequate content. However, buying two or three different books should ensure that you are equipped with all the necessary knowledge and content. How you then convey that knowledge is up to you.

The decision on whether to purchase a complete set of one textbook or create a resource package consisting of a range of texts is an important one. It will inevitably influence your teaching style and the nature of the learning in the classroom. A single set of one particular text will link in well with teacher-focused and directed approaches to learning, while a range of different texts will complement a more pupil-centred research-orientated pedagogy.

ARTEFACTS

You should, of course, supplement the textbooks with the use of relevant artefacts. There are companies which specialise in producing artefacts for educational purposes, sometimes at quite low prices. However, you can also pick up artefacts for a few pence if you know what to look for. Charity shops are a very useful source of all sorts of bits and pieces: candles, rosary beads, prayer books, tiny communion glasses, a pottery chalice, a water stoup, a lapel badge of a dove – these have all been seen in a local High Street charity shop from time to time. It's worth popping in occasionally to see what's available. Admittedly these are all Christian artefacts but maybe a second-hand shop in an area renowned for members of a different faith community would result in similar benefits. You can also learn to improvise: a wooden rattle once bought from Alton Towers could easily represent a Jewish gregger used during Purim.

If your department has some money to invest in buying artefacts think carefully about the content to be covered in the scheme of work before ordering. Prices vary widely. You could pay anything from £2 to £24 for a Seder plate. There are a range of suppliers of religious artefacts, and Figure 13.2 offers recommendations and contact details. Expect to pay around £6 for a *kippah* and around £14 for menorah. Don't confuse the latter with a *hanukiah* used at Hanukkah. Videos tend to be quite expensive (£20+), as are the Torah scrolls complete with velvet mantle – not much change from £30. Whatever you finally purchase, don't order in a hurry and be aware that smaller versions are obviously much cheaper. It may be cheaper still to approach a place of worship explaining your needs.

There is no question that the use of artefacts, whether displayed around the room or given directly to the pupils for examination, brings a religion more pertinence in the mind of a pupil. Not only will pupils remember the purpose of the artefact more clearly if they have actually handled it, their understanding and interest are likely to be much greater. Artefacts allow pupils to be more actively involved in the lesson and are particularly important in deepening awareness and understanding of religious symbolism, a skill that locally Agreed Syllabuses are including more and more. Pupils

Figure 13.2 Recommended artefact suppliers

Artefacts to Order
Telephone: 01945 587452.

Articles of Faith
Resource House, Kay Street, Bury, Lancashire BL9 6BU.
Telephone: 0161 763 6232.

Religion in Evidence
Unit 7, Monk Road, Alfreton, Derbyshire DE55 7RL.
Telephone: 01773 830 255.

should have a clear understanding of the artefact's importance to worshippers from a particular faith tradition. If the pupil is not able to understand more fully the beliefs of a Hindu or Muslim as a result of the lesson then something somewhere is wrong.

It can be more beneficial not to bombard pupils with facts about an artefact but instead encourage them to figure out the purpose and use of an object by themselves. Problem solving is an excellent method of arousing interest and stimulating the imagination, and it should provide an element of fun. If you are fortunate enough to have a number of artefacts from the same religion you could split the class into small groups and ask each group to deduce the use and symbolism of one artefact and report back with its conclusions. A scallop shell used during a baptism service or an Advent candle should instigate some thought-provoking discussion points. Teachers should, of course, use their professional judgement in deciding whether to provide stimulus clues. The artefacts could be placed on different tables around the room and pupils could circulate in groups, spending five minutes at each table, before reaching a decision. This exercise could be set towards the end of a scheme of work when pupils have sufficient knowledge to arrive at a considered answer. Alternatively, used at the beginning of a scheme, the right artefacts could generate enthusiasm for the topic to be studied.

Some artefacts are very easy to acquire. Greeting cards sent at Easter and Christmas, for example, or Muslim Eid cards can be used as a stimulus to display work. I once saw pupils design a Muslim prayer mat, and it was interesting to see them carefully observe the rules of Islamic art – a much easier task once they'd had the advantage of perusing a variety of Eid cards. A colleague of mine often makes plaited bread for her classes when they're studying Shabbat.

Of course, sensitivity should always be the rule when explaining the use of artefacts, particularly if there are pupils from the faith tradition being studied in the class or even in the school. One doesn't want a case of bullying to develop because of misconception or thoughtlessness, nor does one want to offend. This can be a difficult area, subject to much debate. I know some teachers who would always place their copy of the Qur'an on the top shelf of a bookcase in accordance with Muslim practice and others who would disagree strongly with such behaviour. It may be appropriate to ask pupils to consider the extent to which respect should be shown to other religions in the way that artefacts are used. Bear in mind, though, that with some classes this would be a non-starter.

Take care also that artefacts are not abused. Make sure that you know all there is to know about any particular objects, and the possible dangers. Some schools actually superglue a kirpan dagger into its sheath to avoid any possibility of an incident. You should be in a position to emphasise that a Sikh would never withdraw the knife unless he intended to use it on someone. The department should obviously have a lockable cupboard for artefacts. A wise investment would be to replace the cupboard with a secure display cabinet. This allows artefacts to be viewed constantly by your pupils and helps enhance the learning environment.

SCHOOL TRIPS

Taking pupils out of school to visit a place of interest should be both enjoyable and educational. There will be a minefield of organisation to contemplate and work through, and some teachers would consider the whole procedure not worth the bother. However, if you think the destination will fulfil the criteria, then go for it. RE departments, like other oft-overlooked subjects in the school, need to be aware of raising their profile and a visit is one such way.

Many places of worship welcome school parties, but not all will actually be wise to what will be entertaining and useful to your pupils. If pupils are liable to be bored rigid, why spend precious time and money on something they won't enjoy? Do take the time to find out what the place is like and what programme is on offer. A day trip to Bhaktevedanta Manor in Watford, for example, might include a visit to the cow sanctuary, a vegetarian lunch and a performance of Ramayana. A visit to a locked church, listening to the local curate, could be tedious by comparison unless you have organised specific tasks and built more activities into the trip. If you don't have time to visit a place beforehand, then find out from someone who has taken a school party there what to expect. You may decide to rejig the programme on offer, by careful negotiation with the education officer/co-ordinator. Cathedrals sometimes have someone appointed to deal with school visits. Ask what options are available. They may be happy for you to let the pupils loose for an hour or so whilst they research the various aspects of the building. On the other hand, they may not. Make sure you are satisfied with the potential educational value of the visit.

Do ask if there's anything they expect of you and the pupils. A visit to a mosque will require adjustment of clothing. There may be services scheduled to take place at which the presence of thirty Year 8 boys and girls might not be entirely welcome. Check also the safety aspect. Is there good parking? Will you have to walk across a busy town centre? Are there any areas that should be out of bounds because pupils could fall or push each other? Be wise to the pitfalls. Your school will have a policy for school trips, which refers especially to the safety aspects of any out-of-school activity. It is vital to be familiar with it and follow its guidance to the letter.

You will have to send letters home, organise a coach or minibus and driver, collect payment for costs, work out arrival times, sort out the cover for lessons you won't be able to teach and gather additional staff to accompany you. It will be hard work, but it will be worth it.

If you are new to an area and want to find out what is available there are a number of people to ask: the local RE adviser for the county or borough, the heads of RE departments in other schools near by, or the nearest RE resource centre should be able to give you some indication of useful places to visit.

SUMMARY AND KEY POINTS

You should not feel daunted by the task that lies ahead, although most teachers experience more than a little apprehension. The beauty of teaching RE is that so often one is teaching about life, and as such there should never be a shortage of material and resources to draw from. One hopes to facilitate a stimulating educational experience for pupils who may wish to be anywhere but your classroom. Their apathy aside, you can only try and learn from what works and what doesn't. No one expects you to get it perfect first time, and what works in some situations may well fall flat in others. Be patient and keep trying.

FURTHER READING

Gateshill, P. and Thompson, J. (1992) *Religious Artefacts in the Classroom*, London: Hodder & Stoughton. A practical guide for primary and secondary teachers of RE. It lists the main artefacts for each of the six major traditions usually taught in Britain and provides many ideas for you to store away in the back of your mind.

14 Information and Communications Technology

Andrew Clutterbuck

There is a whole range of information and communications technology (ICT). You are likely to be familiar with the more traditional ones (e.g. radio, television, video), and have probably experienced them as part of your own education. This chapter is concerned solely with computer-related ICT. The computer, by virtue of its multi-functional capacities, stands apart from these others. It can be used for writing, reading, viewing, listening, drawing, speaking, thinking, searching and modelling. It is both an educational resource: a provider of information and understanding, and a tool for education: supporting the learning process by promoting thinking, reflection and the organisation of information. Its usefulness in the school curriculum extends to all subjects, including RE, and to all teachers, including the teacher of RE.

The potential of the computer in education is not, however, a quality of the machine *per se*; it is dependent on the presence and skills of the teacher to manage the learning situation, the processes involved and the learning resulting from its use (BECTa 1998a, p. 56). Research shows that, where pupils are left on their own with ICT, their learning potential drops away steeply. This chapter provides practical guidance to support your use of ICT in RE both in the classroom and in your other professional activities.

ICT AND EDUCATION

The world in which we live, teach and learn

Several observers have noted that education in general seems to have been remarkably unaffected by ICT (Dutton 1996, p. 249; Hicks 1998). In itself this need not be a major cause of concern, but such 'immunity' from ICT seems to be at the expense of the benefits ICT is perceived to bring to teaching and learning and to the other professional activities of teachers.

OBJECTIVES

By the end of this chapter you should:

- be aware of the standards expected of newly qualified teachers (NQTs) in ICT;
- have an understanding of the potential of ICT in education and RE;
- have a working knowledge of the ICT available to the RE teacher and the language used to articulate ICT issues;
- begin to understand how current and future ICT can be integrated effectively into your teaching and other professional activities;
- be aware of the opportunities to develop your understanding of ICT and of how ICT can contribute to your professional development in both ICT and RE.

Task 14.1 The generic benefits of ICT

Many benefits are listed for computer-related ICT. Discuss what may be meant by the following benefits. Consider the legitimacy of the claims and their value to the RE teacher.
   ICT is of value in the RE classroom because it:

- is interesting and enjoyable for pupils;
- improves pupils' motivation and the desire to learn;
- is patient and responsive;
- raises the status of the subject;
- is pupil-centred;
- supports open, independent and flexible learning;
- supports discussion, collaboration and sharing;
- is emotionally neutral, blind to gender, race, age and disability;
- promotes deeper understanding;
- improves pupils' presentation and pride in their work;
- improves pupils' creativity;
- encourages pupils to experiment and try things out.

There is a growing sense of a divide between education and the world which our pupils inhabit outside school. Surveys show that some 50 per cent of all primary school children have a computer at home (Straker and Govier 1996, p. 2), and that the figure is set to increase dramatically over the next few years (Stevenson 1997,

p. 9). What this suggests is that our pupils are becoming increasingly familiar with the uses of ICT and the ways in which it can be used to support their everyday activities, including learning. As skills develop and disperse throughout the pupil population it is likely that demands will be made in the school context for these different ways of teaching and learning to be acknowledged. Pupils are already beginning to bring into the RE classroom information on religion they have retrieved from the World Wide Web and to produce word-processed assignments. They may also begin actively to question whether there are alternative, better, ways of researching, producing and presenting their learning than through the traditional methods of teacher talk, textbook and exercise book (Gayeski 1996, p. 442). The responsibility of the RE teacher in this situation is twofold. First, to educate pupils in the use of ICT to maximise their learning potential and, second, to integrate ICT effectively in the teaching and learning of RE.

Competence in ICT will become increasingly necessary as a prerequisite of employment and access to continuing education. Pupils need to be prepared for the world outside school, and in this, RE, like every other subject on the school curriculum, has a responsibility for developing pupils' skills and abilities.

Your teacher education, ICT and you

The Department for Education and Employment (DfEE) makes clear the importance it attaches to ICT in education across all subjects, including RE, when it states that providers of initial teacher education (ITE) must:

> ensure that only those trainees who have shown that they have the knowledge, understanding and skills to use ICT effectively in teaching subject(s) are judged to have successfully completed an ITT course leading to Qualified Teacher Status.
>
> (DfEE 1998b, p. 1)

The same document acknowledges that student teachers enter ITE with a variety of experience in ICT and describes their experience in two senses. Understanding both in terms of levels of competence and levels of confidence, it distinguishes between your personal level and your level in securing pupils' learning within the phase and in the subject(s) you are training to teach (DfEE 1998b, p. 1). What is evident here is that, while the former is a prerequisite of the latter, personal competence and confidence do not readily translate into effective classroom practice. You need, therefore, to gain understanding and experience of both on your teacher education course. Furthermore, your understanding and experience in the use of ICT should be 'firmly rooted within the relevant subject and phase' rather than 'generically or as an end in itself' (DfEE 1998b, p. 1).

Your institution of higher education (IHE) should audit your knowledge, understanding and skills in ICT and, where gaps are identified, make arrangements to ensure you gain the relevant experience during your course such that, on completion, you are competent using ICT within the relevant phase and subject(s) (DfEE 1998b, p. 1). A basis for the audit is given in the DfEE document (pp.9–18), and this can be usefully read in conjunction with the guidance provided in the leaflet *Training Tomorrow's Teachers in Information Technology* (NCET 1998). The audit and any gaps which are identified will serve you well in terms of objectives to be met during your course and will assist you in the construction of your Teacher Training Agency (TTA) *Career Entry Profile*.

These DfEE requirements may appear to be an added burden if you perceive your essential concern as getting to grips with the practicalities of curriculum design, new subject content and classroom management. But the message is not that ICT is an 'added extra'; rather ICT should be an integral consideration for you in all aspects of teaching, learning and management. As you will be among the first entrants to the teaching profession under these DfEE requirements, it is likely that understanding and experience of ICT in the classroom will figure at interview for a teaching post. Indeed, given the current impetus behind ICT in schools, you may even be asked to take on a developmental role in ICT in the school.

Where education's at

The fulfilment of the DfEE requirements is the responsibility of your IHE, working in partnership with your school experience placement(s). Your school placement(s) should provide opportunities for the planned use of ICT in the classroom, and for the assessment of progression and differentiation in pupils' use of ICT. The DfEE documents reflecting the current levels of ICT provision in schools do not, however, specify that ICT competence must be demonstrated in your school experience. It is clearly intended, though, that where ICT facilities exist they should be an integral part of your teaching and learning considerations and, if appropriate, used. Not only will you encounter variable levels of ICT provision in schools, but it is also likely that you will encounter a range of knowledge, attitudes, skills and experience among staff regarding ICT. If, however, predictions and policies hold true, ICT in schools seems set to change and develop, and to do so fairly rapidly. Targets set by government include each Local Education Authority (LEA) preparing development plans for ICT, training in ICT for in-service teachers, the provision of e-mail addresses for pupils and teachers, and the establishing of a National Grid for Learning (NGfL) to make resources accessible to all schools, colleges and universities (DfEE 1997). This chapter is set in the context of change and transformation of ICT in our schools. Some of what follows may not be immediately realisable in your school experience, but you need to be aware of it and, if your IHE offers better ICT facilities, to explore and develop your ICT skills, competences and teaching potential in this context. The following discussion outlines situations likely to become progressively realistic for later entrants to ITE and for your subsequent professional teaching career.

The scope for ICT in RE

We need now to turn our attention to the extent to which RE is expected to integrate ICT and the scope for such integration. With the exception of Physical

Education, all National Curriculum subject orders have a generic sentence stating that 'Pupils should be given the opportunities, where appropriate, to develop and apply their IT capability in their study of *x*.' The RE curriculum, by contrast, is formulated under locally Agreed Syllabuses and, although some may mention ICT, or refer simply to information technology (IT), there is clearly no national or uniform requirement (BECTa 1998b; Stern 1998, p. 8). The non-statutory Model Syllabuses for RE limit their mention of IT to those situations in which pupils have special needs of a particular sort (e.g. aural, visual, motor-skill) (SCAA 1994a, p. 8, 1994b, p. 7). This lack of an explicit requirement in RE-centred legislation and guidance regarding ICT should, however, be seen in the context both of the ICT requirements stipulated for the education of teachers and of the Dearing Report, which stated that all subjects should contribute to the development of IT ability (Dearing 1994). Likewise, OFSTED inspectors are concerned with IT as a Key Skill throughout the curriculum (OFSTED 1995a, p. 117, 1996, pp. 10 f.).

Evidence suggests that RE take-up of ICT has been very slow and patchy. While there may be a variety of reasons for this state of affairs you should be aware that there is nothing inherent in ICT which constitutes a fundamental obstacle to its educational use in RE. Neither information nor communication are newcomers to RE: both have an essential presence in every good teaching and learning situation. *Information* of some sort or other is a necessary basis for understanding, evaluating or criticising the world, including the religious world, in which we find ourselves. *Communication*, again in various forms, describes the process of dialogue between teacher, pupils and sometimes a wider audience, for the purposes of sharing, enhancing and expressing understanding. It is the *technology* component that is comparatively new, yet this, it must be stressed, is not an end in itself but a means by which support is provided for the 'information' and 'communication' aspects of learning and teaching. While there are certainly moral, ethical and social issues concerning ICT which need to be discussed (see Stern 1998, p. 30), there is no reason why RE alone should be concerned with these aspects of ICT or why they should be RE's only concern with ICT.

Task 14.2 Prospects for ICT's impact on RE

Discuss why you think Humanities subjects in general, and RE in particular, have been slow to integrate ICT into their teaching and learning.

Look at the RE skills and attitudes listed in, for example, the Model Syllabuses for Religious Education (SCAA 1994a, pp. 7–8, 1994b, pp. 6–7) or Blaylock and Johnson (1988, p. 33). Consider which you feel ICT is capable of supporting and developing in RE. You might revisit this task later in your course, when your experience of RE and ICT has developed, to see if your assessment has changed.

Given this lack of detail on how, when and where ICT may be integrated into RE, and the ongoing development of ICT provision in schools, effective integration is to some extent down to your imagination and willingness to engage in (calculated) risk. The rest of this chapter is an invitation to consider ICT's practical potential for your professional activities.

PRACTICAL CONSIDERATIONS

Experience, policy and access

Your school should have an ICT policy in force and it is worth while asking your school-based tutor what its implications are for RE and for your teaching. The school's policy may, for example, plan for pupils' ICT skills to be developed or con-solidated in other areas of the curriculum, including, possibly, RE. There may be schemes of work relating to ICT and to its assessment in RE, and these will be nec-essary for your planning and preparation.

You should also ascertain the way in which the school's ICT policy has affected the location of computers: a dedicated suite (the 'computer room'), dispersal throughout the school's classrooms, or a mixed mode, with a dedicated suite and some dispersal. Each has advantages and disadvantages for you and your pupils (Taylor 1996, p.229). The first, for example, means that, although an entire class can be accommodated, it is necessary to book the room at a time convenient for your teaching. The second allows more immediate access but is likely to allow only a small number of pupils to work at any one time. Whatever the case, you need to be sure that you are aware of how and when access is available to you.

Meeting the school's ICT co-ordinator is also a good idea, and the ICT technician, if the school has one. These people, along with your school-based tutor, can not only help you in your planning and preparation, and possibly support your use of ICT, but they can advise you on the software available, the access pupils have to computers (e.g. scheduled lessons, open access, after school, lunchtimes, homework clubs, libraries, cyber cafés, home provision) and the pupils' levels of use, confidence and competence with ICT. It goes without saying that using ICT resources with which pupils are already familiar is easier than having to teach new applications and packages in addition to RE.

> **Task 14.3 Carrying out an ICT audit**
>
> Using this section and the ones following, construct audit forms which you can use to audit ICT in your IHE and in your school experience placement(s). (See Bell and Biott 1996, for suggestions as to the gen-eral dimensions of ICT opportunities in school placements.) These audits should enable you to identify opportunities to gain and consol-idate your experience and progressively fill any gaps identified in your personal audit carried out by your IHE.

Planning and monitoring the use of ICT

As a student teacher of RE your primary concern is with the teaching of RE. The teaching and learning outcomes for RE are your primary planning considerations. However, an integral part of the next stage of this planning process should also be an assessment of whether ICT is capable of *effectively enhancing the quality of teaching and learning*. Unless it fulfils this criterion it should not be used. This assessment demands of you an awareness of what ICT is able to offer and of the ICT that is available to you and your pupils. Including ICT at any cost, either as the primary basis of your planning, or as a final consideration in the planning cycle, has two possible outcomes: the 'bolt-on' ICT experience or the distortion of RE to suit the capacity of ICT.

Where ICT is considered to be capable of enhancing the quality of teaching and learning its proper integration into RE has begun: it is there because it has a worthwhile contribution to make. Your next steps are in the active management and mediation of the role of ICT in the classroom context. Using whiteboard, television, video and overhead projector is reasonably straightforward because we have probably seen them used in our own education and because pupils are familiar with their use in the classroom. ICT presents new challenges. There are, however, constructive steps you can take in order to maximise success: Figure 14.1 gives details.

Figure 14.1 Some suggestions for the successful use of ICT

You should ensure that you:

- are familiar with the ICT resource that your pupils will be using;
- have, if possible, given consideration to the positioning of ICT devices (is there enough room for pupils to take notes, does the layout promote pupil discussion and collaboration?);
- have written down, for pupil use, clear instructions on the operation of the ICT resource;
- have provided pupils with clear details on what the purposes and processes of the ICT activity are and that these are achievable within the time available;
- have an alternative plan should the ICT resource fail or the activity not meet its objectives;
- feel confident, competent and comfortable using ICT with a particular group of pupils.

You might consider:

- working with a smaller group of pupils (you could negotiate this with your school-based tutor);
- asking another teacher, possibly the ICT co-ordinator or an RE teacher, to be present to assist you;
- preparing the ground for ICT in your lessons by asking pupils to complete some ICT-related work outside class time (resources permitting);

Figure 14.1 Continued

- observing teachers, even from other subject areas, in their use of ICT in the classroom;
- awaiting an opportunity to introduce ICT as an incidental part of a lesson for a small group of pupils;
- arranging pupil groups in such a way as to maintain on-task activity (e.g. mix boys with girls, ICT/RE ability levels, friendship groups);
- using ICT with which pupils are very familiar or which is simple and efficient in its operation.

In the context of your pupils' use of ICT there are a number of things you can consider monitoring. Several writers point to ICT bringing about a transformation in the teacher's role, in the relationship between teacher and pupil and in the learning process (Donnelly 1996, p. 89; Harrison 1998; Scrimshaw 1996; Smart 1996, p. ix; Stevenson 1997, p. 12; Straker and Govier 1996, p. 228). It would be worth while considering the nature and extent of any changes which occur during your pupils' use of ICT in RE. For example, you may observe or record the discussions pupils have, ask them to evaluate what they have achieved, whether they would do things differently next time or whether they could jot down some helpful notes for the next group or class. For the moment, it is worth being aware that when using ICT pupils will need you for help and guidance but may wish to retain control of their use of ICT. Considering carefully when and how you intervene also recognises that your pupils may be getting used to a different way of working – a learning experience which may be equally unfamiliar to you.

You should monitor uptake and use to ensure that one gender group is not at a disadvantage and that ICT-competent pupils, whatever their gender, do not exclude others. These are real issues which need action on your part in order to ensure equality of access and opportunity.

Content-free (generic) applications

Content-free applications provide a framework to support an activity but are dependent upon you to supply the information essential to their working. As they are 'content-free', their uses are not restricted to any area of the curriculum, although some may prove more useful in one area than another. They include the following:

- word-processing packages;
- graphics and drawing packages;
- spreadsheet packages;
- database packages.

You are likely to be familiar with some or all of these applications. The more sophisticated packages bring many of these applications together, or allow them to be linked. However they are organised, their utility both to you and to your pupils should not be underestimated. Such packages alone provide a successful basis on which to begin to integrate ICT into RE.

Generic applications possess the general capacity to save on time by cutting out repetitive or difficult labour and by enhancing presentation. The corollary of this labour-saving is that they should allow attention and time to be directed to the more intrinsically valuable learning activities of reflection, experimentation, creativity and analysis. Too often, however, content-free applications are used only for their presentational capacity: the labour is conducted elsewhere in the traditional fashion. For example, asking a pupil to word-process a completed piece of work is using the word-processor as a typewriter, and although that may sometimes be justifiable it is not exploiting the full potential of the application.

To consider their utility in the RE classroom, we need to understand the type of data generic applications require (see Figure 14.2). From this it is clear that some have a more immediate use in the RE classroom than others. The word-processor and graphics/drawing packages, for example, support two types of information commonly used in RE and within religions. Although we shall spend time considering these two packages, it may be useful to consider whether there are times when a database or a spreadsheet could be used effectively in RE.

Figure 14.2 Content-free applications and their information requirements

Application	*Type of information required*
• Word-processor	• Words, text
• Graphics/drawing	• Pictures, diagrams, images
• Spreadsheet	• Numerical values
• Database	• Words or numerical values relevant to a group of similarly structured entities

The word-processor can be viewed as supporting the three aspects of the writing process shown in Figure 14.3. Ordinarily, in asking pupils to produce written work, we ask them to handle all three aspects together. And, unless we allow for the labour-intensive task of redrafting, we often expect the first piece of work to be the final piece of work. Word-processors allow this process to be broken down and the various aspects of writing to be effectively supported. Research points to the word-processor's capacity to facilitate writing and thinking as being beneficial to all pupils, and especially so to those with special educational needs (SEN), for whom writing can often be one of the most demanding of activities (Crawford 1997, p. 98; NCET 1995, pp. 6, 17; Robinson 1994, p. 30; Straker and Govier 1996, pp. 40, 48, 51). In RE pupils are asked to articulate complex, subtle ideas, often expressed through new vocabularies, and this demand can be problematic in the traditional writing process. The word-processor is able to support pupils in their expression by removing some of the labour, allowing the process to be broken down, facilitating revision and creativity.

Figure 14.3 Aspects of the writing process

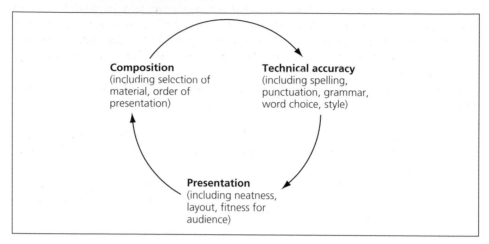

You should consider which aspect(s) of the writing process you wish to support. For example, pupils could use the word-processor to 'brainstorm' their ideas and then experiment with placing them in some kind of order to be written up elsewhere. Alternatively, first drafts may be completed on paper and then progressively revised and checked on the word-processor until a final version is produced. Presentation may be usefully exploited if pupils are asked to produce material for a specific purpose (e.g. a leaflet, newspaper article or review, poster, letter) and/or when an audience is specified (e.g. faith community, parents, other pupils). Here pupils will need to consider layout, size and format, fonts and style of language: the fact that they are engaged in effective communication for an audience will necessitate understanding of the material.

The technical accuracy of writing can be assisted not just by detaching it from other aspects of writing but by the use of checkers for spelling, grammar and style. A thesaurus can be useful in helping pupils to develop and extend their vocabulary and consider their audience and purpose.

The word-processor is not only useful for pupils to use on an individual basis: it is an excellent means by which to produce collaborative work, provided, as for all group work, the activity is sufficiently complex to engender discussion. The word-processor can become the 'mediator' between pupils as they discuss and record their understandings, with ideas easily deleted, added or amended in the course of the work.

From this it should be clear that even the use of the word-processor requires you to think carefully about why, when, how and which pupils are going to use it. To prevent what Robinson (1994, p. 24) refers to as 'fanatical font fiddling' when pupils' focus should be on the composition and structuring of ideas you need to make clear to them the purpose of its use. Establishing a clear purpose encourages your pupils to maximise what the word-processor has to offer, thereby enhancing their learning experience.

Pictures, graphics and drawings can be used by most word-processors, and these add an extra dimension to the pupils' work. There are a variety of ways of getting artwork into documents: clip art is often available as part of a word-processor or drawing package (but it can tend towards the stereotypical), scanners can be used (copyright permitting) to include artwork, or it is possible to have ordinary photographic negatives transferred on to disk by film developers without the use of a digital camera (Fitzpatrick 1994, p. 65).

Finally, content-free applications are very useful for you in your teaching and administration. They can, for example, be used to:

- produce professional print materials that are, clear, attractive, adaptable and reusable, using graphics and pictures to help break up and provide visual cues to the text;
- keep up-to-date records on pupils (marks, assessments, progress, observations) which are easily sorted and calculated. (Note, however, that confidentiality needs to be assured.)

Content-based packages

Content-based packages are most commonly available as CD-ROMs (although it is likely that these will disappear as such packages become available over the Internet). They are essentially databases containing either general information (as in an encyclopaedia-type package) or information specific to RE. Figure 14.4 shows how it is possible to locate what these packages offer along two continua. The first deals with their mode(s) of communication. Truly multimedia packages offer more than a textbook could provide, although this does not mean that their information content will be any better. Such packages are seeking to utilise other media through which learning may take place. Where only text or text and still pictures are used, they are replicating the form of their conceptual forebear: the book. The second continuum shows that such packages can also be understood in terms of the learning processes they offer to pupils. At one end there is the rigidly structured package where 'pages' are turned in strict sequence or a page is selected for the pupil on the basis of the pupil's

Figure 14.4 The dimensions of content-based packages

	X	
Mono-media		Multi-media: text, music, voice, still pictures, video pictures, graphics

	X	
Rigidly structured tutorial	Guided exploration and tutorial	Free exploration and/or experimentation

response to an activity. At the other end are those which permit pupils to explore and/or experiment by inputting information of their own. A good multimedia encyclopaedia, for example, will figure at the point marked x on both continua.

There is no 'better' position for any package to be on these continua, but you need to know that they offer and require different things of pupils and therefore your role in using them in the classroom is different. A rigidly structured package is going to be restricted in its use in the RE curriculum (Smart 1996, p. 11). It is likely to have a highly specific content and to present it in a particular way. A free–exploration package, on the other hand, could be specific or general in content but demands more of pupils in terms of knowing the purpose of their enquiry and how to locate the necessary information. Multimedia packages tend to be very attractive, but you should be able to justify the inclusion of so many media in terms of the content – sometimes the media are just gimmicks. Mono-media packages, such as 'picture galleries', can be very useful and can, for example, allow two or more pictures to be placed side by side for comparative analysis, or for close-ups to be viewed – things a book would not permit with such ease. It is also possible for groups of pupils to work together – again something which wouldn't be so easy with one textbook.

As well as being aware of the purposes of a content-based package you need to ensure that your pupils are aware of why and how they should be using them. Give pupils guidance on how to access the main features of the package and ensure they have enough time to experiment with the way things work. You can minimise your technical input by inducting a small group of pupils into the use of the package and then getting individuals from this group to induct others. Rigidly structured packages tend to be more straightforward: process and content are already determined. By contrast, exploration–type packages demand different, query-based, skills. These skills are akin to those needed for use of the World Wide Web and are dealt with in that section.

Task 14.4 Evaluating content-based packages

Explore several CD-ROM packages which are from a subject area other than RE and/or are general reference packages (e.g. encyclopaedias). Develop a set of generic descriptors and evaluation criteria for the packages to enable you to describe their key features and to evaluate their utility in the classroom context. (Selecting a non-RE package means that you will not be distracted by an evaluation of its content.)

Apply your criteria to several RE CD-ROMs and discuss what further criteria are needed to evaluate their RE content.

Ask a group of pupils to evaluate an RE CD-ROM for you. How do their criteria compare with those you developed? Do you need to amend your criteria?

THE INTERNET

The Internet offers access to information via the World Wide Web (WWW) and the capacity to communicate with others via e-mail. The striking things about this access are that it is both cheap (the cost of a local telephone call) and unrestricted by geographical distance. It is possible to look at the treasures of the Vatican or those at the Victoria and Albert Museum, and to communicate with pupils and teachers in India or in a nearby school. Access to such information and the capacity for communication make the Internet a highly valuable resource for RE: from the classroom the religious world outside becomes accessible and, if you so wish, you become accessible to the outside world. The Internet is especially valuable to RE, given RE's broad nature, its need for resources and its emphasis on communication (Gates 1998, p. 2).

The World Wide Web

The WWW is a vast, expanding, changing and interlinked collection of resources which can draw upon a range of media. There are resources on the WWW which are capable of contributing to all areas of the RE curriculum. When using the WWW (as with using free-exploration content-based packages) you need to be aware of the processes involved in resource-based learning. Figure 14.5 gives a representation of the process.

At the centre of all resource-based learning is the need to establish a purpose. This should be expressed in terms of what is to be researched and how the findings are to be communicated. The 'what' may be thought of in terms of an area, focus, topic

Figure 14.5 The resource-based learning process

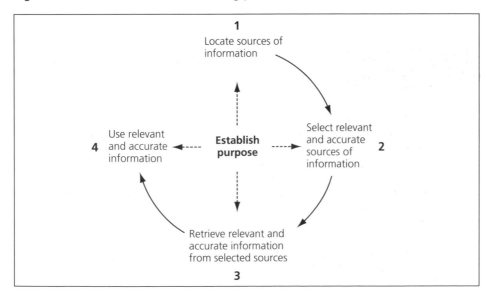

or question(s) and the 'how' as, among others, a written assignment, presentation, discussion, report, synopsis, etc. With the purpose established, it is possible for you to access the process at points 1, 2, 3 or 4. By preparing a hand-out for your pupils, for example, you are asking them to work from point 3: you have already undertaken the location and selection of resources. Alternatively, you might present your pupils with a number of resources (books, video, etc.) and then ask them to select those which they will use. In this case you are asking them to work from point 2. As a resource the WWW differs from other resources in the skills it requires in only two important respects:

- It is vast in size: there are problems in *locating* relevant resources.
- It is unregulated: there are problems in *selecting* relevant and accurate resources.

What this means is that you and your pupils need to have developed the skills associated with points 1, 2 and 3 of Figure 14.5 in a way which is appropriate to the WWW (see Herring 1996, pp. 66–152, for details of information skills). Your pupils' skills should be developed over time, and initially it would be appropriate for you to locate and specify those resources which are relevant and useful for them to work with, so entering the process at point 3 in Figure 14.5. (Cunningham *et al.* 1997, shows WWW resources identified for Year 6 pupils to use in conjunction with worksheets.) As their skills improve you can increase the range of WWW resources available to them, and educate them in criteria for selection of resources, until they are able to conduct full searches on their own.

At the outset, however, you are likely to be the one locating the resources, and this can be tackled in two ways. The first is to use the capacity of the WWW itself, which supports a number of 'search engines'. These respond to your query by scanning the WWW and listing sites of possible interest. Using a search engine needs practice, as entering a query such as 'Islam' will yield thousands of sites, many of which will be of no use to you or your pupils. Alternatively you could go direct to a site which provides links with areas likely to satisfy your query. The WWW sites listed in Task 14.5 have links with resources on most religions, information on social, moral and ethical issues, newspaper items of interest for RE, and discussion groups. If pupils have completed an activity which has involved searching on the WWW you should ask them to evaluate their search strategy, and to share with others any good resources they have located.

The selection of resources is more difficult. You need to reflect carefully on the criteria which you ordinarily use and seek to develop them further. (There are WWW resources which can help you in formulating criteria, e.g. Tillman 1998.) However, it is important to be aware that the WWW is capable of offering access to the living religious world: people's feelings, evaluations and personal reflections. WWW resources may not always present religions as the neatly 'packaged' phenomena we have grown accustomed to in print and video media developed for the classroom: they present both the core and the edges of religions, the controversial and the problematic. This access to the 'unmediated' in religions offers opportunities for pupils to experience the religious world first-hand, to begin to question the 'world religions' construct and to develop a language with which to participate in the ideas religious people articulate. There is also the potential for pupils to experience the need for methodology in their study, and to critically experiment with a variety of methodologies. (See Geaves 1998 and Jackson 1997 for discussions of methodology and the 'world religions' issue.) In short, your selection should, where appropriate, allow your pupils to come into contact with this 'real' religious world.

Task 14.5 Exploring RE and religion on the World Wide Web

Access the WWW sites below and bookmark each to ensure ease of return on future occasions. Explore their opening menu options and note what facilities they offer to users. Some are subscription-based services, but these usually provide a free area so that you may see what is available.

Choose one religious tradition and one Key Stage and, using the WWW sites listed below, compile a list of WWW resources on a topic such as places of worship, pilgrimage, practices, festivals, writings, beliefs, ethics, rites of passage (you may wish to focus on particular aspects of these suggestions). You could explore the menus they offer or, if available, use their search facilities. Working with your intended learning outcomes, select the resources most appropriate to your purposes and construct a lesson and activity outlines which show how you propose to use the WWW resources.

Using the WWW sites below, locate a school RE WWW site. Consider what purposes the site serves and in what ways it enhances pupils' experience of RE and their religious understanding.

- http://re-xs.ucsm.ac.uk/
  The Religious Education Exchange Service based at the University College of St Martin, Lancaster.
- http://theresite.org.uk/
  The RE site supported by SPCK and Culham College Institute.
- http://www.bradford.gov.uk/education/interfaith/frames.html
  The Interfaith Education Centre.
- http://www.angliainteractive.com/
  The Anglia Interactive site.

When considering the use of relevant and accurate information (point 4 in Figure 14.5), make sure your pupils are engaged in an activity requiring them to use the material they have researched. There is sometimes a great temptation to simply copy what they have found. This stems from the assumptions that the location, selection and retrieval of material constitute the totality of the activity, and that copyright and plagiarism are issues they need not consider. By carefully specifying the purpose of their work and how their findings are to be communicated you can challenge your pupils in a variety of ways to use, evaluate and respond to the material. With

It is well presented, highly readable and offers practical classroom ideas and advice. Further information can be obtained from the publishers' web site at http://www.ect.hobsons.com.

Leask, M. and Pachler, N (1999) *Learning to Teach Using ICT in the Secondary School*, London: Routledge. Although not available at the time of writing, this book should prove to be useful supportive reading for those seeking to enhance their skills in the successful development of ICT in secondary schools and in developing their pupils' skills.

Somekh, B., and Davis, N. (eds.) (1997) *Using Information Technology Effectively in Teaching and Learning*, London: Routledge. A very useful series of articles is presented in this book. They serve to show how good writing on ICT in education is still exploratory and how such writing needs to be based on reflective practice informed by theoretical considerations. There is much material here to stimulate further discussion and to inform the nature of future publications on RE and ICT.

Stern, L. J. (1998) *Byting Back: Religious Education Sinks its Teeth into Computers. A Guide and In-service Training Pack for RE Teachers*, London: BFSS National RE Centre. This booklet is intended for in-service teachers and their training in ICT. It usefully presents a wealth of ICT resources, suggests activities for teachers to complete on RE and ICT and gives an insight into the issues which are likely to be discussed by those already teaching RE.

Straker, A. and Govier, H. (1996) *Children Using Computers*, Oxford: Nash Pollock. Although written for the primary school, this is a good, general introduction to ICT, detailing the different types of ICT and their use in schools, the range of skills required by pupils, and practical strategies for using ICT in the classroom.

15 Professional Development

Joy White

When I started teaching my short and long-term aims were simply to survive! I felt I never had time to plan my development, never had time to go on courses, and never had time to read more about my subject. For three years I drifted from term to term, responding to whatever the latest initiatives were but without any sense of ownership of my own growth. When the time came to apply for Head of Department posts I realised I had little more to offer than when I started teaching. True to say I learnt the hard way, 'if you don't know where you're going, you'll never get there'.

(RE teacher)

This chapter charts the various stages in personal and professional development you are likely to be challenged by during your first teaching post. It aims to highlight the many opportunities which exist within the school, the local community and the broader national framework and infrastructure that supports the subject, and seeks to raise your awareness of the range of individuals and organisations available to support you. It reflects upon the importance of the TTA Career Entry Profile and the proposed TTA Standards for Subject Leaders in Religious Education as tools of reflective practice. Throughout the chapter there is a clear emphasis on the necessity of taking ownership of your own development and planning both in the short and long term.

OBJECTIVES

By the end of this chapter you should be able to:

- understand the variety of roles you need to develop as a teacher of RE;

> - reflect on the range of opportunities that exist for your own professional and personal development;
> - develop strategies for keeping yourself up to date in your subject.

OBTAINING YOUR FIRST TEACHING JOB

> I was so proud when I got the first post I applied for, I didn't consider the limited range of opportunities I would be given. The structure of the school meant it was very difficult to get a wider range of experience for me to move on in later years.
>
> (RE teacher)

It is a sobering thought that your first teaching post will have a huge effect on the whole of your teaching career. You will find yourself faced with a wide range of decisions when choosing your first school: City Technology College? Grant-maintained? Education Action Zone? Faith community school? Single sex? Co-educational? Community school? It is in this post that you will be able to learn more about your subject and explore different styles of pedagogy and management. You will need to be a fast learner, as many teachers of RE take up a head of department role as early as their third year of teaching. It is vital to find the right type of school for you and your expertise. It may not seem so when you are applying for posts but RE specialists are in demand and it is important to make an informed choice. It is naturally tempting to jump at the first job offered to you, but it is probably best to observe a little caution and be reflective in any decision you make. You need to do your homework and find out information which then needs to be considered against your own educational and philosophical viewpoints. Very few teachers can work to the best of their ability in a system that they are philosophically opposed to.

Consider the following advertisement:

> *Green Road School.* Required for September, a highly qualified NQT to teach RE and PSE throughout the school. Green Road is a highly successful school with a strong record of academic and extra-curricular achievement. The school is situated in pleasant countryside within easy reach of London and adjacent to woodland and a golf course.

Sounds like an ideal place to spend a holiday but what does the advertisement really tell you about the state of RE at Green Road? The reality may be that the school achieves excellent academic GCSE results in many areas of the curriculum but no status is accorded to RE. The school may be breaking statutory requirements at Key Stages 3 and 4 and, with an OFSTED inspection looming, decides to appoint a newly qualified teacher to act as head of department in an attempt to appease the inspectors. It is, then, vitally important to find out all you can about a school before you get too involved in the application process.

Finding out about schools prior to application

The nature of the school

You need to find out basic information about the school. Information supplied to potential applicants is a good place to start in your search for information. You ought also to look at OFSTED reports and the school's public examination profile. If possible listen to what local people have to say about any school you intend to apply for and if possible visit the school at the end of the day to get some idea of interaction between pupils and pupils and between pupils and staff. Some schools welcome informal discussions and visits prior to the formal interviewing procedure. Information you should search for might include, for example:

- What category of school is it?
- Is it a community, foundation or independent school, or a City Technology College?
- Is it a single-sex school and is it planning to remain so?
- Is there a selection criterion for entry into the school, and if so, what is it?
- Is the teaching contract temporary or permanent?
- What are the terms and conditions attached to the post?
- What is its policy regarding RE and collective worship?
- Is the school ethos likely to fit in with your character, personality and teaching style?
- Is it part of an Education Action Zone?

The status of RE

In addition, you will need to find out about the nature and status of RE in the school. It is vital to understand the structure of the RE department. Many RE departments are located within Humanities departments, where they may be regarded as Cinderella not only in terms of status but also in terms of budget and resourcing allocations. You should make sure that you are aware of any other responsibilities the department may have, e.g. significant contributions to SMSC, charity fund raising, citizenship education. Departments have a wide range of practices regarding lunchtime devotional clubs (e.g. the Christian Union) and collective worship. For some it is an integral part of the role of the department, whereas for others it is something they have no part in. It is important that your own view reflects the common practice. Questions you ought to be asking of the department at this preliminary stage include:

- What is the school's policy regarding RE and collective worship?
- What are the timetabling arrangements?

- What is the take-up of the subject at GCSE and A Level? What does the public examination profile of the RE department look like?
- What is the budget allocation for RE? How does it compare with other Humanities subjects?
- Which Agreed Syllabus is taught?
- What is the philosophical stance behind the Agreed Syllabus?
- How many religions are required at each Key Stage and what are they?

Induction support

Finally, you will need to find out what induction and in-service training support you are likely to receive.

- What does the institution's and the LEA's induction programme consist of?
- Is there an RE specialist who will take responsibility for mentoring you during your induction into the profession? If so, how experienced are they? Are they the kind of person you are likely to work well with?
- What support is there from the Local Authority in terms of a teachers' centre, resource centre or advisory service?
- Is there an RE or Humanities adviser available for you to consult?

OFSTED reports

It would be a grave error to automatically disregard schools which OFSTED has deemed to 'have serious weaknesses' or to be 'in need of special measures'. Some of the most stimulating and rigorous RE departments are in schools which have been 'named and shamed'. When you have decided to apply for a school you need to obtain a copy of the previous OFSTED report. (All reports are easily available on the Internet.) Look carefully at the whole report and consider the implications of the following for RE.

- What are the key points for action?
- What comments are made about the spiritual, moral, social and cultural development of pupils?
- What points are made about the leadership and management of the school?
- How do Key Stage 4 examination results reflect the national picture?
- How do GCSE RE entry numbers and results compare with other subjects in the school?
- What is the ethnic diversity within the school community?
- What issues are raised in the parents' questionnaire response?

When deciding on your first job you need to think about where you want to be in five years' time and ensure the post you are applying for will give you a relevant range of opportunities and experiences. It can be a difficult leap, for example, from a single-sex church school to a multifaith, inner city community school without the appropriate groundwork. Consequently at this initial stage in your career it is important to look out for a post which has the widest range of career opportunities and experiences to draw upon in later years. This will lay the foundation of the rest of your professional and personal development.

The application process

Start looking early. Many schools will have planned their budget a year in advance and will start to advertise in January or February for a post to be taken up in the following September. However, don't panic if no suitable job is advertised immediately. Although jobs appear from the start of the year the vast majority of posts for newly qualified teachers (NQTs) will not be advertised until after Easter, and many not until the second half of the summer term. The most obvious places to look are the *Times Educational Supplement*, published each Friday, and the *Guardian Education Supplement*, published each Tuesday. Take time to consider the advertisement and consider the skills required. If a job looks as if it may suit you don't hesitate to ring or write for further information. You won't lose anything by enquiring, and it is a good rule of thumb, at this stage, to keep as many options open as possible. However, if you decide to apply you should be willing to take time and care over your application. In the end this will save time and money which can be put to better use on a few good-quality applications for the most suitable positions.

It is obviously a compliment when newly qualified teachers are offered a post in the school in which they have done their teaching practice. This can have many positive factors as you begin your job in September, such as knowing the department and school structure, and knowing many of the students. You must, however, establish that a wider range of opportunities will be offered to you than when you were on teaching practice. It would be helpful if you could be offered interview experience so that you will be experienced when you apply for your next post.

It is important to attend any interview with a clear and objective view as to the experiences you are hoping for in your first post. Interviews differ between schools and it is easy to get caught up in the momentum of the day and allow the process to become simply a competition among the various candidates. Delighted as you may feel if selected, always beware that 'morning after' feeling when you wake to realise that perhaps it isn't the school for you.

As part of the interview procedure many schools now offer a chance for you to teach a lesson. This is an excellent opportunity for you to assess the attitudes of the pupils to the subject and for you also to evaluate the resources available. In previous years I have heard of candidates unable to see the school in action, never meeting the head of department, never encountering any pupils and not being given access to the RE resources. Just as many OFSTED judgements are made by observation, so you should take the opportunity at the school to have a good look round and gain a general 'feel' for the place. Look at the quality and quantity of wall displays and the range of books in the library concerned with RE. If possible look at the staff room notice boards to see if there are a range of career development opportunities displayed. You need to avoid schools where staff development is not taken seriously. A teacher recently said to me, 'In the school there was no culture of professional development.

We had no idea of any courses we could attend and if we were "sent" by the head teacher on a course it meant he saw us as a failing teacher.'

Have a good talk with the head of department to try to establish where they see the department going and what your role in its development could be. Unlike many other subjects you may find that the head of department is your only other subject colleague, so it is important that you share a similar philosophy or at least can ensure that your differences won't be to the detriment of the department. Of particular interest is the department's attitude to having students of RE. An opinion I heard expressed recently was that 'They're more trouble than they're worth.' Such a response could certainly be grounds to doubt the level of support a teacher would get in the first year. In my experience no two RE departments are the same. Each has its own ethos and philosophy, its own role in the school, its own links with the community and its own roles in contributing to the personal, spiritual, moral, social and cultural dimensions of the school.

Now for the $64,000 question. What happens if by July you have not found a suitable position? The answer is simple: don't panic. An initial step is to keep looking in the press, particularly, at this time, the local press. Sign on with a teacher employment agency. Doing supply work will give you the opportunity to get more experience in a variety of schools. It will also give you time to reflect on why you have not gained a position. Are your c.v. or references effective? Have you always geared your application to the job specification? How professional is your self-presentation, both on paper and in face-to-face situations? Has all your teaching experience been in a limited environment, e.g. all girls' schools? What have you learnt from the interview feedback which you have been given from earlier interviews?

Task 15.1 Preparing to apply for your first teaching post

It is important to consider your own philosophical and educational rationale. First consider the following types of schools and write down some brief notes reflecting your reasons for wanting/not wanting to teach in each type.

- City Technology College;
- Community school;
- Independent school;
- Single-sex school;
- Denominational school.

Now read the position adverts in the *Times Educational Supplement* and request details from an appropriate school. When you receive the job description read it closely, then write 500 words describing:

- what type of school it appears to be;
- what you will expect to teach;

> - how the department is organised;
> - whether you will be expected to contribute to collective worship.
>
> Finally make a list of three to five key questions which you would need to ask at interview to decide whether it is the right post for you.

ESTABLISHING YOURSELF IN YOUR FIRST POST

> I went from day to day dealing with everything that I needed to. It wasn't until the end of the year that I realised I had done nothing for my own professional development. I made sure that changed the next year.
>
> (RE teacher)

Don't be surprised if by your first half-term you feel the only focus in your development plan is to get through the next half-term. Without doubt this will be one of the busiest times of your life but it is essential that you are proactive in this year when your practical experiences are built more rapidly and critically than at any other time in your career as a teacher.

You will be assigned a mentor but there will be many people within the school community who can help your development. It is important to seek advice actively from the appropriate individuals, as there will be many aspects of school life which have not been covered on your course. Ted Wragg, Professor of Education at Exeter University, wrote that 'any difficulties NQTs experience are usually due to lack of support. Too often relatively few concessions are made, and they're given too much responsibility' (*TES*, 8 January 1999).

An important step during your first month in the school is to take on the responsibility and ownership of your career development. You need to plan your short and long-term programme and the routes you will take to achieve it. It is important that this plan is shared and, if necessary, negotiated with your head of department and your mentor. This will give you a sense of direction and purpose. An obvious support in identifying your professional needs will be your Career Entry Profile.

Your Career Entry Profile

One of the most useful tools in establishing your priority needs is the *Career Entry Profile*. The vivid pink and purple colours should mean that you don't lose it in a hurry. If you haven't already come across this document, you will do before the end of your PGCE programme. You will be expected to fill in the profile before completing your PGCE and take it with you to your first teaching post. Since 1998 the profile has been a crucial tool allowing newly qualified teachers to show their strengths and priorities for further development. It also allows you to take responsibility from the earliest point in your career for your own professional development.

It requires target setting and review, which act as a good foundation for appraisal in latter years. The information contained in it should consist of a number of steps which collectively aim to:

- enable targeted monitoring and support for the newly qualified teacher during the induction period;
- be integral to an action plan for induction which will take account of the newly qualified teacher's own targets, the targets of the school and any nationally identified objectives for induction;
- encourage newly qualified teachers to take account of their strengths and developmental needs, which were identified as priorities at the end of their training.

Creating a personal development plan

You should use your Career Entry Profile as the basis for negotiating a *personal development plan* with your mentor. Your development plan should consist of some small targets which are easily and rapidly achievable as well as the broader focuses of development. It should not be a case of merely making existing skills more explicit but should include needs identification and prioritisation. You will need to look critically and objectively for the gap between your present and your anticipated performance.

Another document to support you in this identification is the *Subject Leader Qualification Document* which clearly specifies the criteria for a successful head of department, detailing the key outcomes of effective subject leadership as well as the professional knowledge, understanding, skills and attributes required. Once you have identified your needs it is important to decide who will support you, how and when. You also need consider when you will review the success of the programme and the next steps forward. For example, an outline personal development plan might contain elements such as those outlined in Figure 15.1.

Figure 15.1 Sample personal development plan

Target	Who involved	How	Start/ review	Indicator of success
Knowledge of A Level teaching	Head of department	• Lesson observation • Team teaching • Read set texts • Attend relevant meetings • Moderate exam marking • Attend one-day INSET course	October– July	• Confidence with subject matter • Successful teaching • Contribution to curriculum development at A Level

The following list contains the most popular needs development areas:

- the development of ITC and RE;
- target setting in RE;
- differentiation and RE;
- implementing effective assessment;
- knowledge of world faiths;
- active learning;
- special educational needs and RE;
- making effective use of educational visits;
- display work;
- spiritual, moral, social and cultural development;
- effective use of resources.

In addition to subject-specific issues you will also need to conduct a needs analysis of your skills and knowledge in generic issues such as pastoral care, pre-vocational training, health and safety requirements and raising standards of achievement.

Many schools have their own structured induction programme which will be utilised for all newly qualified teachers. These will usually contain areas which OFSTED has indicated need to be addressed, and which will be expected to show evidence of progress before the next inspection. You will need to see where there is overlap with your own needs and also where any of your expertise may be offered to support the school in the run-up to the next OFSTED. The majority of schools' induction plans will be based upon three key areas:

- ensuring newly qualified teachers have the basic educational and organisational information that they need to operate as teachers in that particular school;
- including an element based on individual needs as identified in the Career Entry Profile;
- developing a broader professional awareness with a view to long-term professional development.

At the end of each term time must be planned to review your development as a whole and decide the priorities for next term. This record of termly achievement and experience will act as an excellent *aide-mémoire* when applying for your next position. When drawing up your action plan it is important to reflect upon the variety of strategies which will help development and to take the opportunity to draw upon as wide a range of experience as possible. These are just a few suggestions:

- observation by or of other colleagues;
- visits to other schools;
- in-service training courses;
- material resources;
- support from professional advisers and consultants.

Establishing yourself in your school

Your first port of call within any school must be your own department. Tensions can, and often do, exist in hard-pressed departments and it is vital that there is a structured channel of communication and support. Frequently I hear departmental heads lamenting that their new teachers are not showing initiative. Simultaneously new teachers report their frustrations with departmental heads who don't delegate or hold proper meetings. Such simple misconceptions need only time for quality communication; but time is always at a premium in schools. Try to be as enthusiastic, committed and supportive of your head of department as possible, whatever the challenges facing you. Though it is easy simply to mutter and complain about things you are not happy with, the professional option of providing support to change things, though more challenging, is also far more rewarding in the long term.

It is important to negotiate the areas of departmental responsibility you are to develop each term and to discuss what the indicators of success will be. It is also important to negotiate the areas that you will 'shadow'. There should be a balance between departmental and personal needs. One word of warning: be aware of what you can confidently take on. It is by no means rare for newly qualified teachers in their first term to be given the 'challenge' of whole-school collective worship. Normally it is simply because nobody else wants to do it: beware of being taken advantage of because of your newly qualified status. The school will view you as far more professional if you do a few jobs well rather than a range of responsibilities half well. By the completion of your second year of teaching you should have taken responsibility or shadowed all the activities necessary for running a department. In particular, try to gain experience of management issues such as budgeting, resourcing, stocktaking, timetabling, etc.

Since the introduction of the short course GCSE many more pupils are taking a final examination at the end of Key Stage 4. If you are not given an exam group during your first year it is essential to shadow the whole process: planning the course content; ways of promoting the subject with pupils and with parents; strategies for the interpreting and application of an exam syllabus; effective use of resources; setting and moderation of coursework; setting and marking of exam papers; target setting; revision techniques. In doing so you will lay sound foundations for your future involvement in examination teaching.

During this first year it can be extremely rewarding to work on one joint project with colleagues from other departments. All too often RE is marginalised and it is important to look at strategies to highlight the ethos of the subject. Such small-scale projects are often of personal interest and allow you to mix with a wider range of staff than your own department or year group. Recent projects I have observed have included RE and Art departments collaborating on a project concerning local places of worship; RE and Drama departments working on a project called 'Response to the Holocaust' and RE and Science departments holding a lunchtime debate on 'Are humans playing God?'.

Time should be available for you to observe others teaching and for them to observe you. Daunting as this may seem, it is an essential step to be able to discuss with a colleague and reflect on practice. The majority of staff will spend between 170 and 190 days on their own in the classroom in their first year. One newly qualified teacher recently remarked about her first year:

> I felt so isolated in the classroom. Closing the door and just getting on with it. I desperately wanted to discuss with colleagues if I was doing things correctly but I was afraid to ask them to watch in case they thought I was having problems. I just wish that mutual classroom observation had been built into my induction programme.

It is very tempting in your first year to want to take an active role in the many extracurricular activities that schools offer. These can be stimulating and enriching and have the added bonus of allowing you the opportunity to meet students outside the classroom. It is important to remember that your salary is being paid for your conformity to your job description. A recent survey asked teachers what things in their early teaching career they would do differently now: 32 per cent replied that their involvement in extracurricular activities in the first year had had a detrimental effect on their teaching in the classroom.

Task 15.2 Creating a personal development plan

Obtain a copy of *Standards for Subject Leaders in Religious Education*, referred to in the text. Read the document carefully and highlight the areas it refers to in which you personally need further development. Prioritise those areas and draw up a development plan under the following sub-headings:

- your personal attainment target(s);
- the mentors, tutors and other support services and individuals involved;
- the means by which your development will be achieved;
- the starting date and the date(s) for review of your progress;
- any criteria that will indicate your progress.

Remember to be realistic. Don't cram all your development needs into the first term. You also need to think about how to incorporate a wide range of support (school, local, national).

CONSOLIDATING YOUR PROFESSIONAL DEVELOPMENT

Utilising local support networks

> I needed to talk to other RE professionals. Each day was filled with thoughts about my own school and my own teaching. I needed to swap experiences with others.
>
> (RE teacher)

Every Local Authority's Agreed Syllabus must reflect the faith communities of the area. In turn these local requirements will be translated into your school's schemes of work. If you are new to the area you will need to acquaint yourself quickly with the range of resources which will be available to you.

One of the greatest resources for RE teachers will be their local faith community. Links with it will not only enrich any scheme of work, showing the true integrity of the religion as practised locally, but will also be a support in terms of resources. The most obvious way to find the variety of local faith communities within the area is by asking the pupils themselves. Failing that, relevant information will be found in Yellow Pages. For security reasons it is important to contact the faith community prior to your visit. This will also be the time to clarify dress code and practices. It's worth asking whether you will be allowed to take photographs during your visit. These can be an excellent classroom resource – especially if they can be enlarged to A3 size or made into overhead transparencies. Your links with the local communities will support many attributes to your personal and professional development:

- increasing your own knowledge of faith traditions and how they are practised within your locality;
- expanding your range of classroom resources;
- enabling you to invite visiting speakers in from the communities to talk to your classes;
- assisting you in making effective class visits to places of worship.

Another local feature of key importance to your professional development will be the work of the LEA and the Teachers' Development Centre. These usually run a range of INSET courses and professional meetings, as well as incorporating a variety of services such as reprographic and resources. Some include an RE resource centre which will be invaluable for you. Many schools have different funding arrangements with the LEA and it is important to be aware what the arrangements are and how best to use the service.

Most LEAs will provide a central programme to support school induction of newly qualified teachers. This can be very valuable to newly qualified RE teachers, who often come from small departments where there is no other newly qualified teacher. Centrally run programmes enable cross-transfer of skills, initiatives and inspiration as well as enabling you to see practice in other schools.

It is common practice for newly qualified teachers to be allowed to go on a few courses during their first year. The courses need to be carefully selected, bearing in mind your career profile and targets. The average cost of a day course (including supply cover and travel expenses) will be around £300, so the school has a right to see its money used effectively and making an impact on your practice.

Take care when reading course details and ensure the course will fulfil your needs. Remember that any course run from outside the LEA's area may well bear little resemblance to the Agreed Syllabus which your school is following. Certain questions should be reflected upon before you consult your head teacher or mentor.

- How will the course link with my agreed targets?
- What do I expect to gain from the day?
- How will it affect my classroom practice?
- How does the course contribute to department and school development plans?
- How will I disseminate what I have learned to the department and the school?

In addition to day courses many LEAs run twilight courses for teachers. These usually run between 4.30 p.m. and 6.00 p.m. and do not require supply cover. They can be valuable in enabling RE teachers to meet and discuss matters of common interest, consider new initiatives and developments in the subject, and to work together to devise projects, such as baseline assessment for Year 7 entry or review new resources.

An important body to become involved with is your local Standing Advisory Council on Religious Education (SACRE), whose role it is to offer help, support and advice to the teaching of RE in the local schools. The membership of any SACRE is at the discretion of the Local Education Authority but usually consists of representatives of four bodies: local councillors, teachers and head teachers, the Church of England, and other faith traditions represented in the district. Usually a SACRE meets once a term to discuss events affecting RE within schools, including OFSTED reports and other related issues. When a new Agreed Syllabus for RE is to be written many SACREs become transformed into Agreed Syllabus Conferences with the brief to undertake this role. One way of getting on to the SACRE is to contact your union representative and see if there is a vacancy on the teachers' group. If you belong to a faith group you can always contact them to offer your services. Being a member of the SACRE will broaden your knowledge of all aspects of RE.

Utilising national networks

> After three years in teaching I began to feel jaded. Then someone told me they'd got a grant through the British Council for educational research. I sent in an application form and research submission and within four months I was conducting research into Holocaust education in Israel. That experience recharged my batteries and gave me an enthusiasm I thought I had lost.
>
> (RE teacher)

There are many books and publications which will be of interest and use during your early years of teaching. The most commonly read are the CEM mailings that are published three times each year. These include *RE Today*, a high-quality glossy magazine devoted to topical and practical issues in the teaching of RE which includes national and international news concerning RE updates and forthcoming events. Additional magazines and inserts included in the mailing include information on new resources, collective worship support and the *British Journal of Religious Education*, the standard academic journal on the subject. It includes research reports on a wide variety of religious education issues. If you are prepared to set some quality reading time aside then these periodicals will give you many ideas for classroom practice in addition to increasing your own subject development.

To understand the integrity of a religious tradition and its views on contemporary issues there is no better place to look than the range of newspapers reflecting multi-cultural Britain. Do refer to your SHAP calendars, listing all the major religious festivals each year, and make your purchases at relevant times, e.g. the *Jewish Chronicle* just before Pesach, or *Eastern Eye* just before Diwali will throw light on the integrity of the religion rather than the stereotypes and platitudes that abound in many text-books. Similarly obtaining the *Church Times*, the *Tablet* and the *Methodist Recorder* all in the same week will show the different viewpoints on topical issues across a range of Christian denominations.

You need to become aware of the range of organisations that can offer support, assistance and resources to RE teachers and of their differing rationale and strategies. Making an approach in order to obtain support from a relevant organisation should be a part of your development plan. Such contacts can open up 'golden' opportunities but should be made only when you are certain you will be able to respond appropriately to the support offered. Once you have settled into your first school you need to think in terms of more formal ways of increasing you expertise and skills as an RE teacher: attendance at conferences, involvement and even secondment on research projects, further study, including possibly M.A. and M.Phil./Ph.D. research.

The St Gabriel's Trust has been a terrific support and revitaliser of a wide range of teachers. It annually provides grants for teacher-led in-service training, realising the importance of network development to stop teachers from feeling professionally isolated. Past areas of study have included sixth-form RE; producing resource boxes for studying world faiths; photo-packs about local churches and short course GCSE. As one teacher involved said:

> When we were awarded a St Gabriel's grant we knew it might help with the instigation of the short course GCSE, but we had no idea of the other ramifications. Throughout the year I felt inspired about my teaching – the first time in many years. It was invigorating to sit and discuss with other colleagues, to share good practice and good resources. Even when the grant ended our group decided to meet regularly and to take on new initiatives together.

In addition to awarding grants St Gabriel's runs an annual RE Teachers' Weekend where 250 teachers from all phases meet to share ideas and attend seminars on over twenty topics. The two days provide free in-service training with all conference fees and accommodation paid for by the St Gabriel's Programme. For more information or to receive the regular newsletter contact the Development Officer, Culham College Institute, The Malthouse, 60 East St Helen Street, Abingdon, Oxon. OX14 5EB. Or you can visit the web site: http://www.culham.ac.uk/sg.

Other supportive bodies for the developments of religious education include the Farmington Institute. Although its aims are to support, encourage and improve Christian education the institute takes a particular interest in developing good relations with world religions. Each year it awards a number of primary and secondary Farmington Fellowships that release teachers for a term to study an aspect of RE at a university or institution of higher education.

The Stapleford Centre is one of the leading lights in promoting the personal and professional development of teachers from a Christian perspective. In addition to providing a range of courses it regularly publishes Christian resources for the teaching of values across the curriculum.

There are numerous non-subject-specific agencies which may be able to support your development, e.g. the Churchill Trust or the British Council. Some agencies will have a very definite focus for their support such as the Holocaust Education Trust, which subsidises in-service training on the teaching of the Holocaust. It is important to be proactive and realise the potential of some of the declared national/international years of special interest. For example, many teachers of RE were able to take advantage of the International Year of Anti-racism and Anti-semitism (1997/8) to fund national and international projects. An important motto to remember in the fight against fossilisation in RE is that 'if we don't move forward we'll find we're going backwards'.

There is no finer way to get to know a GCSE syllabus than to become an exam marker. It is true you won't get rich quickly (or even slowly) but you will gain an excellent working knowledge of the syllabus content, marking scheme and standards in other schools. Advertisements for external examiners and coursework moderators are regularly featured in the *Times Educational Supplement*. Remember, though, that if you do apply and are accepted it is vital to realise the implications for your time schedule and to plan round a potentially very busy June.

Further research and study

It is so important that the daily grind and the surplus of paperwork don't let you forget the love of the subject that led you into teaching. It is easy to lose touch with the academic rigour and argument that are such a vital part of the subject. Thankfully it has never been easier to further your development through studying for an M.A. There are a wide range of courses available now following a variety of study systems and forms of organisation. It is true the majority of teachers have to fit any further study or qualifications into their working life; gone are the days when schools could offer secondments, although many will still help towards the cost of the fees. Before embarking on an M.A. you must reflect upon your own personality and personal and professional commitments.

The teacher who has a lot of extracurricular activities may be tempted to apply for a distance learning M.A., which will not necessitate attending regular weekly lectures. The disadvantage of this option is that it is easy to feel isolated and miss the valuable discourse resulting from seminars and workshops. Distance learning also necessitates a tremendous amount of self-discipline, as there will be less supervision and personal contact. Again it is important right from the first year of teaching to consider when is the best time to embark on an M.A. Many teachers have regretted not starting during their first two years of teaching, so seeing it as a natural development of their first degree. Some teachers have enjoyed a gap of five or six years, believing they had more to offer in their studies because of the accrued experience. It is important to select what is right for you and to include it in your development plan. Whatever M.A. you choose to do, whenever you choose to do it, you can be sure that the effort in terms of your own development will be well worth while.

Task 15.3 Keeping up the momentum and focusing on further study

You want to teach RE because of your enthusiasm for the subject. It is important this zeal is never lost and that your teaching allows it to be enriched. Here are some suggestions for keeping up your momentum.

- Make a list of professional organisations you will link yourself with, and the magazines and journals you intend to subscribe to. Don't wait till next year to join up: do it now!
- Set yourself targets for keeping your professional reading and study up to scratch – both in the field of RE itself and in the 'subject knowledge' areas of Religious Studies, Theology, Philosophy, Anthropology, etc.
- Set up a mutual support network among your fellow students. Consider having regular e-mail conversations during your first year of teaching, and regular reunions for social as well as professional purposes!
- Write out a medium-term plan for your professional development. Where do you want to be in ten years' time? What INSET courses and HEI study programmes do you need to take up to achieve it? Have you reached the limit of your academic development yet? Have you considered the possibility of a part-time M.A. course in RE, or even of future doctoral research?
- Make a list of the 'wake-up' strategies you intend to adopt next year should the going get tough, your enthusiasm begin to wane, or you find yourself slipping into the trap of simply going through the motions to survive.

SUMMARY AND KEY POINTS

We began the chapter by indicating how important it was to be thinking about your second post when you've only just started your first. Hopefully if you realised the details of your development plan you will:

- increase and keep up to date with your subject knowledge;
- experience or shadow a range of responsibilities within your school;
- develop those areas that need addressing in your Career Entry Profile and National Standards for Subject Leaders (TTA);
- take part in effective in-service training;
- initiate and organise cross-curricular projects;
- experience a wide range of teaching strategies;
- obtain a further qualification.

FURTHER READING

Baumann, A.S., Bloomfield, A. and Roughton, L. (1997) *Becoming a Secondary School Teacher*, London: Hodder & Stoughton. Written to support PGCE students and their mentors. It is in three parts: 'teaching and learning', 'developing your teaching' and 'the learning school'. It contains clear material about the development of a professional development portfolio which is the basis of a Career Entry Profile that trainee teachers have to complete.

Hargreaves, A. and Fullar, M. (1996) *Understanding Teacher Development*, London: Cassell. The nature and development of teaching as a career.

Spackman, F. (1991) *Teachers' Professional Responsibilities*, London: David Fulton. Provides basic information about your legal and professional responsibilities as a teacher.

Weller, P. (ed.) (1993) *Religions in the UK: A Multi Faith Directory*, Derby: University of Derby/Inter Faith Network. An indispensable reference book, packed full of information, contacts, addresses, statistics, etc.

Appendix A
Useful Addresses and Contacts

Compiled by Alison Seaman

GOVERNMENT OFFICES

Department for Education and
Employment
Sanctuary Buildings
Great Smith Street
London SW1P 3BT
Telephone: 0171 925 5000

Welsh Office Education Department
Phase II Building
Ty Glas Road
Llanishen
Cardiff CF4 5WE
Telephone: 01222 761456

Scottish Office Education Department
New St Andrew's House
St James' Centre
Edinburgh EH1 3SY
Telephone: 0131 556 8400

Department for Education for
Northern Ireland
Rathgael House
Balloo Road
Bangor
Co Down BT19 7PR

Qualifications and Curriculum
Authority (QCA)
29 Bolton Street
London W1Y 7PD
Telephone: 0171 509 5555

Teacher Training Agency (TTA)
Portland House
Stag Place
London SW1E 5TT
Telephone: 0171 925 3700

NATIONAL AND REGIONAL RE RESOURCE CENTRES

The following RE centres offer a wide range of support services, including
extensive collections of RE resources, training and advisory services and

publications. The centres provide a good starting point for access to national RE networks. There are also many local RE resource centres, too numerous to list here.

British and Foreign School Society National RE Centre

Brunel University
Osterley Campus
Borough Road
Isleworth
Middlesex TW7 5DU
Telephone: 0181 891 8324

National Society's RE Centre

36 Causton Street
London SW1P 4AU
Telephone: 0171 932 1190

Welsh National Centre for RE

University of Wales
School of Education
Bangor
Gwynedd LL57 2UW
Telephone: 01248 382155

Westhill RE Centre

University of Birmingham, Westhill
Selly Oak
Birmingham
West Midlands B29 6LL
Telephone: 0121 472 7248

York RE Centre

University College of Ripon and York
St John,
Lord Mayor's Walk
York
North Yorkshire
YO3 7EX
Telephone: 01904 716858/7

FAITH COMMUNITY EDUCATION AND RESOURCE ORGANISATIONS

The following organisations provide educational support and resources related to specific religious traditions.

Buddhist

Buddhist Society
58 Eccleston Square
London SW1V 1PH
Telephone: 0171 834 5858

Christian

The Church of England Board of Education/ The National Society

Church House
Great Smith Street
Westminster
London SW1P 3NZ
Telephone: 0171 898 1412

Catholic Education Service
39 Eccleston Square
London SW1V 1BX
Telephone: 0171 584 7491

Hindu

Hindu Council of the UK
c/o 150 Penn Road
Wolverhampton
West Midlands WV3 0EN
Telephone: 01902 334331

ISKCON Educational Services
Dharam Marg
Hilfield Lane
Aldenham
Watford
Hertfordshire WD2 8EZ
Telephone: 01923 859578

Humanist

British Humanist Association
47 Theobalds Road
London WC1X 8SP
Telephone: 0171 430 0908

Jewish

Board of Deputies of British Jews
Fifth floor
Commonwealth House
1–19 New Oxford Street
London WC1A 1NE
Telephone: 0171 543 5400

Jewish Resource Centre
Centre for RE and Development
(CREDE)
Roehampton Institute
Digby Stuart College
Roehampton Lane
London SW15 5PH
Telephone: 0181 392 3349

Muslim

Muslim Education Forum
93 Court Road
Birmingham
West Midlands B12 9LQ
Telephone: 0121 440 3500

Muslim Educational Trust
130 Stroud Green Road
London N4 3RZ
Telephone: 0171 272 8502

Sikh

British Sikh Education Council
10 Featherstone Road
Southall
Middlesex UB2 5AA
Telephone: 0181 574 1902

RE PROFESSIONAL AND RELATED ORGANISATIONS

Association of Teachers of Religious Education in Scotland

c/o Kirkcudbright Academy
Kirkcudbright
Dumfries and Galloway DG6 4JN
Scottish professional RE teacher association.

Christian Education Movement

Royal Buildings
Victoria Street
Derby DE1 1GW
Telephone: 01332 296655
An ecumenical educational charity which works throughout the UK to support RE in schools. Publishes a wide range of teaching materials, a termly magazine RE Today *and the* British Journal of Religious Education.

Interfaith Network for the UK

5–7 Tavistock Place
London WC1H 9SN
Telephone: 0171 388 0008
The Interfaith Network exists to promote good relations between faith communities, and forms links from them to interfaith and educational bodies. The following publication is apposite for all RE professionals. It provides a comprehensive list of contacts and information: P. Weller, Religions in the UK, *Derby: University of Derby/Inter Faith Network (1997).*

National Association of SACREs

c/o RE Centre
University of Birmingham, Westhill
Selly Oak
Birmingham
West Midlands B29 6LL
Develops links between the activities of local SACREs.

Professional Council for Religious Education

Royal Buildings
Victoria Street
Derby DE1 1GW
Telephone: 01332 296655
The subject teacher association for RE professionals.

Religious Education Council of England and Wales

Royal Buildings
Victoria Street
Derby DE1 1GW
Telephone: 01332 296655
Provides a national forum for discussion of matters concerning RE. It promotes the interests of RE at national level.

Scottish Joint Committee for Religious and Moral Education

Education Institute of Scotland
46 Moray Place
Edinburgh EH3 6BH
Telephone: 0131 225 6244
Promotes RE, RS and Moral Education in schools and in further and higher education. Advice is given in these subject areas, and conferences are organised at Scottish and district levels.

SHAP Working Party on World Religions in Education

36 Causton Street
London SW1P 4AU
Telephone: 0171 932 1194
Established to encourage the study and teaching of world religions. Publications include a calendar of religious festivals and an annual journal World Religions in Education.

Welsh Association of SACREs

Curriculum Support Service
County Hall
Mold
Clwyd CH7 6ND
Telephone: 01325 704103
Develops links between the activities of local SACREs in Wales.

EXAMINATION BOARDS FOR RELIGIOUS EDUCATION AND RELIGIOUS STUDIES

EDEXCEL Foundation

Stewart House
32 Russell Square
London WC1B 5DN
Telephone: 0171 393 4500
Fax: 0171 393 4501
E-mail: enquiries@edexcel.org.uk
Website: www.edexcel.org.uk

AQA (Assessment and Qualifications Alliance) (Amalgamation of NEAB, AEB and SEG AQA)

NEAB RE Subject Officer
Devas Street
Manchester M15 6EX
Telephone: 0161 953 1180
Fax: 0161 273 7572
E-mail: pubs@neab.ac.uk
Website: www.neab.ac.uk

NEAB publications:
Aldon House
39 Heald Grove
Rusholme
Manchester M14 4NA
Telephone: 0161 953 1170
Fax: 0161 953 1177

SEG RE Subject Officer
Stag Hill House
Guildford
Surrey GU2 5XJ
Telephone: 01483 506506 (general),
01483 477887(publications)
Fax: 01483 300152

OCR (Previously MEG and OCEAC)

RE Subject Officer
1 Hills Road
Cambridge CB1 2EU
Telephone: 01223 552662
Fax: 01223 460278
E-mail: helpdesk@ucies.org.uk
Website: www.ocr.org.uk

Publications:
Mill Wharf
Mill Street
Birmingham B6 4BU
Telephone: 01223 552662
Fax: 0121 628 2930

WJEC (Welsh Joint Education Committee)

245 Western Avenue
Cardiff CF5 2YX
Telephone: 01222 265000
Fax: 01222 575994
E-mail: exams@wjec.co.uk
Website: www.wjec.co.uk

Appendix B:
GCSE Religious Education and
Religious Studies Syllabuses

Compiled by Angela Wright

EDEXCEL

GCSE full course syllabus		*GCSE short course syllabus*	
Religious Studies		*Religious Education Syllabus A: Religion and Life*	*Religious Education Syllabus B: Religions: Faith and Practice*
(One unit from Alternative A and one unit from Alternative B)		*(One unit to be studied)*	*(One unit to be studied)*
Alternative A	*Alternative B*	Religion and Life from the Viewpoint of Christianity and at least one other Religion	Buddhism
Religion and Life from the Viewpoint of Christianity and at least one other Religion	Buddhism		Christianity
	Christianity		Catholicism
	Catholicism	Religion and Life from a Christian Perspective	Mark's Gospel
Religion and Life from a Christian Perspective	Mark's Gospel		Hinduism
	Hinduism	Religion and Life from a Catholic Perspective	Islam
Religion and Life from a Catholic Perspective	Islam	Religion and Life from a Muslim Perspective	Judaism
	Judaism		Sikhism
Religion and Life from a Muslim Perspective	Sikhism	Religion and Life from a Jewish Perspective	
Religion and Life from a Jewish Perspective			

See notes at end.

NEAB

GCSE full course syllabus			GCSE short course syllabus	
Religious Studies Syllabus A: World Religions	*Religious Studies Syllabus B: Christian Belief and Practice*	*Religious Studies Syllabus C: Christian Belief and Practice (Modular)*	*Religious Studies (short course) Syllabus A: World Religions*	*Religious Education Syllabus D: Thinking about God and Morality*
Two units to be studied from six	*One unit from Section 1 and one from Section 2*	*One core module plus two modules for test and two pieces of coursework from these modules*	*One unit to be studied from six*	*Both parts to be studied*
Section 1 Buddhism	*Section 1* (A) Christianity, or	*Core Module* Section 1, The Human Condition	*Section 1* Buddhism	*Part A* *Thinking about God* The existence of God
Section 2 Christianity	(B) Christian Belief and Practice with reference to the Roman Catholic Tradition, or	Section 2, Jesus Christ Section 3, New Testament Principles of Christian Living and	*Section 2* Christianity	The nature of God How God may be known
Section 3 Hinduism			*Section 3* Hinduism	*Part B* *Thinking about Morality*
Section 4 Islam	(C) Study of the Person and Ministry of Jesus, *and*	*Module 1* Christian Mission or	*Section 4* Islam	Ways of making moral decisions; issues of life and death;
Section 5 Judaism	*Section 2* (A) Effects of Christianity in lifestyles, or	*Module 2* Christian Spiritual Life or	*Section 5* Judaism	relationships; global issues
Section 6 Sikhism			*Section 6* Sikhism	
	(B) Effects of the Roman Catholic tradition upon lifestyle	*Module 3* Christian Vocation or *Module 4* Topics from the Bible and Church History		

See notes at end.

OCR

GCSE full course syllabuses		*GCSE short course syllabuses*	
Religious Studies Syllabus A	*Religious Studies Syllabus B: Jewish Studies*	*Religious Education Syllabus A*	*Religious Education Syllabus B*
One of twenty-seven options! – combinations of two of the following, with some restrictions plus coursework		*Thirteen options, one to be chosen*	*Four or five of the following units, depending on whether coursework is included*
Christianity through a Study of Luke and Acts	*Section 1* Jewish Studies	Christian Perspectives on Issues *plus* (a) Luke and Acts	*Unit 1* Existence of God *Unit 2*
Christian Perspectives on Personal, Social and World Issues	*Section 2* Jewish Texts	(b) Christianity (c) Hinduism (d) Islam (e) Judaism	What is Truth? *Unit 3* Religion and Spirituality *Unit 4*
Christianity		(f) Sikhism (g) Buddhism	Religion and Science *Unit 5*
Hinduism		(h) Hinduism	Good and Evil *Unit 6*
Islam		Christianity *plus* (j) Islam	Religion and Human Relationships
Judaism		(k) Judaism (l) Sikhism	*Unit 7* Religion and Conflict/
Sikhism		(m) Buddhism	Reconciliation *Unit 8*
Buddhism		(n) Jewish Studies *plus* Jewish Texts	Religion and Materialism *Unit 9*
		(p) Christianity (Roman Catholic) *plus* Christian (RC) Perspectives	Death and Dying *Unit 10* Religion and the Environment

See notes at end.

SEG

GCSE full course syllabuses		GCSE short course syllabuses	
Religious Studies Syllabus A: Christianity	*Religious Studies Syllabus B: Interfaith Studies and Ethics*	*Religious Studies Syllabus C: Christianity: the Roman Catholic Tradition*	*Religious Education (short course)*
Two from three options	*Any two options in Section A; any two of Section B (the same religions in each)*		*Sections A, B and C to be studied; either coursework or exam on Section D*
Option 1 The Christian Church	*Section A* Buddhism Christianity	*Unit 1* Jesus Christ	*Section A* Christianity
Option 2 Christian Perspectives on Contemporary Issues	Hinduism Islam Judaism Sikhism	*Unit 2* The Passion and Resurrection of Jesus	*Section B* *One from* Buddhism Hinduism Islam
		Unit 3	Judaism
Option 3 Christianity through the Life and Teaching of Jesus, as demonstrated in the Synoptic Gospels	*Section B* *A study of the ethical teachings of* Buddhism Christianity Hinduism Islam Judaism Sikhism	*Either* St Luke's Gospel *or* Issues in Christian Living	Sikhism Christian Ethics
		Unit 4 The Church	*Section C* Ultimate Questions Questions of Meaning Life and Death Issues Planet Earth
		Unit 5 Life, Marriage and the Family	
			Section D Religion in Action

See notes at end.

WJEC

GCSE full course syllabuses	*GCSE short course syllabuses*	*Certificate of Educational Achievement*
Religious Studies Two options to be chosen – options arranged in three groups. One option to be taken from any two groups	*Religious Education* Five units (Unit 5 is either examined or submitted as coursework)	*COEA* Any two options but not option 9 with 2 or 3
Group 1 Christianity (1) Christianity: the Roman Catholic Tradition	*Unit 1* Relationships	1 Jesus and the Foundation of Christianity
	Unit 2 Our World	2 Christian Life in Contemporary Society
Group 2 Christianity (2) Christianity through the Gospels	*Unit 3* Looking for Meaning	3 Christian Life and Worship
	Unit 4 Identity and Belonging	4 Sikhism in Contemporary Society
Group 3 Judaism Buddhism Islam Hinduism Sikhism	*Unit 5* Is it fair?	5 Hinduism in Contemporary Society
		6 Buddhism in Contemporary Society
		7 Judaism in Contemporary Society
		8 Islam in Contemporary Society
		9 Christian Practice and Morality

See notes at end.

NOTES

1 Some full course syllabuses are considered to meet the requirements of the short course criteria.

2 The EDEXCEL full course combines both the short course focus on philosophy and ethics and the more systematic RS consideration of individual faiths. This allows the short course to be taught alongside the full course option group with ease.

3 Those which allow for any easy combination of the short and full courses to be taught in tandem are: OCR RS A and OCR RE A (short course – full course style); NEAB syllabus A and NEAB short course syllabus A (full course style); either of EDEXCEL RS syllabuses A or B with either of EDEXCEL RE (short course) syllabuses A or B (offering the possibility of a combination of RS/RE).

4 The SEG short course in itself offers a combination of a full-course style coverage of Christianity alongside considerations of ultimate questions and ethical issues.

5 The information is correct for examination in the year 2000. You should be aware that syllabus arrangements change on a regular basis.

Glossary

Accreditation The recognition of a programme of study by an institution, normally through certification on the successful completion of a course, thus providing it with value through formal public recognition.

Assembly A meeting of the school community for purposes of administration and/or to celebrate an aspect of the life of the school, but not involving any dimension of collective worship.

Child-centred education See Progressive education.

Cognitive learning Learning rooted in reason and critical reflection rather than in the enhancement of experiential sensibility and/or practical behavioural skills.

Collective worship A form of school-based worship stipulated by the 1944 and 1988 Education Acts, in which the *collective religious beliefs* of the school community are celebrated.

Concept cracking A method of exploring religious *concepts* in the classroom associated with the work of Trevor Cooling.

Conditioning A process or regime whereby a pupil is moulded, or *conditioned*, to adopt particular habits or beliefs without having much choice in the matter.

Confessional RE A form of religious education which derives from a particular religious tradition's *confession* of faith. Its commitment to religious nurture and the transmission of faith is often taken by opponents to be anti-educational.

Critical realism The philosophy that there is an objective reality external to our minds 'out there' waiting to be discovered, but that access to it is not immediately given; rather, it requires an ongoing exploration of the world by human wisdom and intelligence.

Curriculum The subjects and programmes of study taught in schools. The 1988 Education Act distinguishes between: (1) the *whole curriculum*, all learning activities that take place in school, including cross-curricular themes; (2) the *basic curriculum*, RE plus the National Curriculum; and (3) the *National Curriculum*, those subjects prescribed for study at national level.

Developmental education (1) All education that takes account of the variety of psychological models of child-development associated primarily with Piaget and his followers. (2) Education concerned with and for social, economic and cultural inequality and the Developing/Third World.

Differentiation Pedagogy that seeks to take account of the variety of ability ranges represented in the classroom by presenting material and setting tasks *differentiated* to meet the specific needs and aptitudes of individual pupils.

Emotivism The doctrine that our inner feelings and *emotions* reflect what is ultimately true or real, and consequently are the most appropriate guides of our actions.

Empiricism The philosophy that human knowledge is grounded in our sense experience.

Enlightenment Eighteenth-century philosophical movement, standing at the dawn of the modern era, in which the potency of reason was emphasised as the means of obtaining knowledge over against obedience to religious authority.

Experiential RE RE which attempts to give pupils a foundational *experience* of what religion entails, by engaging them in activities which emphasise reflection, the use of the imagination and the development of an inner life.

Faith development An approach to religious education grounded in James Fowler's belief that the universal phenomenon of human faith commitment and formation develops in sequential stages.

Formative assessment The process through which the performance of pupils, programmes of study, schools and teachers is evaluated and reported in order to support and enhance further development.

Generic religion The belief that religion as a phenomenon constitutes a distinct entity, and that specific religious traditions are alternative forms of a common *generic human religiosity*.

Hermeneutics The science or art of human understanding.

Implicit RE A form of RE, flourishing in the 1960s, grounded in the assumption that the capacity for religious experience and insight was implicit in all pupils and simply needed to be drawn out of them. It would often begin by unpacking general moral, cultural and aesthetic topics before attempting to relate them explicitly to religious themes.

Indoctrination A process in which someone attempts to influence another to accept particular *doctrines*, or beliefs, without regard to whether they understand them and accept them voluntarily. The concept of indoctrination is often contrasted with the concept of education.

Interpretative RE An approach to RE associated with Robert Jackson which focuses on the process of *interpreting* an individual or group's religious way of life. This approach draws particularly on ideas from anthropology and ethnography and arises partly through balanced criticism of phenomenology.

Liberal education (1) Education rooted in the liberal values of freedom, tolerance and reason. (2) Following Paul Hirst, the term is also used in the more restrictive sense of education focusing exclusively on the acquisition of knowledge.

Logical positivism A now largely defunct philosophical tradition that claimed that only statements capable of verification and testing through sense experience could be meaningful. Religious, moral and aesthetic language was held to be neither true nor false, but quite literally nonsense.

Multicultural education Education largely within the liberal tradition concerned to teach about cultural diversity as a means of enhancing mutual understanding and toleration.

Multifaith RE (1) In its soft form, any approach to RE that takes account of the diversity of religious traditions; (2) in its harder form the principle of the absolute equality of all religious traditions is brought into play.

Naturalism The philosophical belief that the *natural world* as described by natural science constitutes the sum of reality and that no transcendent religious realm lies beyond it.

Nominalist religion The belief that 'religious' traditions, with their distinct truth claims, are essentially individual entities, each of which must be interpreted on its own terms. The imposition of universal generic religious categories on any single tradition merely serves to undermine authentic understanding. 'Religion' is merely a *nominal* category that does not reflect actual reality.

Non-realism (1) In its soft form, the belief that it is impossible for us to move beyond our own subjective perceptions of reality to achieve an understanding of the **real** objective world. (2) In its hard form, the belief that no objective reality exists beyond our own subjective world view.

Nurture A process whereby those who hold particular religious beliefs attempt to teach and transmit them to others, often children, in ways that encourage understanding and commitment.

Objectivism The philosophical doctrine that both reality and our understanding of reality must, if they are to be considered authentic, transcend our inner subjective feelings and desires.

Open RE An approach to RE that asserts the value of pupils' freedom to decide their response to religion. It is opposed to any form of indoctrination and deeply suspicious of closed forms of confessional religious teaching.

Phenomenological RE An approach to teaching religion associated particularly with Ninian Smart and closely allied with multifaith RE. It seeks to balance an objective study of the world's religions with an empathetic understanding of the world view of the religious believer.

Phenomenology A philosophical movement associated with Edmund Husserl that attempted to understand reality through the twin processes of description and empathetic understanding of the *phenomenological world* that presents itself to our senses.

Pluralism (1) In its soft form, the basic reality of cultural diversity. (2) In its hard form, the claim that truth is to be found in the plurality of cultural contexts.

Postmodernism A broad contemporary philosophical and cultural movement that, in opposition to the rationalism of modernity, stresses the value of relativism, pluralism, emotivism and cultural diversity.

Progression The structure built into a programme of study that enables learning to progress through ordered, appropriate and coherent stages.

Progressive education A form of child-centred education that flourished in the 1960s and has its roots in the thoughts of the French philosopher JJ. Rousseau. It is concerned with allowing the pupil the freedom to develop naturally and tends to be opposed to the imposition of any traditional subject-based curriculum and suspicious of formal schooling.

Realism The philosophical and religious belief that objective reality exists independently of the observer. Whether God exists, or does not exist, is not affected in any way by our decision to believe or not to believe.

Relativism (1) In its hard form, the belief that truth is not universal but is relative to particular groups of people or individuals. 'This is our truth, now tell us yours'. (2) In its soft form, the recognition that all human claims to true knowledge are always partial, contingent and relative. 'We think this, you think that, but which of us is right?'

Religionism A term popularised by John Hull in reference to pathological forms of religious belief which treat their own claims as exclusively true and all other forms as false, and consequently tend towards sectarianism, bigotry, intolerance, oppression and even violence.

Religious pluralism (1) In its soft form it simply indicates the reality of religious diversity. (2) In its hard form it refers to a particular interpretation of that reality, in which all religious traditions are held to contain some element of religious truth.

Religious Studies The academic study of religion, normally from a neutral or scientific perspective, concerned primarily with the understanding of religious culture rather than the reality and truth of God.

Revelation A category of theological epistemology in which knowledge of God rests not in human endeavour, experience and reason, but in the act of *divine revelation*.

Romanticism A broad cultural movement that arose in reaction against the technical rationalism of the Enlightenment. It stressed the importance of feeling and intuition over against reason, and was deeply influential in shaping liberal forms of religion, progressive child-centred education and experiential religious education.

Scientism The philosophy that the only valid form of knowledge is that gained through the exercise of the scientific method.

Formative assessment The process through which the performance of pupils, programmes of study, schools and teachers are evaluated and reported in order to indicate their actual standard of achievement.

Theology The study of religion, normally from the perspective of faith commitment, concerned primarily with the understanding of the reality and truth of God, rather than religious culture understood as merely a human phenomenon.

Bibliography

Albans, P. (1998) 'Effective Questioning in Primary Religious Education and the Assessment of Pupils' Learning from Religion', *Resource*, 21 : 1, pp. 3–6.

Astley, J. (1994) *The Philosophy of Christian Religious Education*, Birmingham, Alabama: Religious Education Press.

Bacon, A. (1969) 'Foreword', *Learning for Living*, 8 : 3, pp. 4–5.

Baumann, A.S., Bloomfield, A. and Roughton, L. (1997) *Becoming a Secondary School Teacher*, London: Hodder & Stoughton

Baumfield, V., Bowness, C., Cush, D. and Miller, J. (1995) 'Model Syllabuses: The Debate Continues', *Resource*, 18 : 1, pp. 3–6.

BECTa (1998a) *Connecting Schools, Networking People*, Coventry: British Educational Communications and Technology Agency.

BECTa (1998b) *Information Sheet on Religious Education, IT and the National Curriculum*, http://www.becta.org.uk/info-sheets/re.html

Beesley, M. (1990) *Stilling: A Pathway for Spiritual Learning in the National Curriculum*, Salisbury: Salisbury Diocese.

Bell, M. and Biott, C. (1996) 'Experienced Teachers and Students as Co-workers,' in Somekh, B. and Davis, N. (eds) *Using Information Technology Effectively in Teaching and Learning*, London: Routledge.

Best, R. (ed.) (1996) *Education, Spirituality and the Whole Child*, London: Cassell.

Bigger S. (1998) 'The Dumbing Down of RE?', paper presented at the Annual Conference of NATFHE Religious Studies Section, Bath Spa University.

Blaylock, L. (1995) *Input 5: RE at Key Stage 4*, Derby: CEM/PCfRE.

Blaylock, L. and Johnson, C. (eds) (1988) *A Teacher's Handbook of Religious Education*, Derby: Christian Education Movement.

Blaylock, L. and Mayled-Porter, H. (1996) *Input 6: GCSE RE Short Courses*, Derby: CEM/PCfRE.

British Humanist Association (1975) *Objective, Fair and Balanced*, London: BHA.

Brown, A. (1996) *Between a Rock and a Hard Place*, London: National Society.

Capel, S., Leask, M., and Turner, T. (1995) *Learning to Teach in the Secondary School*, London: Routledge.

Central Subject Panel for Religious Studies (1994) *A Religious Education Syllabus for Independent Schools 5–18 Years*, n.p.: Central Subject Panel for Religious Studies.

Chadwick, P. (1997) *Shifting Alliances: Church and State in English Education*, London: Cassell.

Child, D. (1974) *Psychology and the Teacher*, London: Holt-Blond.

City of Birmingham Education Committee (1975) *Living Together: A Teacher's Handbook of Suggestions for Religious Education*, Birmingham: City of Birmingham District Council.

Clinton, C., Lynch, S., Orchard, J., Weston, D. and Wright, A. (1998a) *Religion in Focus: Christianity in Today's World*, London: John Murray.

Clinton, C., Lynch, S., Orchard, J., Weston, D. and Wright, A. (1998b) *Religion in Focus: Christianity in Today's World. Teacher's Resource Book*, London: John Murray.

Clinton, C., Lynch, S., Orchard, J., Weston, D. and Wright, A. (1999a) *Religion in Focus: Islam in Today's World*, London: John Murray.

Clinton, C., Lynch, S., Orchard, J., Weston, D. and Wright, A. (1999b) *Religion in Focus: Islam in Today's World. Teacher's Resource Book*, London: John Murray.

Coles, R. (1990) *The Spiritual Life of Children*, Glasgow: Harper-Collins.

Cooling, M. (1996) *Toolkit: Creative Ideas for Using the Bible in the Classroom*, Volumes 1, 2 and 3, Swindon: Bible Society.

Cooling, M. (1998) *Jesus through Art: A Resource for Teaching Religious Education and Art*, Norwich: Religious and Moral Education Press.

Cooling, T. (1991) 'Review of 'New Methods in RE Teaching: An Experiential Approach', *British Journal of Religious Education*, 13 : 2, pp. 122–4.

Cooling, T. (1994a) *Concept Cracking: Exploring Christian Beliefs in School*, Nottingham: Stapleford Project Books.

Cooling, T. (1994b) *A Christian Vision for State Education*, London: SPCK.

Cooling, T. (1997), 'Theology Goes to School: The Story of the Stapleford Project', *Journal of Christian Education*, 40 : 1, 47–60.

Cooper, D. (1986) *Metaphor*, London: Blackwell.

Copley, T. (1989) *Worship, Worries and Winners: Worship in School after the 1988 Act*, London: National Society/Church House Publishers.

Copley, T. (1997) *Teaching Religion: Fifty Years of Religious Education in England and Wales*, Exeter: University of Exeter Press.

Copley, T. (ed.) (1998) *RE Futures: A Reader in Religious Education*, Derby: Professional Council for Religious Education.

Cox, E. and Cairns, J.M. (1989) *Reforming Religious Education: The Religious Clauses of the 1988 Education Reform Act*, London: Kogan Page.

Crawford, R. (1997) *Managing Information Technology in Secondary Schools*, London: Routledge.

Cunningham, M.F., Kent, F.H. and Muir, D. (1997) *Schools in Cyberspace: A Practical Guide to Using the Internet in Schools*, London: Hodder & Stoughton.

Davis, N. (1994) 'Electronic Communication', in Underwood, J. (ed.) *Computer Based Learning: Potential into Practice*, London: David Fulton.

Davis, N. (1996) 'Do Electronic Communications Offer a New Learning Opportunity in Education?', in Somekh, B. and Davis, N. (eds) *Using Information Technology Effectively in Teaching and Learning*, London: Routledge.

Dearing, R. (1994) *The National Curriculum and its Assessment*, London: School Curriculum and Assessment Authority.

Dearing, R. (1996) *Review of Qualifications 16–19*, London: SCAA.

DES (1989) *Circular 3/89. The Education Reform Act 1988: Religious Education and Collective Worship*, London: HMSO.

DES/HMI (1977a) *Curriculum 11–16*, London: HMSO.

DES/HMI (1977b) *Supplement to Curriculum 11–16*, London: HMSO.

DFE (1994a) *Circular 1/94. Religious Education and Collective Worship*, London: HMSO.

DFE (1994b) *Circular 6/94. The Organisation of Special Education Provision*, London: HMSO.

DfEE (1997) *Connecting the Learning Society*, London: HMSO.

DfEE (1998a) *Circular 4/98. Teaching: Higher Status, Higher Standards*, London: HMSO.

DfEE (1998b) *Initial Teacher Training National Curriculum for the Use of Information and Communications Technology in Subject Teaching (Circular 4/98 Annex B)*, London: HMSO.

Donaldson, M. (1992) *Human Minds*, London: Allen Lane/Penguin Press.

Donnelly, J. (1996) *IT and Schools: The Head's Legal Guide*, Kingston upon Thames: Croner Publications.

Downes, T. (1993) 'Student Teachers' Experiences in Using Computers during Teaching Practice', *Journal of Computer Assisted Learning*, 9 : 1, pp. 17–33.

Duncan, G. and Lankshear, D.W. (1995) *Church Schools: A Guide for Governors*, London: National Society.

Dutton, W.H. (1996) *Information and Communication Technologies: Visions and Realities*, Oxford: Oxford University Press.

Erricker, C. (1998) 'Spiritual Confusion: A Critique of Current Educational Policy in England and Wales', *International Journal of Children's Spirituality*, 3 : 1, pp. 51–64.

Erricker, C., Erricker, J., Ota, C., Sullivan, D. and Fletcher, M. (1997) *The Education of the Whole Child*, London: Cassell.

Farrell, M. (1998) *The Special Educational Needs Handbook*, London: David Fulton.

Fisher, R. (1990) *Teaching Children to Think*, Oxford: Blackwell.

Fisher, R. (1998) *Teaching Thinking: Philosophical Enquiry in the Classroom*, London: Cassell.

Fitzpatrick, S. (1994) 'Using Graphics Packages', in Underwood, J. (ed.) *Computer Based Learning: Potential into Practice*, London: David Fulton.

Fowler, J. (1981) *Stages of Faith: The Psychology of Human Development and the Quest for Meaning*, San Francisco: Harper & Row.

Francis, L. and Thatcher, A. (eds) (1990) *Christian Perspectives for Education*, Leominster: Gracewing.

Gains, C. (1996) *The Special Educational Needs Coordinator*, Stafford: National Association for SEN.

Gates, B.E. (1989) *The National Curriculum and Values in Education*, Frinton: Hockerill Educational Foundation.

Gates, B.E. (1998) 'The Value of the Internet for Religious Education', *Resource*, 20 : 3, pp. 1–4.

Gateshill, P. and Thompson, J. (1992) *Religious Artefacts in the Classroom*, London: Hodder & Stoughton.

Gayeski, D. (1996) 'Multimedia Packages in Education', in Plomp, T. and Ely, D.P. (eds), *International Encyclopedia of Educational Technology*, Cambridge: Pergamon.

Geaves, R. (1998) 'The Borders between Religions: A Challenge to the World Religions Approach to Religious Education', *British Journal of Religious Education*, 21 : 1, pp. 20–31.

Gipps, C. (1990) *Assessment: A Teacher's Guide to the Issues*, London: Hodder & Stoughton.

Goldman, R. (1965) *Readiness for Religion: A Basis for Developmental Religious Education*, London: Routledge & Kegan Paul.

Grimmitt, M. (1973) *What Can I Do in RE?*, Great Wakering, Essex: Mayhew-McCrimmon.

Grimmitt, M. (1987) *Religious Education and Human Development: The Relationship between Studying Religions and Personal, Social and Moral Education*, Great Wakering, Essex: McCrimmon.

Hammond, J., Hay, D., Moxon, J., Netto, B., Raban, K., Straugheir, G., and Williams, C. (1990) *New Methods in RE Teaching: An Experiential Approach*, Harlow: Oliver & Boyd.

Hargreaves, A. and Fullar, M. (1996) *Understanding Teacher Development*, London: Cassell.

Harrison, M. (1998) *The Enhancement and Development of Learning Opportunities in Religious Education Using Information Technology*, http://re-xs.ucsm.ac.uk/schools/cupboard/ict/maureenreport.html

Harrison, M. and Kippax, S. (1996) *Thinking about God*, London: Collins.

Hay, D. (1982) *Exploring Inner Space. Is God still Possible in the Twentieth Century?*, Harmondsworth: Penguin Books.

Hay, D. (1985) 'Suspicion of the Spiritual: Teaching Religion in a World of Secular Experience', *British Journal of Religious Education*, 7 : 1, pp. 140–7.

Hay, D. (1990a) *Religious Experience Today*, London: Mowbray.

Hay, D (1990b) 'The Bearing of Empirical Studies of Religious Experience on Education', *Research Papers in Education*, 15 : 1, pp. 3–27.

Hay, D. and Nye, R. (1996) 'Investigating Children's Spirituality: The Need for a Fruitful Hypothesis', *International Journal of Children's Spirituality*, 1 : 1, pp. 6–16.

Hay, D. with Nye, R. (1998) *The Spirit of the Child*, London: Fount.

Herring, J.E. (1996) *Teaching Information Skills in Schools*, London: Library Association Publishing.

Hick, J. (1997), 'Is Christianity the Only True Religion?', *Resource*, 19 : 3, pp. 3–7.

Hicks, B. (1998) 'Blair's Paper Tiger', *TES Online Education*, 9 January.

Hirst, P. (1974) *Knowledge and the Curriculum*, London: Routledge.

HMI (1989) *The Curriculum from 5 to 16*, London: HMSO.

HMSO (1944) *Education Act*, London: HMSO.

HMSO (1981) *Education Act*, London: HMSO.

HMSO (1988) *Education Reform Act*, London: HMSO.

HMSO (1992) *Education (Schools) Act*, London: HMSO.

HMSO (1993) *Education Act*, London: HMSO.

HMSO (1996) *School Inspections Act*, London: HMSO.

HMSO (1998) *School Standards and Framework Act*, London: HMSO.

Hughes, F. (1986) 'Religious Education and Christian Nurture', *RS Today*, 11 : 3, pp. 2–4.

Hull, J.M. (1989) *The Act Unpacked: The Meaning of the 1988 Education Reform Act for Religious Education*, Derby: CEM.

Hull J.M. (1991) *Mishmash. RE in Multicultural Britain. A Study in Metaphor*, Derby: Birmingham University/CEM.

Hull, J.M. (1992) 'Editorial: The Transmission of Religious Prejudice', *British Journal of Religious Education*, 14 : 2, pp. 69–72.

Hull, J.M. (1995) 'Spiritual Education and the Money Culture', *British Journal of Religious Education*, 17 : 3, pp. 130–2.

Hull, J.M. (1996) 'God, Money and the Spirituality of Education', *British Journal of Religious Education*, 18 : 2, pp. 66–8.

Hull, J.M. (1998) *Utopian Whispers*, Derby: CEM.

Hyde, K. (1990) *Religion in Childhood and Adolescence: a Comprehensive Review of Research*, Birmingham, Alabama: REP.

Jackson, R. (1992) 'The Misrepresentation of Religious Education', in Leicester, M. and Taylor, M. (eds) *Ethics, Ethnicity and Education*, London: Kogan Page, pp. 100–13.

Jackson, R. (1997) *Religious Education: An Interpretive Approach*, London: Hodder & Stoughton.

Jones, N. and Docking, J. (1992) *Special Edcuational Needs and the Education Reform Act*, Stoke on Trent: Trentham Books.

Kay, W. and Francis, L.J. (1996) *Drift from the Churches*, Cardiff: University of Wales Press.

Keep, R. (1991) *On-Line: Electronic Mail in the Curriculum*, Coventry: National Council for Education Technology.

Kelly, A.V. (1986) *Knowledge and Curriculum Planning*, London: Harper & Row.

Kennedy, H. (1997) *Learning Works: Widening Participation in Further Education*, London: FEFC.

Kerry, T. (1980) 'The Demands made by RE on Pupils' Thinking', *British Journal of Religious Education*, 3 : 2, pp. 46–52.

Keswick Hall RE Centre (1997) *Directory of Agreed Syllabuses for RE (England, Wales and Northern Ireland), produced in partnership with AREIAC and NASACRE*, Norwich: University of East Anglia.

Kincaid, M. (1991) *How to Improve Learning in RE*, London: Hodder & Stoughton.

Kyriacun, C. (1998) *Essential Teaching Skills*, London: Stanley Thornes.

Leask, M. and Pachler, N. (1999) *Learning to Teach using ICT in the Secondary School*, London: Routledge.

Leicester, M. and Taylor, M. (eds) (1992) *Ethics, Ethnicity and Education*, London: Kogan Page.

Loukes, H. (1961) *Teenage Religion: An Enquiry into Attitudes and Possibilities among British Boys and Girls in Secondary Modern Schools*, London: SCM.

Lovelace, A. and White, J. (1996) *Beliefs, Values and Traditions*, London: Heinemann.

MacIntyre, A. (1985) *After Virtue: A Study in Moral Theory*, London: Duckworth.

Malone, P. (1998), 'Religious Education and Prejudice among Students taking the Course "Studies of Religion" ', *British Journal of Religious Education*, 21 : 1, pp. 7–19.

Mayled, J. (1977) *People and their Gods*, London: Nelson.

Mercier, S.C. (1996) *Interpreting Religions: Muslims*, Oxford: Heinemann.

Munro, H.H. (1976) *The Complete Works of Saki*, New York: Dorset Press.

National Society (1972) *The Fourth R*, London: National Society/SPCK.

NCET (1995) *Differentiation: Taking IT Forward*, Coventry: National Council for Educational Technology.

NCET (1998) *Training Tomorrow's Teachers in Information Technology*, Coventry: National Council for Educational Technology.

NEAB (1997) *NEAB GCSE Coursework Guide*, Manchester: NEAB.

Nussbaum, M. C. (1997) *Cultivating Humanity: A Classical Defense of Reform in Liberal Education*, Cambridge, Massachusetts: Harvard University Press.

OFSTED (1994) *Framework for the Inspection of Schools*, London: HMSO.

OFSTED (1995a) *Guidance on the Inspection of Secondary Schools*, London: HMSO.

OFSTED (1995b) *Review of Inspection Findings 1993/94*, London: HMSO.

OFSTED (1996) *Subjects and Standards: Issues for School Development arising from OFSTED Inspection Findings 1994–1995: Key Stages 3 and 4 and Post–16*, London: HMSO.

OFSTED (1997) *The Impact of New Agreed Syllabuses on the Teaching and Learning of Religious Education*, London: HMSO.

OFSTED (1998) *Secondary Education: A Review of Secondary Schools in England 1993–1997*, London: HMSO.

Ogden, V. (1997) *The Role of Religious Education at 16–19 in the Ascendancy of Work-related Learning and a New Framework for Post-compulsory Education*, Abingdon: Culham College Institute.

Parker-Jenkins, M. (1995) *Children of Islam: A Teacher's Guide to Meeting the Needs of Muslim Pupils*, London: Trentham Books.

Parsons, G. (ed.) (1993) *The Growth of Religious Diversity: Britain from 1945*. Volume One: *Traditions*, London: Open University/Routledge.

Parsons, G. (ed.) (1994) *The Growth of Religious Diversity: Britain from 1945*. Volume Two: *Issues*, London: Open University/Routledge.

Priestley, J. (1996) *Spirituality in the Curriculum*, Frinton: Hockerill Educational Foundation.

Priestley, J. (1997) 'Spirituality, Curriculum and Education', *International Journal of Children's Spirituality*, 2 : 1, pp. 23–34.

Qualifications and Curriculum Authority (1997) *Guidance for Schools: the Promotion of Pupils' Spiritual, Moral and Cultural Development*, London: QCA.

Qualifications and Curriculum Authority (1998a) *Exemplification of Standards in Religious Education: Key Stages 1 to 4*, London: QCA.

Qualifications and Curriculum Authority (1998b) *Religious Education Update. Issue 1*, London: QCA.

Ramjhum, A. F. (1995) *Implementing the Code of Practice for Children with Special Educational Needs*, London: David Fulton.

Rizzuto, A. (1979) *Birth of the Living God*, Chicago: University of Chicago Press.

Robinson, B. (1994) 'Word processing and desk-top publishing', in Underwood, J. (ed.) *Computer Based Learning: Potential into Practice*, London: David Fulton.

Robson, G. (1995) *Interpreting Religions: Christians*, Oxford: Heinemann.

Robson, G, (1996) 'Religious Education, Government Policy and Professional Practice 1985–1995', *British Journal of Religious Education*, 19 : 1, pp. 13–23.

Rudduck, J. (ed.) (1995) *An Education that Empowers: A Collection of Lectures in Memory of Lawrence Stenhouse* (BERA Dialogues 10), London: Multilingual Matters.

Rudge, J. (1989) Unpublished personal record of a seminar held at Homerton College, Cambridge at the invitation of the Keswick Hall Trustees, April 1989.

Rudge, L. (1998a), 'I am Nothing – Does it Matter? A Critique of Current Religious Education Policy and Practice in England on behalf of the Silent Majority', *British Journal of Religious Education*, 20 : 3, pp. 155–65.

Rudge L. (1998b) 'To Live is to Change: A Reflection on the "First S" (Spiritual Development) in the School Curriculum', paper presented to the Australian Association of RE conference, September.

Satterley, D. (1989) *Assessment in Schools*, Oxford: Blackwell.

SCAA (1994a) *Model Syllabuses. Model 1: Living Faiths Today*, London: School Curriculum and Assessment Authority.

SCAA (1994b) *Model Syllabuses. Model 2: Questions and Teachings*, London: School Curriculum and Assessment Authority.

SCAA (1994c) *Religious Education Glossary of Terms*, London: SCAA.

SCAA (1995a) *Spiritual and Moral Development*, SCAA Discussion Papers 3, London: School Curriculum and Assessment Authority.

SCAA (1995b) *Religious Education 16–19*, London: School Curriculum and Assessment Authority.

SCAA (1996a) *Education for Adult Life: The Spiritual and Moral Development of Young People*, SCAA Discussion Papers 6, London: School Curriculum and Assessment Authority.

SCAA (1996b) *Findings of the Consultation on Values in Education and the Community*, London: School Curriculum and Assessment Authority.

Schools Council (1971) *Religious Education in Secondary Schools*, Schools Council Working Paper 36, London: Evans/Methuen.

Scrimshaw, P. (1996) 'Computers and the Teacher's Role', in Somekh, B. and Davis, N. (eds), *Using Information Technology Effectively in Teaching and Learning*, London: Routledge.

Scruton, R. (1985) *Education and Indoctrination*, London: ERC.

Smart, L. (1996) *Using I. T. in the Primary School*, London: Cassell.

Smart, N. (1973) 'What is Religion?', in Smart, N. and Horder, D. (eds), *New Movements in Religious Education*, London: Temple Smith, pp. 13–22.

Smart, N. and Horder, D. (eds) (1973) *New Movements in Religious Education*, London: Temple Smith.

Snook, I.A. (1972a) *Concepts of Indoctrination: Philosophical Essays*, London: Routledge.

Snook, I.A. (1972b) *Indoctrination and Education*, London: Routledge.

Somekh, B. and Davis, N. (eds) (1997) *Using Information Technology Effectively in Teaching and Learning*, London: Routledge.

Somerset SACRE (1998) *Awareness, Mystery and Value: The Somerset Agreed Syllabus For Religious Education*, Somerset: Somerset SACRE.

Spackman, F. (1991) *Teachers' Professional Responsibilities*, London: David Fulton.

Starkings, D. (ed.) (1993a) *Religion and the Arts in Education: Dimensions of Spirituality*, London: Hodder & Stoughton.

Starkings, D. (1993b) 'The Landscape of Spirituality', in Starkings, D. (ed.) *Religion and the Arts in Education: Dimensions of Spirituality*, London: Hodder & Stoughton, pp. 9–18.

Stern, L.J. (1998) *Byting Back: Religious Education Sinks its Teeth into Computers. A Guide and In-service Training Pack for RE Teachers*, London: BFSS National RE Centre.

Stevenson, D. (1997) *Information and Communications Technology in UK Schools: An Independent Inquiry*, London: Independent ICT in Schools Commission.

Straker, A. and Govier, H. (1996) *Children Using Computers*, Oxford: Nash Pollock.

Tate, N. (1996) Unpublished address at SCAA conference Education for Adult Life: Spiritual and Moral Aspects of the Curriculum, London, 15 January.

Taylor, C. (1996) 'Organising IT Resources in Educational Institutions', in Somekh, B. and Davis, N. (eds) *Using Information Technology Effectively in Teaching and Learning*, London: Routledge.

Teece, G. (1998) 'Citizenship Education and RE: Threat or Opportunity?', *Resource*, 21 : 1, pp. 7–10.

Thatcher, A. (1990) 'The Recovery of Christian Education', in Francis, L. and Thatcher, A. (eds) *Christian Perspectives for Education*, Leominster: Gracewing, pp. 273–81.

Thatcher, A. (1991) 'A Critique of Inwardness in Religious Education', *British Journal of Religious Education*, 14 : 1, pp. 22–7.

Thiessen, E.J. (1993) *Teaching for Commitment: Liberal Education, Indoctrination and Christian Nurture*, Leominster: Gracewing.

Thompson, P. (1991) 'Spirituality and an Experiential Approach to RE', *Spectrum*, 23 : 2, pp. 125–36.

Tillman, N.N. (1998) *Evaluating Quality on the Net*, http://www.tiac.net/users/hope/findqual.html

Torrance, H. and Prior, J. (1998) *Investigating Formative Assessment*, Buckingham: Open University Press.

UEA (1996–99) 'Curriculum and Professional Development in RE: Syllabus Implementation Studies 1996–99'. Unpublished research project, part funded by the Keswick Hall Trust and St Gabriel's, due for public report 1999–2000.

Underwood, J. (1994) 'Introduction: Where are we now and where are we going?', in Underwood, J. (ed.) *Computer Based Learning: Potential into Practice*, London: David Fulton.

Watson, B. (1987) *Education and Belief*, Oxford: Blackwell.

Watson, B. (1993) *The Effective Teaching of Religious Education*, London: Longman.

Watton, V. (1996) *Religion and Life*, London: Hodder & Stoughton.

Wayne, E. (1996) *Interpreting Religion: Hindus*, Oxford: Heinemann.

Webster, D. (1991) 'School Worship', *Theology*, XCIV : 760, pp. 245–54.

Webster, D. (1995) *Collective Worship in Schools: Contemporary Approaches*, Cleethorpes: Kenelm Press.

Weller, P. (ed.) (1993) *Religions in the UK: A Multi-faith Directory*, Derby: University of Derby/Inter Faith Network.

Wertsch, J. (1985) *Vygotsky and the Social Formation of the Mind*, Cambridge, Massachusetts: Harvard University Press.

Wilde, O. (1983) *The Complete Works of Oscar Wilde*, London: Collins.

Williams, B. (1997) *One World, Many Issues*, London: Stanley Thornes.

Wintersgill, B. (1995) 'The Case of the Missing Models: Exploding the Myths', *Resource*, 18 : 1, pp. 6–11.

Wright, A. (1993) *Religious Education in the Secondary School: Prospects for Religious Literacy*, London: David Fulton.

Wright, A. (1996a) 'Language and Experience in the Hermeneutics of Religious Under-standing', *British Journal of Religious Education*, 18 : 3, pp. 166-80.

Wright, A. (1996b) 'The Child in Relationship: Towards a Communal Model of Spirituality', in Best, R. (ed.) *Education, Spirituality and the Whole Child*, London: Cassell, pp. 139–49.

Wright, A. (1997a) 'Embodied Spirituality: The Place of Culture and Tradition in Contem-porary Educational Discourse on Spirituality', *International Journal of Children's Spirituality*, 1 : 2, pp. 8–20.

Wright, A. (1997b) 'Hermeneutics and Religious Understanding. Part One: The Hermeneutics of Modern Religious Education', *Journal of Beliefs and Values*, 18 : 2, pp. 203–16.

Wright, A. (1998a) 'Hermeneutics and Religious Understanding. Part Two: Towards a Critical Theory for Religious Education', *Journal of Beliefs and Values*, 19 : 1, pp. 59–70.

Wright, A. (1998b) *Spiritual Pedagogy: A Survey, Critique and Reconstruction of Contemporary Spiritual Education in England and Wales*, Abingdon: Culham College Institute.

Wright, A. (1998c) 'Religious Education, Religious Literacy and Democratic Citizenship', unpublished paper presented to the International Seminar on Religious Education and Values, Carmarthen.

Wright, A. (1999) *Discerning the Spirit: Teaching Spirituality in the Religious Education Classroom*, Abingdon: Culham College Institute.

Wright, C. (1995a) *Key Christian Beliefs*, Oxford: Lion.

Wright, C. (1995b) *Delivering Collective Worship*, Bury St Edmunds: Courseware.

Author Index

Subject Index